TRADE SECRETS

Tips & Hints from the Pros

By Gene Schnaser

 Rodale Press, Emmaus, Pennsylvania

Printed in the United States of America on recycled paper, containing a high percentage of de-inked fiber.

Book design by Jeanne E. Stock
Illustrations by Marlyn Rodi and Sally Onopa

Library of Congress Cataloging-in-Publication Data

Trade secrets : tips and hints from the pros / [edited] by
  Gene Schnaser.
        p.   cm.
  Bibliography: p.
  Includes index.
  ISBN 0-87857-767-X   ISBN 0-87857-768-8 (pbk.)
  1. Dwellings – Maintenance and repair – Amateurs' manuals.
I. Schnaser, Gene.
  TH4817.3.T73   1988
643'.7 – dc19   88-1579
                                                        CIP

2 4 6 8 10 9 7 5 3 1   hardcover
2 4 6 8 10 9 7 5 3 1   paperback

To Gustav Pete Schnaser, a dad who appreciated the worth of letting a kid fritter away time in the shop when there was real work to be done; Ruby Schnaser, a mom who understood a kid's need to build potentially dangerous structures and mechanical devices; Roger Erickson, a 12-year-old boy mechanic who uncovered the wonders of hay rope pulleys, Maytag engines and Model Ts; Herb Friedrich, an ingenious uncle who made the shop a special place; Vernon Van Winkle, a faithful helper and supplier of found welding rods, pitchforks and 2 × 4s; Bernard Hoidahl, a whistling mechanic who demonstrated the virtue of patience when turning a perfectly good '37 Ford coupe into a stock car; Harold M. Johnson, an editor of the old school who opened my eyes to the extraordinary in the common place; Jim Stanley, a friend who helped make connections between pounding nails and computer programs and most of all, Jeanne and Steve, a family who enthusiastically accept my vocational excursions, and cheer me on during the storms.

CONTENTS

ACKNOWLEDGMENTS

It is something special when folks in this fast-paced, money-driven society freely give a chunk of their time to help a writer help the unknown masses. I know some of the providers of information in this book truly feel the value of passing shop, construction and mechanical lore along to future generations. All, I know, have a deep appreciation of the value of tricks, tips and shortcuts that can loosely be called trade secrets. They know there is no one place where all the answers can be found and how hard it is for the beginner to accumulate the information others have spent a lifetime discovering.

My deepest gratitude is extended to each and every person who lent their time and talents to the making of this book. I also am deeply indebted to a fellow by the name of Roger Rawlings who, as a writer for what's now called *Rodale's Practical Homeowner,* collected material for a number of the chapters. Much credit is also due to the dozens of other professionals who helped in smaller, but important, ways to make this book a reality.

Portions of this book have been previously published in *Rodale's New Shelter, Fine Homebuilding* and *Homestyles* magazines. Grateful acknowledgment is also made for permission to excerpt, and in some cases condense, from the following sources: The 1984 *Garrett Wade Tools Catalog* and *Old Houses: A Rebuilder's Manual* by George Nash (Prentice-Hall, 1979).

INTRODUCTION

This book is a collection of tips and ideas from some pretty savvy folks. Most of them, it's fair to say, don't even realize how much they know that the rest of us don't. And, still, most will tell you that they have a lot to learn themselves. I guess the point is that we never stop learning, never stop climbing the ladder toward our own idea of perfection. As you look through this book, you may find there are some tips you've already picked up, but there should be plenty that you can add to your own personal toolbox of tricks and techniques.

While working on this collection of how-to ideas, I happened to mention it to Art, one of my neighbors. He looked at me for a while, then said he hoped I wouldn't try to get too fancy with it. He said if it's not very technical (highfalutin was what he said), he won't feel like he needs to be an expert in order to read it.

Art's shop is in a corner of his basement. He has some tools. More than half came from his dad's collection, before they had the big auction a few years back. Some of the tools are pretty beat-up and are what you might call depreciated-out. Still, Art has them all hanging up there on the wall and wouldn't part with a single one, even if you tried to trade him "even up" for new tools.

Sure, when he pulls down his rusty old square, he knows it'll be a little hard to read the numbers. But, you see, that beat-up old square has a history of its own. It's a history that only Art and a few others know about, one that connects him to his own personal heritage of sawing, hammering, nailing, gluing and making something out of nothing.

Whenever he uses that square, he finds himself thinking back to when he used it to help his dad build their machine shop and that little shack that his dad used for years to smoke-cure fish from the river with apple wood. It reminds him of a whole raft of early projects, including the "stagecoach" he and his brother built to fit on top of the coaster wagon that Grandpa gave to the boys the Christmas of '54. He loves his old tools and uses them on his projects whenever he can.

Art is a computer programmer and is as sharp as a razor about computer codes, endless loops, that sort of thing. But one day we got to talking about certain projects, and Art confessed he's often embarrassed by what he doesn't know about building and shop work. He says he finds it hard to learn how to do new things. He says he thinks it's mostly his own fault because he doesn't like to let on how "dumb" he is when talking to the so-called experts. He says he has the feeling that a real pro might have a good laugh if he actually saw his shop down there in the basement.

Well, we know that in this day and age, just about everyone is sort of an expert on something or other. (My dad used to say you could learn something from anyone if you just kept your ears open.) But in the old days, I suspect it was a little different. I suspect folks didn't worry about being "experts" before going ahead and working raw materials into what they needed. For one thing, they didn't have the money to hire a specialist to do it for them. And not many could take the time to attend a class, even if there was one nearby, to learn how to do what needed to be done.

Years back it seems there used to be more of an open tradition of passing craft lore down from older craftsman to younger apprentice. It seems you had more of a chance to learn by doing, under the watchful eye of some old guy who had a lifetime of experience in his head. Unfortunately, a lot of that know-how got lost with the passing of those old fellows. And today people tend to keep that kind of knowledge more to themselves instead of freely passing it on to the next generation.

Art and I talked about how tricks of the trade tend to become status symbols to some folks who know about them and hoard them as their leg up on the world. This is probably part of human nature, but it is unfortunate. It tends to divide folks into categories of "those who know" and "those who don't." To make matters worse, a few of those "in the know" tend to project themselves as the high priests of how-to knowledge. Because of this, a natural fear arises in each of us that the "experts" are going to discover that on some things we're about as dumb as a box of rocks.

Well, while Art and I were talking, we decided that maybe the best thing is to just admit that no person can be an expert on everything, and realize that you shouldn't have to feel intimidated just because someone else knows more about something than you do. We decided that the best approach is just to go ahead and ask those dumb questions.

Not long after our visit, I happened to notice that James Thurber, who lived from 1894 to 1961, once said, "It is better to know some of the questions than all of the answers." I hope you'll find this book valuable reading, partly because I've been out there asking some of those dumb questions for you, but mostly because there are still fellows out there who are willing to unselfishly sit down and go over what they know in order to help out the rest of us.

Gene Schnaser
St. Paul, Minnesota

PART 1

A GUIDE TO TOOLING UP

CHAPTER 1

DON PESCHKE:

BUYING TOOLS

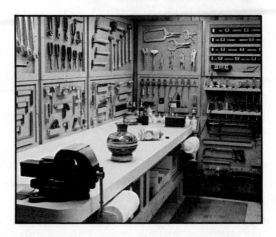

One of your neighbors who builds furniture in his spare time buys the most expensive tools he can find. The guy next door does some remodeling and repair work and picks up bargain tools wherever he can find them. Who is right?

"They both may be," explains Don Peschke, editor and founder of *Woodsmith* magazine, a bimonthly published in Des Moines, Iowa, and read by thousands of woodworkers. "It's just that they have different needs and different points of view."

Don got the idea to start up *Woodsmith* magazine in 1978. The publication now has its headquarters in a converted Des Moines mansion. *Woodsmith* has more than a dozen employees, and some have the job of testing tools and techniques in a shop many would call a woodworker's paradise.

Don says that hardly anyone will argue that higher priced tools offer you more features, more power and generally longer life. The real challenge when buying tools, he emphasizes, is to get as much tool quality as you're willing to pay for.

Good tool-buying strategy starts with determining what your needs are. For example, if you are going to put an addition on your house or build a garage, then buy those tools that will adequately do the job. And figure in the cost of the tools as part of your expense of making the improvements.

Cheaper tools will work fine if you're just starting to set up a shop or are planning only light-duty projects. A $9 drill can last for years if it's only used occasionally, but the same drill in the hands of a professional remodeler could be burned up in a day. The key is your level of expectation. If you buy tools off the bargain table and expect them to do heavy, professional work day after day, there's no question you will be disappointed.

BUYING STRATEGIES

Generally I would advise buying the best tools you can afford, with one major caution, and that is to go slow on tool buying if you're just starting, either in remodeling or in woodworking. I know of several cases where someone has gotten excited about becoming a woodworker, bought $1,500 worth of equipment, then made the discovery that he or she didn't have enough time or didn't enjoy it enough to pursue his or her projects.

If you're just beginning, consider buying tools at the middle of the price scale – a $30 to $50 drill instead of a $120 drill, for example. If you find you're getting a lot of use out of that tool and you need more power or features, then you can go ahead and buy the more expensive tool. You'll have the confidence that it will be used and that its extra features will be worthwhile.

What I find, with few exceptions, is that the tool market is so competitive that it almost becomes a rule that you get what you pay for. But even if you make a few mistakes along the way, you aren't going to go bankrupt. Sometimes you have to look hard to see the differences between what are called professional tools and what are called consumer tools. Both will accomplish what they were designed to do, but the features designed into a professional tool will allow it to perform better under constant punishment over a longer period of time.

What features do you get for the extra buck? Among hand tools, cost factors can include size, weight, balance and material used. Other factors are how the tool is processed, assembled and finished. A good hammer, for example, will have a head of drop-forged steel instead of cast iron. It will be ground and polished instead of painted. The face will be beveled and rim-tempered to avoid chipping or breaking. It will have tempered claws with edges designed to get a good grip on nails.

Quality hammers can have steel, fiberglass or wooden handles; which you choose is a personal matter. Plastics and fiberglass don't necessarily indicate low quality – in many cases manufacturers have used better grades to produce superior tools for the dollar.

How much a power tool costs can depend on the tool's amperage, RPMs, horsepower and torque, as well as the manufacturer's reputation. As price goes up, you can expect longer and better cords, heavier-duty switches and housings of supertough nylon instead of lower-grade plastics. Inside, you can expect more use of ball bearings, copper windings, brass brush holders and hardened wrought steel gears. Overall, you can expect a higher power-to-weight ratio and more special features such as case-hardened drill chucks, variable speed and higher-quality accessories.

There's nothing wrong with a tool made in another country; in many cases you can get quite superior quality. However, occasionally you need to be a more savvy tool buyer to make sure the price you are paying is actually fetching the quality you think you're buying.

WHERE TO INVEST

I personally like to stay away from low-end stationary tools, and put out the extra money to get a professional tool. I've found that the lower-priced bench-top tools simply don't have the features of more expensive stationary tools. The problem is that you still spend enough on them so you feel like you have to get some use out of them. But if you use them hard, they wear out much faster. Plus, I think they're harder to sell when you want to trade up to higher quality.

Three tools for general woodworking that I would spend more money on include a good table saw, drill press and router. Most of the projects we run in *Woodsmith* magazine can be built with just these three power tools. With these in your shop, along with some hand tools, you can build just about anything. As for hand tools, I would spend the money to get a good plane and a good set of chisels.

To use either the plane or chisels successfully, the key is keeping them sharp. I used to get frustrated with these tools until I learned how to sharpen them. Consider buying a cheap set of chisels to practice your sharpening technique. After you've perfected your skill, then go ahead and buy a more expensive set. You will still find uses for the cheap chisels.

When I want new tools, I try to decide what I need, then wait for that tool to go on sale. The first part of the year is usually a good time to watch the ads. For used tools, I like to stick to classified ads or garage sales. You can get some good bargains at auctions, especially on heavy, specialized tools that other bidders aren't that familiar with. But people at auctions often get caught up in the bidding so much that they wind up paying more for the tools than they should.

If I am buying tools secondhand, I try to stick almost exclusively to the industrial-quality tools. The service life of a low-priced tool can be quite short. Most of its life can already be used up, but you can't tell by looking at it. When a cheap drill or sander dies, there's not much you can do but toss it in the garbage. Repairs can run as much or more than its original price. But repairs may be worthwhile on a higher-priced, industrial-quality tool, and service is more available for these tools as well.

The depreciation factor also favors buying more expensive tools. Once you use a new tool, its value drops and hovers around 50 percent of its original price. You may be able to resell a higher-quality tool for 60 percent or more of its cost, but a cheaper tool might only sell for 30 percent or less of its cost. This is why a good-quality tool can be a decent investment. You use it over the years and, depending upon inflation, you may be able to resell it eventually for close to its original price.

OUTFITTING TOOLS

Accessories and attachments are critical to tool performance, sometimes more so than the tool itself. You can even have problems with industrial-quality tools if you equip them with cheap blades or bits. If you try to get by with a $10 saw blade instead of a $50 blade, for example, a table saw won't perform as well no matter what you paid for it. I go with carbide-tipped blades and bits. They're expensive-a set of eight good carbide bits for a router can run you $150 – but they're well worth it if you are serious about doing good work.

There is still something to taking care of your tools. Not many carpenters today use their lunch breaks to sharpen their tools. But a good workman will know when, for example, a saw blade should be sharpened. Anyone concerned about tool performance will keep cutting edges sharp, replace blades and bits when necessary and store or transport his tools with reasonable care.

One final tool-buying tip: don't overlook tapping the experiences of others. Talk with other tool owners about tool performance. It's pretty easy to strike up a conversation about tools almost anywhere someone is working. Sometimes what they say can be tainted by pride of ownership, but most often they will give you the straight scoop about what they think about their tools.

CHAPTER 2

GARRETSON WADE CHINN:

THOUGHTS ON HAND TOOLS

There's little that could be more important to your enjoyment, accomplishment and satisfaction of working on most any household project than your attitude toward your tools. In a way, the most important tool of all that you possess could be how you think of the tools you use.

For example, think of a wood turner who spends hours sharpening his chisels, polishing them to a fine edge and studying the wood to be turned. He realizes that working wood is almost more rehearsal than performance, yet he looks forward to hearing the living sounds of the stone against the chisel, the lumber whirring on the lathe and the edge of the chisel against the wood.

On the other hand, you might think of someone just learning to build houses. You might watch him work and discover that he views both his tools and materials as elements to be dominated and subdued. His tools are just tools, separate from himself and what he is trying to do. He might try to keep his mind off what he is doing with a blaring radio. He manhandles the boards, saw and hammer, leaving a trail of debris as he tries to "force the project done."

Which person do you think will turn out the better work? Which will suffer more lost time because of accidents, work that needs redoing or searching for misplaced items? Which will enjoy his work, his finished results or his life more?

"It all starts with attitude," explains Garretson Wade Chinn. "It's almost a state of mind." Garretson is principal owner of one of the largest fine woodworking-tool supply houses in the world. The *Garrett Wade Tools Catalog,* in fact, has become an institution among the best craftsmen. The tools it offers, from Old World workbenches to precision backsaws, are among the best available.

Going to Garrett Wade for tools is like going to the Mercedes factory to buy a car, to "21" for dinner, or to Abercrombie & Fitch to procure a double-barrel 12-gauge shotgun. It's not the place to look if your mind is set on a bargain tool to use and throw in a heap in the corner of your shop.

Garretson has thought about tools in practical and even metaphysical terms. If you talk to him, you can tell he has a definite feeling for tools, an eye for excellence and a passion to help folks discover the real enjoyment tools have to offer, by exposing the inner beauty of tools that have made his company so successful. He also has some good suggestions for anyone equipping a shop for working with wood.

Our personal commitment has always been to search out the finest tools and woodworking products available. We work hard at it. If a tool doesn't meet our demands for quality, durability and function, you won't find us offering it. The reason behind it is this. Our goal is basically to help people who work with wood avoid disappointment. What our business is all about, really, is helping people derive more satisfaction from using tools.

OUTFITTING YOUR SHOP

There are many variables that determine what tools you need in your shop. Often it's just a matter of taste, budget and function. But one thing is certain. If you have the proper tool for each job, you will find yourself doing much better work. This is the absolute truth.

Good tools can help you do better work with more confidence, but it's how you think about your tools that counts most.

THE WORKBENCH

A good workbench is a "must" tool for any woodworker, cabinet-maker or wood sculptor. Any woodworker who has had to work on an unstable surface with small, inadequate vises knows what I mean. Our ancestors used the classic benches (still available) in making the fine Colonial furniture we are so proud of today. If you are a new woodworker, such benches will help you learn hand work with new confidence. You will find that your bench will become an extension of yourself – like an extra pair of very strong hands. And if you're an experienced woodcrafter, you will be able to work with more speed and flexibility.

The key requirements in any good bench are (1) sturdiness (weight and quality of construction), (2) the ability to hold your work piece firmly in a variety of positions (the bench vises and bench dog system), (3) a large, smooth work area (the top) and (4) an adequate tool tray. A good workbench will have either a single or double row of bench dogs, against which work can be held; a shoulder wood vise on one side of the bench and a tail vise on the end of the bench.

When choosing a workbench, I'd suggest you first decide how much you can afford to spend. Second, determine how much space you have available. Third, decide whether the type of work *you are likely to want to do in the future* requires a large bench or a small bench. A workbench is an important investment, so buy one wisely. A proper bench will make the greatest difference in your enjoyment of your work and in helping you do your best.

MARKING-OUT TOOLS

Wood turners can, of course, make use of special marking-out tools. However, for most workshops, I'd suggest the following to start: a gradu-

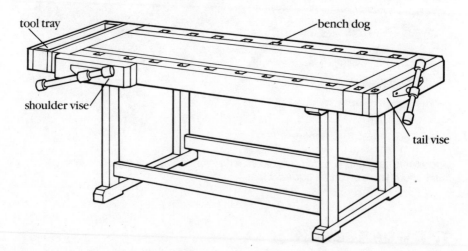

For fine woodworking, a good workbench is essential. It's an important investment, so take a close look at what you can get for your money. The illustration shows some features you should look for.

ated try square, an engineer's square, a marking and/or mortise gauge, a marking awl, a measuring tape and steel rules of several lengths.

For particularly exacting work, it is a good idea to use the same measuring tools throughout the job because, in many cases, two apparently identical rules can vary as much as $1/32$ inch in one foot. (This is not true of those specifically called precision rules, but can be the case with more generally available products.) Also, switching from a rule to a tape to a square may create errors during the job that cannot, in the end, be traced.

A few more tips: try practicing reading rules upside down – this can be a very handy skill in some situations. Also, for greatest accuracy when using a tape, tip one edge down against the stock.

There are a couple of good books available that offer a wealth of detailed information on workshop geometry and drafting: *Encyclopedia of Furniture Making* by Ernest Joyce (Sterling, 1979) and *The Victorian Cabinet-Maker's Assistant* by Blackie and Son (Dover, 1970).

HANDSAWS

The difference between an adequate saw and the best lies in the balance of the tool, the ruggedness and comfort of the handle, the quality of the steel (plus the accuracy and sharpness of the teeth) and, in general, ease of use. There are many different types (both in size and design) of excellent saws made in Europe, Japan and this country. As you might expect, each will perform its own special function best. For example, you can crosscut a board with a ripsaw but it will work much slower and produce a very rough finish. In contrast to a ripsaw, where the teeth are set and filed to cut with their points, crosscut saw teeth are filed to cut with their edges and shaped with no hook, which prevents snagging on wood fibers.

Choosing the right saw is usually as much a matter of taste (and budget) as anything else. However, I would suggest the following basic assortment: ripsaw, fast-cutting crosscut saw, fine-cutting crosscut saw, stiff backsaw (tenon, dovetail or Dozuki), a small fine-toothed detailing saw and a hacksaw. Other saws can easily be added as you complete and fill out the range in your shop.

Western saws cut on the push stroke and Japanese saws on the pull stroke. The tooth styles of Japanese and Western saws are different on both ripsaws and crosscut saws. But both Japanese and Western tenon saws function like crosscut saws. The brass back on the Western tenon saw gives the saw weight so you don't have to "press" on it. The Japanese tenon saw (known as a Dozuki) relies on its special tooth pattern, rather than the weight of the blade, to do the work.

A few tips on preparing handsaws for more effective use. First, uneven teeth on a saw make for slow cutting, not only because fewer teeth have to do the work, but also because sawdust piles up in front of the long teeth, causing the saw to "ride." Keeping teeth well filed to level position will help the teeth cut evenly and carry an equal amount of sawdust in each gullet.

It's easy to forget about your stance when sawing. Putting your feet in the right place is as important as using the correct tool. A proper stance will allow your hand, shoulder and elbow to be in a straight line with the saw blade. With a proper stance and a sharp saw, you can make the blade cut with little effort, and the sound will tell you so. If excessive force seems to be needed (assuming the blade is reasonably sharp) or the cut "sounds" bad, the culprit is most probably a bad stance.

STEEL AND WOODEN PLANES

Until 30 or 40 years ago, a craftsman could obtain literally hundreds of types of planes. In this day of power-driven tools, we are apt to forget how important hand planes are for precision work. They are the violins of woodworking.

Each plane has its own special purpose, work that it can do more easily and accurately than any other. Not only can you usually do more careful (and better) work with a hand plane, but also – often because of power tool set-up time – work faster.

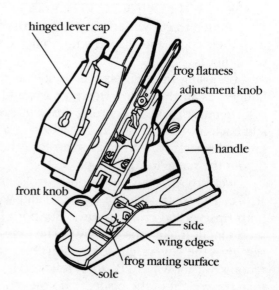

A hand plane is a more forgiving tool than a power tool is, and experience with a hand plane will help you better understand your power tools. A good plane has these components.

hinged lever cap

frog flatness adjustment knob

handle

front knob

side

wing edges

frog mating surface

sole

Skill at hand planing is one of the most important abilities of any craftsman. Experience with hand planes will help you understand exactly what a power tool is doing when you use it for a particular job (an important and subtle appreciation if you are to achieve consistently good results with power tools). Also, a hand plane is a far more forgiving tool. Careful work sacrificed for speed can ruin more otherwise good work than anything else.

Here are a few hints about using any plane. First, keep the blade as sharp as possible (bench stones and honing guides are excellent for this purpose). Second, *generally* plane with the grain (though there are some exceptions to this rule). If you don't work with the grain, you run the danger of "catching the grain," lifting chips of wood and producing a rough surface. When planing end grain, push the plane one way to the middle of the board only; then repeat this process going in the other direction. This prevents splitting the board at the edge.

The variety of planes available is usually confusing to the inexperienced woodworker and sometimes even to more experienced craftsmen. All planes are divided into two groups: bench planes and specialty planes. Bench planes (whether steel or wooden, Japanese or Western) have wide blades and a large, flat sole. They are used for flattening, smoothing or leveling wide surfaces or long edges. They vary greatly in width, length and weight. You will probably find it useful to have at least one short-, medium- and long-length plane in your shop.

An example of a specialty plane is a block plane, which is shaped like a small bench plane, but is used one-handed. Its function is general trimming (made possible by its small size) or cutting end grain. It comes in several different styles and one has a special low angle to make end-grain work more effective. Every shop should have at least one.

Other specialty planes include the relatively long-sole trimming planes. Bullnose planes are among the shortest of this style and the Record shoulder planes, the longest. They are extremely useful and I recommend that your shop have a minimum of two with different lengths and blade widths.

I'd also recommend that you have one or two smaller trimming planes such as the palm planes and the various brass planes. The variety is extensive, and you are likely to use them often. Other planes I'd buy when they are needed include rabbeting planes, side rabbet planes, router planes, spokeshaves and multicutter planes.

Use a modest amount of common sense and your planes will last a lifetime – even more. Be careful not to drop a steel plane because the casting may crack, break or dent. When metal is dented there will be some metal displaced from the dent and pushed outward, causing a raised ring or bump around the dent. The dent won't cause a problem, but the metal raised around it can. You can rub the surface with a fine honing stone to remove the bumps from around the dents so they don't leave small scratches in the wood surface. Once the bumps are removed, you can ignore the remaining dent. Keep a light coating of oil on the unplated surfaces to prevent rust spots and stains from the natural acids on your hands. Try, of course, to avoid denting the soles of your wooden planes. But if you get a dent or two (almost inevitable after a number of years) just ignore it. It won't have the slightest effect on a wooden plane's function.

A planing tip: the most common fault when using bench planes is "dipping." For accurate results, it is critical to avoid this. Just pay attention to this simple rule: at the beginning of each stroke, put slightly more pressure on the front of the plane. At the end of the stroke, keep slightly more pressure on the back.

FILES AND RASPS

Filing is one of man's oldest arts. A good file or rasp used properly should cut cleanly and smoothly. The teeth should not catch the wood fibers. The right file does the work you want to do better and usually faster.

Files are formed by raising a continuous tooth evenly across the file. There are two basic kinds of files: single cut and double cut. The teeth run in only one direction on single-cut files, but run in two directions on the double-cut files. Double-cut files cut quicker and more coarsely.

Rasps differ from files in that the teeth are formed individually and are not connected to one another. Files will cut smoother than rasps but when used on wood will work much slower and are susceptible to clogging.

In order of ascending smoothness of cut, files are graded coarse, bastard cut, second cut and smooth cut. Rasps are graded, in ascending order, wood rasp, cabinet rasp bastard and cabinet rasp second cut. In general, a longer file or rasp will have somewhat coarser teeth than a shorter one.

Use file handles with your files and rasps. Hold the file or rasp at the handle end with your thumb along the top edge. Grasp the other end with the thumb and forefinger of your other hand. Hold the stock firmly in a vise or clamp. For general filing, keep the stock at about elbow height. If the work requires heavier filing, it should be lower; if it is finer, it should be near eye level.

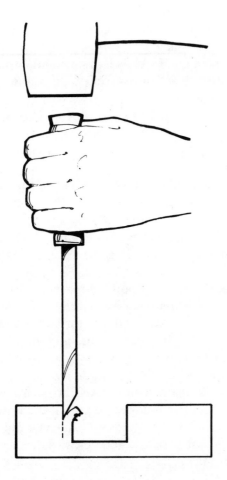

Always begin chiseling inside your marked lines. Chisel so chips fall into an open area–the result will be a square shoulder.

CHISELS AND KNIVES

A good chisel will be nicely balanced, properly designed for the work it is asked to do and will hold a keen edge for a long time. I would recommend three basic kinds of chisel: the bevel-edged cabinetmaker's chisels, the square-edged framing chisels and the mortise chisels.

Bevel-edged and square-edged chisels are used for all general forming work and are usually struck with a mallet. Mortise chisels are narrow chisels with thick heavy blades and a very broad bevel angle that serves to break waste when the chisel is used to cut deep square holes (mortises). These chisels are also meant to be struck, often with considerable force. Conversely, a chisel *not* designed to be struck is a paring chisel. These are usually longer and more delicate and are always kept shaving-sharp, because they are moved solely by hand pressure.

Many times I get asked what kind of chisels to get and which type of steel is better. With the exception of the Japanese chisels, which have the hardest edges of any, the steel in most quality chisels is substantially the same. So I'd suggest that you choose a chisel for yourself on the following basis: length, type of handle and balance.

For some craftsmen, a shorter chisel may be preferable. Others may prefer a plastic handle or a wooden one that is reinforced at the top because of its unique "handle heavy" balance. In any case, your choice is truly a matter of personal preference.

I'd suggest you consider having a full range of bevel-edged chisels. You will also probably find that several sizes of mortise chisels, and at least one cranked-neck chisel, will be needed in your shop. (Keep them very sharp and store them boxed, in a rack on a wall or in a tool roll. Just putting them in a toolbox will inevitably result in some damage to the cutting edges.)

Although many craftsmen like a hollow-ground chisel edge, I recommend a flat bevel or perhaps a double bevel (or micro bevel). Twenty-five degrees is generally correct for softwoods and 30° for hardwoods. Using any chisel requires a knack, one easily acquired but, nonetheless, a knack. Practice makes perfect, but here are a few hints: first, mark out your work carefully, using a solid square of the right size for easy handling. Second, always begin work inside your marked lines and cut into the waste wood. Third, rough out the whole cut, pare away the waste carefully and then pare carefully down to the mark for your final finish trimming. Using these basic rules, you'll have a nice clean-sided, flat-bottomed hole when you are finished.

CARVING TOOLS

What constitutes the best set or selection of individual carving tools? Again, it's a matter of personal style. The kind of work you do, or want to do, and the way in which you use the tools will, for the most part, determine this for you. But carving is very much a matter of personal choice and equally experienced carvers can legitimately disagree on what tools are best.

The major kinds of carving tools include parting tools (V-cutting shape), chisels (flat, no curvature), gouges (have curvature in blade), bent gouges (also have long bend in blade), spoon-shaped tools (curved like straight gouge, but end is shaped like a spoon), back bent-shaped tools (like spoon gouge, but for convex rather than concave shapes), fishtail-shaped tools (blade shaped like fishtail), wing parting tools, veiner gouges, macaroni tools and fluteroni tools (these last four types are comparatively rare).

All carving tools should be kept very sharp. This is even more important for beginning carvers than for experienced ones. A truly sharp carving tool will be easier to use and more satisfying to handle. It will let you concentrate on the line the tool is cutting rather than on how much force is going to be needed to make the cut.

TURNING TOOLS

The best group of turning tools for you will depend on the kind of work you do and the size and power of your lathe. The best turning tools are made from high-quality steel, forged with care and hardened and tempered to give a long edge life, yet retain the flexibility to withstand sudden shock. The handles should be of substantial length and diameter, and the ferrules strong. These are qualities I don't think you will find in the cheap grades. There are basically three different kinds of turning tools: gouges, chisels and scrapers.

Gouges are for roughing, long curves, coves and hollows. Chisels (either straight or skew) can be used on convex surfaces, for beading, for making V cuts or on end-grain work. Scrapers have very blunt bevels. They are used extensively on faceplate and bowl work, and where you can't use a cutting tool.

Scrapers are, in some ways, safer tools to use than chisels or gouges. For this reason, the scraping technique is more often taught in schools than is cutting with chisels or gouges. Scrapers, however, generally do not leave as smooth a finish as do the cutting tools.

Traditional high-carbon steel tools have been available for a long time, whereas the high-speed steel tools are a recent innovation. High-speed steel tools will hold a usable sharp edge much longer than plain carbon steel tools. The laminated steel turning tools from Japan have a superhard edge that can be made the sharpest of all turning tools.

SCREWDRIVERS

Lastly, just a word about screwdrivers. The screwdrivers generally available in this country, in my opinion, are badly designed for use with wood screws. The tapered tip simply doesn't fit a wood screw slot well. It depends on a wedge fit and supplies torque only at the top of the slot. And due to its wedgelike shape, the common tapered screwdriver tends to move upward and slip when maximum force is applied.

To avoid these problems, look for parallel-sided screwdrivers. Also look for screwdrivers with oval handles – they are easier to turn than those with round handles. To select the right screwdriver for the job, try to match the thickness and width of the blade as closely as possible to the size of the screw slot. Hold the screwdriver plumb to the screw; the tip of the screwdriver should reach the bottom of the slot.

CHAPTER 3

HOWARD SILKEN:

CHOOSING THE RIGHT SAW

If you thought about it, you might wonder why woodworkers and carpenters make such a big deal about sawing techniques and the tools used for sawing wood.

Cutting wood, sometimes into very precise units, is rivaled only by nailing (and other methods of fastening it back together) as the most talked-about subject in the general area of home and shop construction. The reason sawing ranks high, points out Howard Silken, is that it accounts for more than 90 percent of woodworking operations. He should know. His whole working career has revolved around tools. He's the kind of guy you wish you could take along to the store whenever you've saved up enough to buy a major workshop tool.

Howard ran a tool sales, service and rental shop for years, then went on to become a leading expert on the fine points of workshop tools. He also has several tool inventions under his belt, one a revolutionary new kind of radial arm saw. Because of his experience, he is often called on to testify as an expert witness in lawsuits involving tool accidents.

On a balmy winter day at his home in Delray Beach, Florida, Howard talks about some things to think about before buying a stationary saw.

"Howard, I just moved into my new house and I want to set up a shop in my basement. What's the first tool I should buy?" I bet you I've been asked that question a hundred times. Fortunately for me, I knew how to go about answering that kind of question. That was how I made my living. I was a power-tool dealer, knew my tools and was successful because I tried to sell my customers what they needed instead of what I could have made the most money on.

BUYING YOUR FIRST SAW

You might imagine that suggesting a list of tools to outfit a home shop might be very simple. It is to start with. For example, straight sawing is about 80 percent of woodworking, curved sawing is about 10 percent, sanding about 5 percent and turning, jointing, shaping and drilling all account for about another 5 percent. So the answer to the original question is that the first tool to get is a circular saw.

After that, it gets more difficult. You must ask yourself some important questions to fish out more facts. For example, I'd suggest that before you lay out any money to purchase a shop saw or any other tool, you give some thought to these questions:

• What exactly do you want to do with this saw? Do you just want to putter around? Build things to save money? Create useful or artistic things? Satisfy your urge to work with your hands?

• What experience and training have you had with power tools, especially saws?

• Are you the type of person who will go out of his way to learn from others and books? Do you always read the instruction manuals that come with almost every appliance on the market?

• What are you willing to pay for your tools? Most important, are you willing to purchase fewer, but better quality, tools to keep within your budget? Or do you like owning fine tools even if you hardly ever use them?

Don't laugh at the last question, I'm that type of person myself and I've sold to hundreds of customers who would buy any new tool if it was good quality and they did not already own one! But to get on with making some decisions: If you answered "Yes" to any one of the above questions, you should definitely own a stationary saw. Your answers to some of the questions will help you decide what type of saw you should own. For example, if you are a know-it-all, don't buy a radial arm saw. The radial arm saw is a beautiful, complicated, versatile, multipurpose tool. The average purchaser, even an experienced woodworker, utilizes only about 20 percent of the machine's capabilities (mostly by using the self-teach method).

If, however, you are willing to put the time into reading as much as you can about the tool, the radial arm saw is the best bet. A radial arm saw is very safe to use if you follow ALL the rules about setting the guards. It is extremely dangerous if you do not.

SAW DRIVES

All radial arm saws are direct drive. That is, the blade (or other accessories) mounts directly on the motor shaft (the arbor). There are a few table saws that are direct drive, but they are rare. Most table, floor or bench saws are belt driven. Some use standard V belts and others use timing belts.

Almost all table saws that use universal motors also use timing belts as opposed to V belts. Universal motors are high speed and have carbon brushes. Timing belts are flat belts with molded rubber teeth. They work like the sprocket and chain link on a bicycle. Because timing belts cannot slip, there is no loss in drive power.

On any saw, too big an arbor pulley will cut down on the depth of cut. A one-inch arbor pulley is about standard size. A 3,450 RPM motor would have a one-inch drive pulley. A 1,725 RPM motor would use a two-inch drive pulley. This poses a slight problem with V-belt saws. Small drive and driven pulleys have little surface on their walls to transfer the power to the V belt. In spite of this, they work quite well. The Delta Unisaw overcomes this problem by using pulleys with three grooves and three matched belts.

Saws with timing belts solve this problem but cause another. When the belt breaks, or the teeth wear away, where are you going to get a replacement? If you do purchase a saw with this type of drive, be sure to buy a spare belt or two at the time of your purchase – if the dealer has one, that is. Chances are good he may not. If, on the other hand, you buy a saw with a standard V belt, you can easily get a replacement at any auto or tool supply store. The same is true with the motor. On a V-belt drive saw, almost any motor of the right horsepower can be used. Most universal motors, however, are in special castings. If the motor goes bad, you might have a very difficult time replacing it.

Almost every stationary saw on the market has a tilt arbor. That is, if you want to cut (rip or crosscut) at a bevel angle, it is the blade that tilts, not the table. One such tool that still uses a tilt table is the Shopsmith. The Shopsmith is a great multipurpose tool, but works best only with small pieces of material. It would be my suggestion that any saw you purchase not have a tilt table. (All radial arm saws are tilt arbor.)

SIGNS OF QUALITY

When buying a table saw, check out its construction – the heavier the saw, the better. Heavy saws have less vibration and better accuracy of fence and miter gauge alignment. They also have less runout. Runout occurs when the end of the arbor shaft turns as if it were bent. This makes the blade whip back and forth, causing vibration, as well as causing the saw to cut a wider kerf. Most runout comes about when the arbor bearings wear. A good saw should have heavy-duty sealed ball bearings. Stay away from saws with sleeve bearings.

In my tool store, I sold one particular brand (Powermatic) to professional contractors because I always said, "If you melted down this saw you could build two of the competitors' saws from the same amount of steel." These professionals, because of their experience, knew the importance of a heavy, rigid tool. So, if you see a price of $59.95 for a 10-inch bench saw, the first thing you should do is pick up the carton (with the saw in it) and see if it feels as if the carton has something in it besides Styrofoam. If it doesn't, don't buy the saw. Manufacturers of saws keep the price and weight down in several ways, mostly in the tabletop of the saw. On some saws, the top is made of sheet metal. Others are, believe it or not, plastic. It looks like metal, but it is not. One good whack on a corner and off it will come. The better saws have cast-iron tables. Some have solid cast-iron or cast-aluminum extensions. Either is good.

Other things to look at are the motor mount, the table mount and the method of blade tilt and elevation. You may have to turn the tool upside down to check these out. This is easy to do on the cheap saws. On the better saws, you usually can see from the rear.

If the castings, under the table, are made of "white" metal (usually zinc), watch out! White metal gears and drives will abrade very quickly, particularly if sawdust gets onto the teeth or threads. Sawdust from plywood, particle board or Masonite is very abrasive. If the mechanism underneath is cast iron and machined, it should be a better tool.

TELLTALE BLADES

The saw blade that comes with the saw can tell you a great deal about the reliability of the manufacturer. First of all, it will probably be a combination (rip or crosscut) chisel-toothed blade. If it has a painted surface, watch out – it is most likely an untensioned blade.

Always ask a salesperson if the blade is "tensioned." If he says, "I don't know," buy your saw somewhere else. All saw blades are made from flat steel discs. The steel itself is under stress and strain in different locations of the blade. When the blade spins at high speed it will vibrate and not cut true. Tensioned blades are relieved of their stresses by a sawsmith. His job is to hammer the blank with a special hammer and anvil. He can feel and hear when the blade has been properly tensioned. Tensioned blades, when they rev up at high speeds, run without vibrating. They snap out and run true even if they have a slight bit of natural runout. Small blades (under eight inches) need not be tensioned.

If the blade is Krome Edge or Chrome Finished, stay away from it. Although chromium-coated blades do hold their cutting edge longer than regular blades (because the chrome coating is very hard), the first time you have that blade sharpened, the file will remove the chrome surface and you are left with a sharp, but relatively soft, metal blade. From then on, the blade will have to be sharpened after *every* use.

If you are convinced that the right saw for you is a table, bench or floor saw, you must next decide whether you want a small one or a large one (an 8-inch or 10-inch). To make this decision, you have to have a good idea as to what you want to do with it.

Small saws are good for model making, small artistic plastic work, framing and small woodworking such as toys, chairs and small cabinets. Large saws are needed if you will be doing any construction, making large furniture, using plywood sheets or doing work that will need a three-inch depth of cut.

One thing to remember is that a 10-inch saw will do everything an 8-inch saw will do, but an 8-inch saw will not do what a 10-inch saw will do.

CHAPTER 4

PATRICK SPIELMAN:

LEARNING TO USE A ROUTER

The router is a Johnny-come-lately to the home shop. It was during World War I that patternmaker R. L. Carter of Syracuse, New York, fashioned a bit from a hair clipper and attached it to an electric motor. He had a winner on his hands. In the next 10 years, Carter sold 10,000 of what he called his Electric Hand Shaper.

Routers still sell like hotcakes, ranking number three in the power tool Top Forty, right after electric drills and circular saws. The reason, says veteran router-user Pat Spielman, is that, with a

little practice and a touch of imagination, it puts the equivalent
of an entire workshop of tools in your hands.

During the 28 years he taught high-school woodworking,
Spielman used his routers (he owns five) to churn out crafts as
well as custom wood signs of all sizes. He believes a router
should be the second power tool, after a table or jig saw, that you
should consider buying. In fact, not long ago he wrote a 224-page
book called *The Router Handbook* (Sterling Publishing, 1983) to
help people get going with a router.

One afternoon, in his shop (called Spielman's Wood Works)
outside of Fish Creek, Wisconsin, he talks about his favorite shop
tool — one he admires but admits is not magic. He says it's
important not to fall into the common trap of expecting to bring
home your router, plug it in and turn out wonderful work. He
says that it's going to take some experimenting and some time to
put that router to work.

If your projects now look like they were made by an amateur, I'd take
a good look at buying a router. It has the potential to springboard you into
the ranks of the professional woodworker. Instead of confining yourself
just to simple projects, you can tackle just about anything with a router.
And the best thing is that with more professional results, you'll feel a lot
better about your work!

USING A ROUTER

It only takes a trip to price molding at a lumberyard to drive home
how a router can really save you money. But more than that, the best
reason to learn to use a router is that it can unlock a lot of doors for you in
woodworking. I think it's one of the most versatile woodworking tools
ever invented!

Making perfect joints can be a breeze with a router, even difficult
jobs such as through and half-blind dovetails, mortise and tenons, stopped
dadoes and grooved joints. You can make letter-perfect wood signs,
raised panels, louvered cabinet doors or decorative panels. Plus, with
some inexpensive attachments and jigs, you can use it to duplicate all
types of carving, from simple designs to intricate shapes such as gun
stocks. You can make some unbelievable wood turnings, including router-
cut spiral turnings of table legs, lamps, bowls and dowels. Or you can use
it to fit and trim plastic laminates for counters or furniture, even cut soft
metals. For the average woodworker, it can do the work of the more
expensive (and dangerous) spindle shaper. Many woodworking joints

usually done with radial and table saws can be cut with a router – often faster and better.

Besides using a router in the normal (vertical) position, you can use it sideways (horizontally) or mount its base upside down. You can take off the base and use it for freehand carving. You can use it as a stationary tool and bring the work to the router or as a portable tool and bring the router to your work. I'm still finding new ways to use it!

BUYING A ROUTER

The toughest part of getting set up can be buying a router you'll be satisfied with. Most mistakes I've made with router equipment have been bad buys. Based on my own experience, I wouldn't hold back when buying a router or a good set of bits. If you stick to the low-end price range, you can find yourself frustrated and can miss out on all the router has to offer.

You should feel good enough about yourself to realize you deserve quality tools. Be prepared to pay that extra $50 or $75 to get the best you can find. But, before you buy, do some research. If possible, check with friends and any professionals you know. See what they like and are honestly satisfied with. Ask if they will let you try out their routers so you can see how they handle.

I personally would go with a brand name router. Even if you just drop it on the floor, you may need service and/or replacement parts. Don't buy a router out of a catalog just because it's on sale. The way it looks in the picture and the way it can feel in your hands can be two different things. Check these features before you buy:

Horsepower: Definitely choose a router with at least 1 HP. You want enough power to make aggressive cuts. I use a 1½-HP router for practically everything. You'll find that as soon as you get comfortable using the router, you'll want to do more and more with it. Don't be misled by high RPMs – routers with the highest RPMs will generally have less horsepower.

Bit changing: Go to the store and check to see how easy it will be to change bits. Some routers require two wrenches, others only one. The easier, the better. Also check the power cord where it attaches to the router. If the cord comes out on one side, rather than at the top, you'll be able to lay the router flat on its top for easier bit changing.

Switches and handles: A poorly positioned switch can be the weak link in router design. Whenever you are handling your router or changing bits, you don't want it to turn on accidentally. I like double switches, one on the motor and one on the handle – you need to trip both before the router

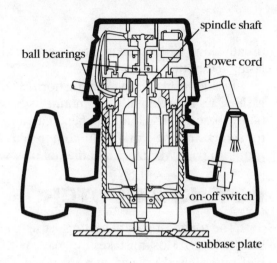

ball bearings

spindle shaft

power cord

on-off switch

subbase plate

When investing in a router, consider buying the best or near-best. Horsepower, switch and handle positions, bit changing and depth adjustment are features to check.

starts up. To be safe, pull the plug before working on your router. When you're using your router, it's convenient to have a pressure switch on the handle. It can be operated while you have both hands on the handles, enabling you to shut the router off fast if you have to.

Depth adjustment: Various types of depth adjustments are available, including, (1) clamp systems where the motor slides vertically in the base, (2) threaded systems where spiral grooves on the motor turn inside the base and (3) rack-and-pinion systems. I prefer the threaded type. The reason is that the motor won't drop down accidentally and damage an expensive bit. With this system you have to intentionally turn it down.

CHOOSING ACCESSORIES

Routers continue to be a popular tool because more accessories are becoming available. Just 10 years ago, you'd see only a few bits in the catalogs; today you'll find dozens that allow the average person to do intricate, professional work. Get an idea of what you need, though, before buying a lot of accessories. Read up on routers to get an idea of the various operations you can use it for and find books that will show you the jigs and fixtures you can make yourself.

Once you become familiar with your router, you'll find you have a whole world of accessories to experiment with. They range from lettering kits and pantographs for sign making, to hinge templates and special jigs to make table legs or decorative posts. You can even buy devices that let you duplicate figures in three dimensions, make bowls or sharpen your own bits. Essential accessories include an assortment of bits, some type of router table, a template guide and eye and ear protection. You might also want to invest in a shop vac, if you don't have one, to help clean up dust and chips.

ROUTER BITS

Sometimes I think there's too much emphasis put on the quality of the router and not enough on the quality of bits. That's where the action is. I'd advise buying fewer high-quality bits rather than a drawerful of low-quality ones. Cheap bits get dull fast and getting them resharpened can cost you more than the bits themselves.

The shape of the bits you buy depends on what kind of work you plan to do. For forming edges, I'd select a round-over bit, cove bit, ogee bit and rabbet bit. If you plan to do surface work such as carving wood signs, then a good arsenal would include a round-nosed bit, a V bit and a straight (flat-bottomed) bit. Later on you might want to get a straight trimmer bit for working on veneer or Formica, or for doing pattern work.

Here are some bit buying tips:

• A good size straight bit is one that's ¼-inch wide. You don't need various sizes unless you need them for production work. With the ¼-inch bit you can make several passes to widen the cut out to ⅜ or ½ inch.

A router pantograph, such as this one from Black & Decker, can be used to duplicate patterns when engraving designs and other flat work. Pantographs that adjust to give different ratios of reduction are also available.

• Buy carbide-tipped bits. They cost double or triple what high-speed steel bits cost, but I think they're worth it. I don't have much patience in woodworking. With carbides I can be reasonably sure they will be sharp and give me good work. High-speed steel bits can dull up fast if you hit a nail, or use them on plywood or particle board.

• For edge-forming bits, I'd recommend getting the two-piece bits: integral cutter and shank with a replaceable ball-bearing pilot guide. Pilot guides can wear out or get gummed up and mess up your work; I like to be able to change them. I don't think much of arbor sets where the shank, cutter and pilot are separate. It's just too easy to bang them up when taking them apart.

A ROUTER TABLE

One of my first jobs working with wood was at a cabinet shop in Prior Lake, Minnesota, during the 1950s. It's where I first got excited

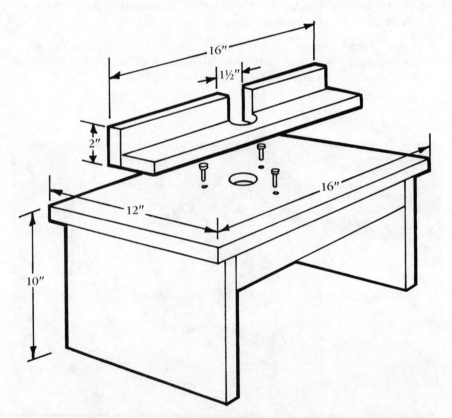

An example of a simple, inexpensive router table you can build yourself. Other styles include those that sit on top of a bench and those that clamp onto the bench's edge.

about what a router could do. Floyd Johnson, the cabinetmaker, could turn out fabulous cabinets with a minimum of tools. His router table was a piece of plywood with a hole in it, resting on two sawhorses, with the router bit sticking through and a piece of scrap wood nailed on for a fence.

You can buy ready-made router tables. Or, like Floyd, you can easily make your own. The fence doesn't have to be square; the only thing you have to watch is the distance from the bit to the fence. You can screw the base of your router to the bottom of the table, and consider buying another base when you want to take the router to the work. You can even rig up the router table sideways, so its surface is vertical, and use it in conjunction with another table for a neat edge-forming setup.

ROUTER GUIDES

You can buy edge guides to attach to your router. I've got them, but I don't use them much. For edge work I like to use the router table and for joints, such as dadoes, I'll just clamp a straightedge to the work and run the router against it. With edge guides you're limited on reach. And, the farther away from the edge you are, the less accuracy you get.

I'd recommend getting a template guide for your router. It fits into the center of the base and the bit goes through it. It allows you to duplicate projects from a pattern. Just cut out a pattern with your jigsaw, fasten it down and the template guide lets you reproduce it easily. It comes in various sizes, is inexpensive and is very handy.

LEARNING ROUTER TECHNIQUES

After you experiment for a while, you'll start to sort out a number of techniques that make for better results. Here are some examples.

FASTENERS FOR SMALL PIECES

For edge routing, you need a way to keep work from slipping and causing kickback. One of the best and quickest ways to hold pieces too small for clamps is to simply fasten them with hot-melt glue onto a larger piece of scrap plywood clamped to your bench. The trick is to use short beads. The glue holds but doesn't penetrate, so it can be cleaned up with a chisel. On other work, you can rig up a frame-type holding fixture to make routing safer and easier.

RABBETING SHORTCUT

Routers are great for machining joints and construction details. Basic cabinet and box construction requires various rabbet joints (cutting out a section of the corner of the material). I've found that for many jobs I can make the rabbet cuts for box bottoms and cabinet backs *after assembly.* I use a ball-bearing guided rabbeting bit that leaves the inside corner rounded. These can be chiseled square, or the corners of the bottom or back can be rounded to fit.

A BOX FRAME

Routers can be used to level rough-cut slabs, but this can be difficult if you don't get set up right. Build a box frame and attach an extended base to your router. This is simply a board long enough to fit across the

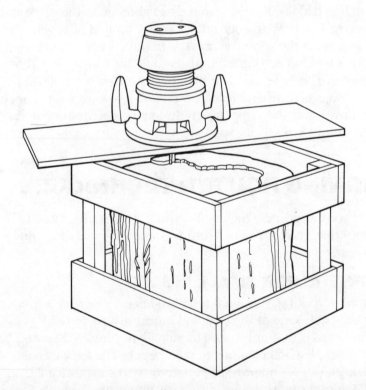

Rough-cut slab can be surfaced by building a box frame that's used with an extended router base (the board under the router). The slab can be held with nails or wedges.

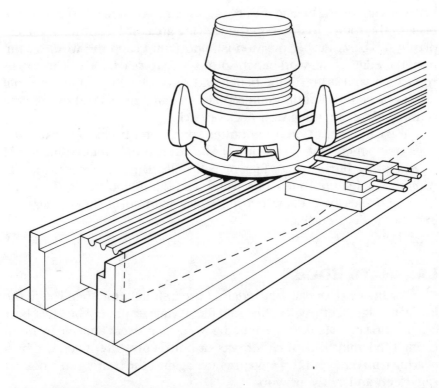

With a homemade jig, you can make square, tapered table legs. The leg is marked for taper, then wedged up so the router takes off the proper amount.

frame. The frame keeps the router bit at a uniform level above the work as long as the wood is secured so it doesn't move. I often need to make the ends of rough-cut logs perfectly flat and parallel to each other. I do this with a box frame built up so I can stand the log on end.

You can set up a similar device with wedges to make taper-cut surfaces. Mark the small end of the piece with layout lines, and wedge the piece up until the bit matches the lines at both ends of the tapered surface. Then run the router over the surface of each of the four tapered surfaces. The same kind of device can be used to cut flutes or other surface decoration into the tapered surfaces.

FREEHAND ROUTING AND CARVING

Once you learn to use the router freehand, you'll end up throwing out many of your templates and patterns. Start on scrap wood and make sure you can see the bit and the area around the cut. Remove the sub-base plate of the router to open up the viewing area, or buy or make a clear plastic sub-base. Proper position is important: clamp the work well in from the edge of the workbench so you have to reach for it. This forces you to put your arms on the bench and/or work (if it's large) so you'll have better control of the router. Position your stool so you can see the action without straining your neck or back.

You can carve wood by mounting your router horizontally near the edge of a bench. But, if you do this, be sure to use suitable high-RPM metal-cutting burrs, rotary files or ball mills. Don't use standard two-wing or single-flute router bits. These can dig in and throw the work. Burrs and files have many cutting edges with small flutes that limit excessively deep cutting.

LAMINATE EDGES

For my work on laminate edges, I use a straight bit, then round the laminate edge lightly with a fine mill file. If you use piloted bits that bear against the laminate during trimming, you can prevent damage by lubricating the laminate with either wax or petroleum jelly. If you use ball-bearing trim bits, apply enough pressure against the bearing so it doesn't spin freely and mar your work.

SHORTCUT FOR SIGNS

Many people, including myself, use their routers to make wood signs. After engraving a sign, I paint the entire board with fast-drying spray paint. Then I use a Surform rasp to clean off the top surface, leaving the letters perfectly painted. You can leave some paint over the board's surface if you want a more rustic effect.

DOOR-HANGING HELP

Many doors end up swinging open or shut because of binding hinge pins. To avoid this, use a door template with your router. Predrill and countersink the holes so the screws will center themselves in the hinges. Start installing the hinges to the door and jamb using only one center screw. Then put the door and jamb hinges together, using a dry lubricant on the pins. Next, with the door open, install the rest of the screws. You'll be surprised at how well the door will work!

MAINTAINING YOUR ROUTER

Once you get a router, track down a local service that can sharpen your carbide bits. The shop should also be able to retip carbide bits for you and sell you ball-bearing pilot guides.

Try to keep the base waxed and free of pitch and gum. You can use lacquer thinner on a small cloth to clean up your bits. I know a person who keeps his bits in a jar of Fantastik all-purpose cleaner. The cleaner helps dissolve the pitch and grime on the bits. I don't like fishing for bits in a jar and prefer having my bits in a drawer, all standing on end.

SAFETY CONSIDERATIONS

Wear goggles or a full face shield, along with good ear protection, when using your router. I'm having problems with my hearing now because I spent too many hours with my head down by a router without proper ear protection. Here are some other safety tips:

- Always unplug the router before making adjustments or changing bits.

- After making adjustments, trigger the router for a quick rev-up. If anything is wrong, this lets you find out before starting any work.

- Don't try to work very small pieces, especially on a router table. Secure small pieces for edge routing with clamps, nails or hot-melt glue.

- Always start the router in the air, not in the work. If you lay it on the work, you will be trying to make the cut in only one revolution instead of several thousand.

- To avoid splitting on edge work, do the end (across-the-grain) edges first. Then do the sides. Experiment on scrap pieces to find the right feed rate. The feed rate on end grain will be slower than when you're going with the grain.

- Feed the work against the rotation of the cutting blade, which is clockwise as viewed from above the router. This means moving the router counter-clockwise around the work on outside edges and clockwise around inside edges.

- Don't use the wood to try to stop a coasting blade. Let the router stop by itself, up and away from the work.

- Figure out a way to control dust and chips. Breathing sawdust is unhealthy. Sawdust also can keep you from doing accurate work by building up under the router or between the router and a straightedge or stop. Investigate router vacuum attachments, or rig up your own system.

A router is a tool anyone can learn to use. I've had seventh-graders turning out projects with it. A router may even launch you on a new career – I get hundreds of letters from people who tell me they've successfully gone into business making custom wood signs with the help of their routers.

CHAPTER 5

MARLYN RODI:

TIPS ON MODIFYING TOOLS

The maxim that you can judge a workman by his tools may be only half right. For example, a beginner tends to think of a tool as a device that does something for you. Experienced craftsmen won't argue with that, but over time they tend to look at tools from a slightly different angle: they realize that a tool is worth more if it lets you get a job done faster, better or in less time.

"There's nothing sacred about it," says Marlyn Rodi, a Los Angeles, California, woodworker. "A tool is only as good as the results it gets you. Since early man first tied a rock onto a stick, he's been figuring out ways to improve tools. We wouldn't have the tools we have today if no one experimented to see if changing them would improve their performance."

Marlyn has what probably could be called the world's smallest complete woodworking shop, built into a 13-by-17-foot single-story garage. A complete array of hand and power tools in such a small area puts a premium on bench top and storage space. His tools are not only selected for their utility, but also for their value versus the storage space they require.

I have a pretty hard-line attitude toward tools. This not only influences what tools I buy, but also what I do with them after I get them home. If there's a way to make a tool easier to use, perform better on a project or more convenient to store, I don't think twice about making alterations or adjustments.

ALTERING TOOLS AND GEAR

If I buy a new sledge or axe, one of the first things I do is slip a short section of pipe, four to six inches long, over the handle up to the head. Then I weld it on to protect the handle right behind the head. Everybody misses the target once in a while, and the most vulnerable part of the handle is right behind the head. This way if I miss, chances are good the pipe guard will keep the handle intact. It's best to use pipe for the guard if you use both sides of the head. If only one side is used, you can get by making a guard of angle iron with the outside corner pointing down. One thing you have to watch when adding pipe or angle iron is that you don't ruin the temper of the tool's edge when you weld the guard into place. I usually keep the edge in a pan of water when I weld; if I get it too hot, I retemper it myself. (Most professional welders can do the job for you without ruining the tempering.) Some folks avoid the problem by wrapping the handle behind the head with ¼-inch welded wire mesh and then applying epoxy cement over it to provide "hazard insurance."

HAMMERS

Smaller tools such as hammers, of course, don't need this kind of doctoring. But with my wooden-handled hammers, I like to bore a hole into the end a couple of inches deep, a little larger than a 16d nail. Then I fill the hole with beeswax. When I'm building and I start to split boards or have trouble driving nails, I first stick the nails into my beeswax reservoir. This usually solves the problem. Sometimes I even use the beeswax for screws that are hard to drive.

Smooth and polished hammers look nice. But when the striking face of the hammer is smooth and slippery, either because it's new or because it's been used a lot, it can slip off from nail heads and cause bent nails left and right. When this happens, I use a piece of emery cloth to roughen up the face. Sometimes I just rub the striking face against a concrete floor or block to roughen it up. Another thing I do with a new hammer, especially cheaper ones, is check the inside edges of the V slot of the claws. If they are not sharp, I use a file to touch them up. This helps me get a grip on nails I want to pull out.

In addition to "touching up" my tools, I also make some modifications. For example, I modify small prybars that are used to remove window and door trim. These tools work best if used in pairs. But the biggest problem is getting the first one in behind the molding or trim. So I buy a cheap one and grind it down quite thin so I can get it behind trim with very little damage. When grinding, I'm careful not to get the tool so hot that its temper is destroyed.

DRILLS AND DRILLING EQUIPMENT

One hassle for just about everybody who uses a power drill is keeping the chuck key handy. Often new drills come with some kind of device to attach the key to the power cord. But the problem is that many of these allow the key to slide down to the end of the cord, just out of arm's reach. You end up wasting time by having to retrieve the cord to get

Attaching a vial level to the top of your hand drill can help you gauge yourself when drilling holes in upright lumber. Small stick-on levels are available for a few dollars.

the key. The solution is to either buy a chuck key holder that stays in one place, or fashion your own improved version. I simply tape the key directly onto the cord, a couple of feet down from the drill. I've seen other people use scrap electrical wire to do this. One thing you don't want to do is damage the cord. For one drill, I made a chuck key holder by welding the key to a washer with a hole just large enough to fit over the cord. I made a cut in the washer so I could bend it open to put it on the cord, then bent it back to a normal position.

I made one addition to a drill that can be considered a luxury. I bought a small stick-on level vial and attached it to the top of the drill. This helps me keep a hole square when I'm drilling into an upright piece of lumber, and it's easier than holding up a square as a guide.

SAWS AND OTHER CUTTING TOOLS

As soon as I got my band saw, table saw and miter saw, I put a good coating of floor wax paste on top of the work tables. This not only protects them from rust, but also helps keep lumber from sticking and binding. Every few months I put another coat on, and these saws look just like new. I also use the wax treatment on my hand saws.

I have a special trick to help me get better use of my circular saws. I scribe lines onto the top of the base, straight out in front of both sides of the blade. From then on I always know where the saw kerf will be. To scribe the lines, I put a square flat up against the blade and make the lines with a sharp awl.

On a saber saw it's helpful to make sure the Allen wrench used for changing blades *is somewhere on your saw* at all times. Newer saber saws come with a clip to hold the little wrench. Mine didn't, so I welded

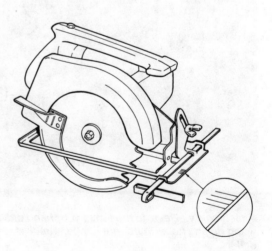

If you take the time to mark your circular saw, you'll always know where the saw kerf will be.

on a metal clip of the kind used to hold screens and storm windows. You could fashion some other holding device, or at the very least, even tape the wrench to the cord. Just make sure it's always there if you need it.

Sawdust is a natural by-product of sawing, and it can be a mess to get rid of. I use a simple disposal system for my stationary table and band saws. I clip ordinary plastic trash can liners under the saws with snap-type clothespins. What doesn't fall into the bags, I just scoop up and throw in. I've experimented with using my shop vac, but found that I can't stand the noise.

SCREWDRIVERS AND FILES

I make it a habit never to throw away an old screwdriver – they come in handy if I need to remove a special type of screw. Screws on some equipment now have square, diamond or other style heads besides the regular plain slot or Phillips slot. If I have screws like these to remove, I fashion my own tool from an old screwdriver. I cut the end off, then use a file to make the end I need. I've even made a tack puller by heating up the end, bending it over about 35°, then filing a V slot into the blade. I've also made my own brake tool from an old screwdriver.

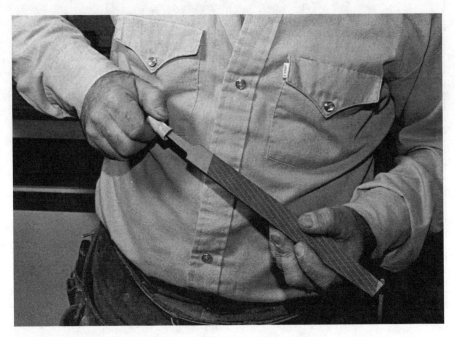

Most files come without handles. You can use a short section of doweling to protect yourself, or even electrical wire nuts of the appropriate size.

Files could use some improvements, too. Though wooden handles are available, most files you see have the bare tang. Bare tangs are not only dangerous, but they also make it difficult for you to use the tool. I drill out sections of wooden dowel to slip over the tangs. You can also use metal door knobs or even large electrical wire nuts to get rid of that sharp point. It's worth the bother.

BUILDING
A GRINDER-POLISHER

It's getting harder to find a good reason to make your own tools these days. But one exception, says Marlyn Rodi, is a grinder-polisher. He made one about six years ago.

My grinder-polisher works just great for all kinds of sanding, sharpening and polishing jobs, and I find myself using it at least once just about every week. Its simple design doesn't require an engineering degree to build. And if you already have an electric

One of the easiest, and most helpful, tools you can make yourself, for less than $20, is a grinder-polisher. With coarse grit, medium grit, emery and leather-covered wheels, it comes in handy for many shop projects.

LADDERS, SAWHORSES AND WORKBENCHES

After falling off a ladder once when a step broke, my advice is to toss out any ladder that isn't 100 percent stable and solidly constructed. Buy heavy-duty ladders, even if they take a little muscle to move around.

I've found it's helpful to put a mark at the center balance point on the sides of both legs of a ladder. This way I can just grab the ladder near

motor and some oak scrap wood, it shouldn't cost you more than about $15 altogether. It might cost you about $3 each for the pillow blocks, then you'll need a couple of pulleys and a shaft.

The housing measures about 30 inches long, 12 inches wide and 12 inches high. The wheels, which I made up myself, are 8 inches in diameter and turn at a low speed of between 500 and 600 RPM. The motor I used was salvaged from a discarded appliance. Unlike a conventional grinder, which has the top part of the wheel turning toward you, this grinder is set up so the top part of the wheels turn *away from you*. If the top of the wheel turns toward you, items can catch and cause injury.

The rod across the front of the housing is to lay a tool against as you use the rig. You really can set up as many wheels as you want; I use four – two with sandpaper of medium and coarse grit, one with emery cloth and one with leather on it. I use the last two quite often for sharpening and polishing things such as knives. I use jeweler's rouge with the leather wheel. It works sort of like a leather strop and puts a mirrorlike finish on whatever I put against it. I sharpen and polish my homemade knives with the rig, sharpen my carving tools and polish metal such as brass parts and decorations. It also works great for polishing and sanding small pieces of wood.

If you want to build a grinder-polisher yourself, but don't want to make your own wheels, check with lapidary supply houses. I've seen them offer wheels of aluminum, padded with rubber, that have a special clamp for attaching sandpaper. If you make your own wheels, the trick is to get the surface of the wheel as smooth and as flat as possible. You want to eliminate the high spots, because these spots wear out first and you'll need to overhaul the wheel in a short time.

I use a ⅛-inch-thick strip of flat rubber over the wheels before attaching the sandpaper. I buy 3-by-23-inch sanding belts, cut them in half and use contact cement to put the strip on the wheel. I roll it on until it overlaps, then cut it so the ends just meet. Then I use a hacksaw to cut off the excess (about ½ inch) on one or both sides.

the mark and it is always in balance when I carry it. Another worthwhile idea is to pad the end of the legs of an extension ladder with foam rubber, old socks or towels to protect your house inside and out.

Sawhorses get cut into and nicked up. No matter what kind you have, you can fasten another 2 × 4 across the top to protect the sawhorse from abuse. You can nail small wooden cleats on the 2 × 4s to hold them in place. I have two wooden sawhorses; one is made a little larger than the other so they will stack nicely in my shop.

Over time most people with a workshop make a number of modifications around the workbench. One thing that works great for me is to have a ceiling outlet in the center of my little shop. This allows me to cluster my stationary tools in the center and plug them in without extension cords running through my work area. I use ordinary screen-door springs over my workbench to keep power cords of portable tools out of the way. If I'm using extension cords, I always tie the two ends into half of an overhand knot before I plug them together. This saves a lot of running and replugging because the cords won't come apart.

WORK GEAR

I don't like the common cloth nail aprons that stores sell for a dollar or two. But if you use them, I've found it helps to put small metal or plastic containers in the pockets so you can keep various nails, screws or small tools separated. I've also found that you can save a pile of money by making your own leather bib-type shop aprons. They're not that difficult to make.

I've also come to pay attention to what I wear when working on projects. Good work clothes have lots of pockets to carry things in. The right kind of footwear is important, too. If, for example, I am working on an extension ladder, I wear good work boots that have a separate heel. The boots protect my arches much more than tennis shoes, and the heels can help me catch the rung in case of a slip.

CREATING THE MOVABLE SHOP

I outfitted my stationary saws and drill press with casters so I can easily move them around my little shop. If you can't afford casters, you can mount a steel rod to the outside of the legs on one side to use as an axle for small wheels. Position the axle so the wheels nearly touch the floor. Then to move the tool, all you do is lift the side opposite the wheels.

I built a cart for my small gas welding outfit and attachments. It rides on casters and when it's not being used I just slide it under my workbench. A small two-wheel utility cart is also handy to have around the shop. I'm

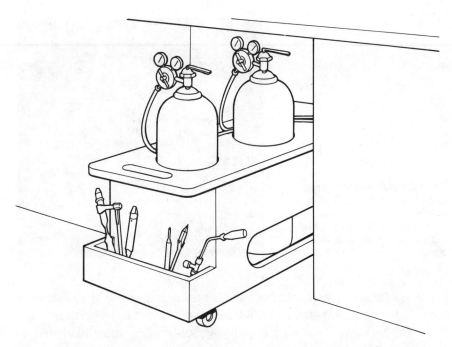

Small roll-around carts with casters can help keep a shop organized and tidy. A cart like this can be made up to house and carry welding supplies, and it stores neatly under a workbench.

continually surprised at how often I use mine. I even strap my shop vac onto the cart when I need to use it in different locations around the shop.

I used to hate my shop vac. I would pull on the hose and the casters would catch on the cord on the floor and the whole thing would tip over. My solution was to simply tie a length of elastic cord around one of the caster legs, up to the hose, about a foot from where it connects to the vac. Now when I pull the vac by the hose, the elastic lifts the casters just enough to hop over the cord.

STORING TOOLS

To make large striking tools such as sledge hammers easier to store, I drill holes in the handles so I can hang them up in a spot that's out of the way, yet convenient. I drill the hole crosswise an inch or so from the end so the head will be flat against the wall. Because the hole is near the end, it doesn't weaken the handle. Before I started doing this, these tools were always in a pile and I wasted time finding what I wanted.

Depending on the design of your shop vacuum, you may find that it tips over easily. One solution is to use elastic cord tied from the hose to the front caster.

The challenge with wrenches and other small tools is to not only keep them organized and accessible, but keep them from getting lost! I finally came up with the idea of painting some of my most likely-to-be-lost tools a bright red. I've also used bright tape and stickers.

TOOLBOXES

Many toolboxes sold for sockets seem as though they were designed to keep sockets mixed up and lying all over. If your box is this way, there's probably too much space above the sockets when the lid is closed. You can fix this with a little foam rubber. With an electric knife, cut a section of foam rubber to fit inside the lid, thick enough to keep the sockets tight in position when the box is closed.

If your sockets are in a pile in a toolbox, take a look at some of the newer, plastic fishing-tackle boxes. I found one that works perfectly as a see-through socket box. I made up label strips to show the size of each of the sockets. I love it!

One thing no one should do without is a drill-bit index box. Before I bought mine, I wasted a lot of time searching for the right bit and trying to read sizes marked on the shank. If you have more than a half-dozen bits, buying an index box will pay for itself many times over in time saved.

One last thought: marked tools, as well as good fences, make good neighbors. I give all my tools an identifying mark with an engraver. If someone borrows a tool, the mark helps remind them to bring it back. I have a five-pound sledge my mother bought for me at a flea market, so I gave that one a big "MOM" on the side of the head!

CHAPTER 6

JOHN JURANITCH:

KEEPING THE EDGES SHARP

    "Let me see your jackknife," John Juranitch says. I draw out my well-worn Schrade Old-Timer and hand it to him. John produces a special edge tester, an invention of his that resembles a pocket pen. In the next few minutes he uses it to tell me how desperately my knife needs sharpening and exactly what is wrong with its edge.

John should know. In certain circles he is known as "the man of edges." His 30-year search for a sharper edge began in a library in Japan. It has culminated in not only the world's first complete book on sharpening edges, but a family consulting and manufacturing business as well. It also led John to gain the world's record for shaving his face with an axe in 14 minutes. He's listed in *The Guinness Book of World Records.*

We sit inside the terminal of the airport in Minneapolis; John is on his way to do some consulting with a large meat-packing firm in the Deep South. With so much to know about honing stones, bevels, stone lubricants and technique, it's a rare person who ever manages to use all of the often conflicting advice to advantage. Yet John pulls out a book he wrote, *The Razor Edge Book of Sharpening,* that tells, in 145 pages, how to put a keen edge on the dullest tool, from plane blades to skinning knives.

We live in a world of edges. But the sad fact is that most of us are so used to dull edges – in the workshop, kitchen and outdoors – that we almost start to believe the tools we use were meant to work that way! But anyone can learn to put a true shaving sharpness onto any edge with the right technique. Learning how to do a good job of sharpening is a worthwhile endeavor. Working with truly sharp edges is much easier, much less tiring and much, much safer than working with dull edges.

DISPELLING THOSE SHARPENING MYTHS

What's the key to a razor-sharp edge? One of the most critical is what I call relief, the gradual tapering of the blade above the edge. Under a microscope a knife edge that might look sharp to the naked eye may actually look like a chisel. To really sharpen that edge, you have to remove some of the blade above the edge before fine-sharpening it.

The ideal is .02 inch thick, ¼ inch above the cutting edge, or as thin as you can get it without having the blade chip. My personal mission in life is to put to rest all the gimmickry and old wives' tales about sharpening, once and for all. Here are some examples of what I mean:

New tools are as sharp as they can be. Wrong. Knives and other tools with cutting edges would be considered dull by a pro as they come from the factory. The reason is that manufacturing and sharpening are really two different professions. An experienced meat cutter, for example, would never use a new blade before sharpening it.

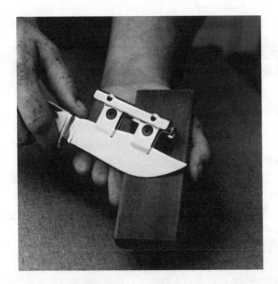

A special guide developed by John to give the perfect angle for sharpening. It's mounted on a blade, which is first ground on a coarse hone in a circular pattern until the burr is felt. Then the sharpening is completed on a fine hone by stroking the blade toward the cutting edge at a 45° angle, flipping over the blade after each stroke. For an extra-keen edge, the guide is moved toward the cutting edge and used with light pressure.

Sharpening stones must always be lubricated. Another myth. This may come as a shock, but if you use oil in sharpening it will (1) cost you money, (2) make a mess and (3) give you an inferior edge. When you use oil in honing, you get a sort of grinding compound, a mixture of oil, grit and metal filings. This passes over the top of the edge, ruining it. The same applies to water.

Precise bevels are critical. To that I say bunk! Show me even a professional who can eyeball the difference between a 19° and a 22° bevel. Just keep the blade at less than a 25° angle when sharpening. Generally, the smaller the angle, the better the edge. To get an idea, take a piece of paper with square edges. Fold it in half at the corner; that's 45°. Fold that angle in half and you have a 22½° angle.

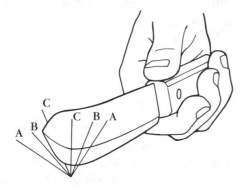

John says that if you plan to use a knife to open up 55-gallon drums or otherwise abuse it, you might want to grind it to a relief such as angle AA. But if you want a sharp knife that's easy to use, he suggests grinding the relief more like CC.

Avoid buying stainless steel. This idea probably got started because Grandma's first stainless steel butter knives weren't very good. I've tested high-carbon steel knives against stainless steel, and stainless can outlast high carbon by as much as four times, plus, they don't rust!

An Arkansas hone is a must. People told me you couldn't sharpen anything without an Arkansas hone. But I've found there's no magic in any hone – it's all in the abrasive. And it doesn't matter if the abrasive is natural, man-made, diamond or anything else. What really counts is grit size, bond hardness and application!

Only butchers need a "steel." A steel is a rod-shaped tool with an abrasive surface. A butcher slides his knife down the surface to touch up the knife. If you don't have a good edge to begin with, steeling won't do much good. But if you have a good edge, steeling will make it better. Just work the blade very lightly on a smooth steel. (The best steel will reflect your face when you look at it.)

All sharpening tools are "gimmicks." The old saying is that if it won't sell, just call it a knife sharpener! Drawers are full of gadgets claimed to sharpen anything. But there are big differences between sharpener kits. Check the hones. One should be very coarse for rapidly cutting a blade; the other, fine for setting the edge. Pass by hones smaller than 5 inches long by 1½ inches wide; you can't get a proper stroke on them.

I run across a lot of people who won't give up the "oil myth." I believed in it myself about 25 years ago. But unless dirt has found its way onto a hone, I've never seen a hone that was plugged up with metal. We have many central sharpening systems in packing plants all over the world, and each is responsible for sharpening hundreds of knives each day. The sharpening machines all run dry. There's been only one or two problems, when the knives were being sharpened without first being cleaned.

Many sharpening stones in hardware stores come with oil. But then, hardware stores don't sharpen knives, they just sell the stones. Years ago, after I discovered better edges with dry sharpening, I asked the head engineer of the largest manufacturer of sharpening stones in the world why he recommended using oil with his stones. He said he didn't really know.

THE THREE MAGIC WORDS

The three magic words in sharpening are *angle, abrasive* and *technique.* If you use them properly, you can get unbelievable results. But it does take practice to learn how to tell *when* an edge is really sharp; in fact, not all professional butchers can do it. That's why I came up with my little

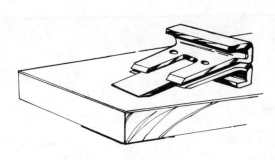

Even single-beveled blades used for wood planes, chisels and jointers come with a poor relief. Only one side of a single-beveled blade is sharpened. To put better relief on the blade, first grind until the edge angle is 25° or less. Then increase the angle of the blade to grind in a good burr. Increase the angle again for a final touch on some fine abrasive. Use the abrasive on the straight side only to remove the burr, and always hold the blade flat.

edge tester. In four simple steps anyone can gauge the sharpness of any edge.

You might think an edge is sharp if you can shave the hair on your arm with it. Not true. Sharp is when the hairs literally pop off your arm without the blade touching the skin!

I think one of the most misunderstood edges is the single-beveled blade such as those in your wood plane, scissors, wood chisel and jointer. In trying to sharpen them, everyone throws up their hands and goes out to buy new ones. But this kind of blade is easy to sharpen once you understand it. Most single-beveled blades come from the manufacturer with too sharp an angle, what we call poor relief, and need to be tapered back more. Instead of about 30°, it should be more like 20° or 25°. The real secret is to *never* touch a hone to its back side. Grind a burr on one side only, then remove the burr by gently working the blade flat on a fine abrasive.

CHAPTER 7

ARNOLD KASTRUP:

MEETING PROJECT CHALLENGES

   One of the best compliments a tradesman can get is when
onlookers remark, "Boy, you sure make that look easy." Practiced
craftsmen will tell you that being able to complete a job
smoothly, and without wasting time, effort or materials, is the
result of years of confronting and solving project problems.
   It's partly the ability to avoid common problems in the first
place that lets a tradesman get jobs done fast, with professional
results. But it's also the ability to solve snags that can develop on
any task, regardless of experience, that separates the men from
the boys.

No one can read enough to know how to solve every possible problem that might crop up on the many projects around the home, at least according to veteran project-tackler Arnold Kastrup. But he believes that anyone can take a creative approach to solve problems as they occur. The idea, he says, is to look problems square in the face and figure out a solution. If it works, you'll be miles ahead the next time around.

Arnold Kastrup is an old-timer who has no degree or impressive paper credentials beyond years of experience. His grandfather was a master woodworker who excelled at making wooden wagon wheels. His own father was another type of craftsman, a harness maker. During World War II Arnold served as a truck mechanic in the Army. Later he worked for a major oil company, repairing everything from hydraulic jacks to domestic oil burners.

At his home in Richfield, Ohio, Arnold talks about the ways he's used tools and other devices to help him get things going right. He says if one thing's helped him more than anything, it's the problem-solving approach he inherited from his family and fine-tuned both on his job and on projects around his home.

Snags can pop up anywhere or anytime, but certain projects will have more than their share. When this happens, you have to haul out one of the best tools you possess – your mind. Lot of times if you just sit back, have a cup of coffee and think about it, you will come up with a way to get it done.

As long as you don't endanger yourself, don't be afraid to come up with your own solutions. Remember, imagination can be more important than knowledge!

IMPROVISING WITH TOOLS

There's no question that having the right tool for the job is best. But often problems that crop up can be solved by using what you already have in a different way. As they say, necessity is the mother of invention. For example, let's say you are drilling holes into masonry, either on the floor or up on a wall, so you can install some kind of anchors. For the anchors to hold well, you must get the dust that results from the drilling out of the holes. The last time I ran into this problem, I came up with a handy solution. I used a piece of old air hose about two feet long. By blowing through the hose I could get the dust out easily without getting it into my eyes.

Using tools and materials in a nonconventional way is how project problems are often solved. For example, silicone sealant can be used to fasten loose wires on cars or trailers.

Or let's say you need to remove shingles from a roof before reshingling. What works great is a flat garden spade. Not only is the spade flat enough to get up under the old shingles, but it has enough of a curve in its handle to give you prybar action. The spade will also let you pop most of the nails out of the roof boards.

There are times when the right tool must be used, and you have no other out. For example, I've found that you can make excellent steak knives, paring knives or even knives for carving wood out of old hacksaw blades. The kind of steel used for the blades holds a cutting edge for a long time. But the problem is how to drill a hole into them for riveting on a handle. If you try a regular steel drill bit, it only burns up. The key is a tungsten drill bit, the kind used to drill holes into glass.

Many other tricks of the trade have to do with using tools in a different way. For example, sometimes you will find you simply cannot get enough leverage with a Crescent adjustable wrench. The first time I ran into this problem, I thought about how plumbers gain leverage on pipe wrenches by using a cheater bar, a section of pipe slipped over the wrench handle. I tried doing the same thing with a Crescent wrench, but found the handle too flat and wide for the pipe. I solved the problem by flattening the end of the pipe into an egg shape so it would fit over the handle. I now keep my leverage pipe in my shop, ready for the next emergency. (If you try this, use caution. With too much pressure, you can hurt yourself or break the wrench.)

Sometimes you don't have a tool and have to figure out how to do without it. Say you are trying to drill a hole in metal, but the bit keeps dancing all over the place because you don't have a center punch. What can you do? You can turn off the drill and push the bit to the metal where you want the hole. Then, while holding the drill firmly down with one hand, use your other hand to rotate the bit clockwise a few turns. This makes a starting hole in the metal, and you're back in business.

SOLVING FASTENER PROBLEMS

It seems that what snags the average handyman most often is problems with fasteners. But here again, certain tricks can get you through the tough spots. For example, if you want to start a screw in a tight place, you can try folding a small piece of paper over the screwdriver blade. The paper may provide enough of a wedge to hold the screw for a "no-finger" operation. Another way is to wrap a turn of roll solder or soft wire around a screw, near the head. When the screw starts, pull the wire away.

You can also start a screw or nut in a hard-to-reach place by putting a small piece of chewing gum on the end of your screw or nut driver. Another way is to use an awl to make a hole big enough to make the screw stick by itself. Still another option is to use tape wrapped sticky-side-out around your finger. Stick the screw or nut to the tape so you can position it with one finger.

Another common problem is driving nails in close or hard-to-reach places. I've found that a good way to manage this is to use a bolt or piece of solid steel rod about ½ by 8 inches. A mechanic calls this sort of device a drift. Put one end of the drift onto the nail head and hit the other end with your hammer. Presto, the nail is driven home, even in impossible situations. This kind of tool comes in handy wherever you can't get a good swing on the hammer because of close quarters, including trying to nail inside gutters. Just remember to wear proper eye protection whenever you're doing this type of work.

NUTS AND BOLTS

Sometimes you need to remove a nut from a bolt in close quarters, but have only open-end wrenches with you. And you find you can't get the wrench onto the nut in the normal fashion because there's no room. What to do? Try standing the open-end wrench up on its end over the nut. Then use either a large screwdriver or another wrench to turn the first wrench. It's worked well a number of times for me, though it can be hard on the wrench.

Taking carriage bolts apart can be a nightmare, too. In the old days these bolts worked fine because they were placed solidly into hardwood. But say you built a picnic table with these bolts a few years ago, and now you have to repair it. As you try to take off the nut, the other end turns in the softwood. What can you do? One thing I've found that works is to cut

Hard-to-reach places can be head-scratchers. You can make oiling electric motors in tight areas easier by soldering a small washer ¼ inch back from the end of your oil can spout. To use with one hand, lift up the cover of the oiler tube with the washer, which also holds the cover back so the spout can be inserted.

a slot in the bolt head by using two blades in a hacksaw. The groove will be wide enough so you can use a screwdriver to hold the bolt as you take off the nut.

Keep your mind open to all the possibilities. When loosening nuts, for example, most of us think of wrenches, not hammers. But if I can't soak a large nut on a rusty bolt with oil or use heat to loosen it, I reach for *two hammers*. It works like this: Hold one hammer against a flat side of the nut, then hit the opposite flat side with the second hammer. This helps expand the nut a wee bit to break it away from the rusty threads. Other ways to free a nut from a rusty bolt include drilling, hacksawing or chiseling. But using two hammers does the job and also saves the nut so you can use it again.

Some projects will really get your mind rolling, especially those involving working alone in high or tight places. But if you think the project through, you'll probably find at least one way to get the job done on your own.

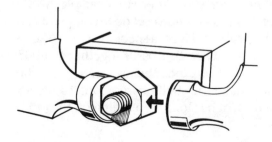

Frozen nut on a bolt? Try using two hammers. Hold one against one side of the nut and strike from the other side. This often will break the nut loose.

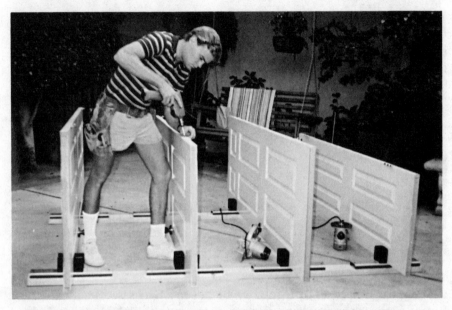

Working alone can take planning and ingenuity. These special BTS (built-to-suit) holders of ⅛-inch aluminum were designed by Marc Archambeau to hold up sheet materials and items such as doors and windows.

WORKING IN HIGH PLACES

The first time I shingled a house, I had a problem getting the shingles up on the roof. I had to hold the bundle on my shoulder with one hand. This left only one hand free to grab onto the ladder. Besides almost breaking my neck, the arches of my feet were killing me.

The second time I shingled a roof, I figured out an easier way: I built myself temporary wooden steps reaching from the ground up onto the roof. That way I could carry the bundles up with both hands, and my arches didn't get sore because I had flat stair treads to walk on. It cost me a buck or two, but was worth it. The steps weren't all that fancy or as wide as regular steps. I made them by fastening treads onto cleats nailed to a pair of 2 × 12s.

Roofs provide challenges in other ways, too. For example, when painting a dormer from my roof, I found I couldn't set down my paint can because of the slope. To solve the problem I built a special holder to keep the can level. I simply nailed two 10-inch-wide boards together at a 90° angle. The end of one board served as a leg, the other as a shelf to set the can on. You can make one easily. Make the shelf board about 10 inches long and the leg board about 5 to 8 inches long, depending on the pitch of your roof.

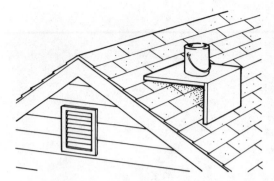

Keeping paint or other cans upright on a sloping roof is easier if you take the time to build yourself a "can holder." You can use scrap lumber, such as two sections of a 10-inch board.

Sometimes working in high places by yourself can make a job seem impossible. For example, I wanted to put drywall on the ceiling of my garage, but I didn't have any help. Believe it or not, I did it by myself! I decided that a pair of "high horses" would do the trick. I built them about three feet wide and high enough so they reached within three inches of the ceiling. To avoid damaging the drywall, I covered them with carpet scraps. Next I made four blocks, about a foot long, out of 2 × 4s, as well as four wedges, also about a foot long, and tapered from less than an inch to about three inches thick.

I then positioned the horses about six feet apart, under where I wanted to put a 4-by-8-foot sheet of drywall. I would slide the drywall on top of the horses. Then, at each corner of the horses (not the drywall), I pushed up with a wood block, at the same time driving a wedge between the block and horses to push the drywall tight up against the ceiling joists.

Once in place, I nailed the sheet at the ends and middle to hold it up. Then I could remove the wedges, blocks and horses and finish the job. I admit it was slow, but it shows that you can do just about anything if you put your mind to it.

PART 2

SETTING UP AND USING A SHOP

CHAPTER 8

ED JACKSON:

ORGANIZING YOUR HOME SHOP

Setting up a good shop can be a lifelong challenge. In fact, it can be five times the job of planning a bathroom and twice as hard as planning a conventional kitchen. The reason is that the best arrangement for you depends on many more factors, such as the space you have available, where it's located, the tools you have now, tools you plan to buy, your interests and how much you can invest as time passes.

How you set up your workplace may actually be influenced by that first power tool you bought 10 years ago, says Ed Jackson, a veteran handyman from St. Paul, Minnesota, who's rearranged his shop dozens of times over the years. "There are always plenty of ways to make better use of the space you have. One thing I've

found is that it's good to realize your workshop doesn't have to look like anyone else's. If it works for you, that's all that counts!" Ed's message is to first consider your own needs, then feel free to be creative.

Basically, shop space is where you find it. Like most "North Country" folks, I set up my home shop in an 11-by-17-foot corner of my basement, just to the side of the stairs. A couple of things that I like are the wide, sliding door to the shop and the large picture window I put in that looks into our family recreation room. The door is 50 inches wide so I can get some pretty big items through it, and it helps keep sawdust and noise from the rest of the basement. And I really appreciated the window when the kids were small. I could get on with my projects and still keep an eye on what they were doing. Now it's great with grandchildren!

SEARCHING OUT SPACE

When space is scarce, every square inch counts. Look for unused space in unconventional places. I purposely left the space between the joists above my basement workshop open for storage. I also use space under the stair treads next to the shop for tool storage. Other places to

Space between the joists of your basement ceiling can be used for storage.

When you're short on space, the idea is to make space do double duty. For example, this table saw extension was adapted so it could also be used as a router table.

look include between open studs, behind doors, under stationary benches, and in rarely used rooms and closets nearby.

With a full complement of hooks, brackets and accessories, pegboard is one of a shop organizer's best tools. I use it wherever I can on my shop's walls. You could even make up pegboard sections that hang off the wall like pages in a book. For an example of how to do this, check the swinging panel displays at lumberyards and home centers. You can use the swinging pegboard for both tools and materials. Instead of buying pegboard hooks, which can be expensive, you might try using short sections of ¼-inch dowels pounded into ¼-inch pegboard to hang your tools.

COMBINATION TOOLS

If you are short on space, consider multifunction tools of the type sold by Shopsmith. One such tool can let you do multiple operations and take the place of a shop full of big power tools: table saw, drill press, horizontal boring machine, lathe and disc sander.

If such a tool is out of your price range, look at the smaller bench-top tools such as table saws, band saws and sanders. You can store these scaled-down versions under the bench and pull them out as needed.

Another option is to make your own combination tools. You could make yourself a sanding table with a disc sander and two belt sanders set up to draw power from a single motor. Another combination tool you can build is a grinder-polisher. You can attach various grit sandpapers and leather onto wooden discs that are fastened to a single jack shaft.

Accessory manufacturers are also coming to the rescue of shop owners who are short on space. In fact, one power drill outfitted with accessories can give you drill press capability and provide power for band saws, sanders, bit sharpeners, wood lathes and other basic tool operations.

Compact work centers let you clamp portable tools onto one table for light-duty work in small spaces. The Work Center, sold by Sears, for example, turns your drill into a drill press, your circular saw into a table saw and your router into a shaper – all on a compact bench, complete with woodworking vise, bench dogs and power switch. Router accessories likewise give you full shop capabilities in minimal space.

PORTABLE WORK SURFACES

You can never get enough work surfaces in a shop. I've found that mobile work surfaces can be handy, especially in a small shop like mine. I converted a metal table to a portable workbench by adding casters. I pull it to where it's needed, or push it out of the way when I need more room for a different project. In addition to the portable workbench, I also have a fold-up bench that's handy for a small shop.

Efficient workshops have one thing in common: plenty of casters to keep everything portable. Consider putting locking casters under all your power tools. They cost money, but pay off big dividends in flexibility. Wheeled tools are easy to rearrange, plus can be dollied over to the workshop door for special operations such as ripping long lumber, or to take advantage of daylight or good weather.

You don't have to get fancy. You could pick up a sturdy used kitchen table, for example, and position it as needed around your shop. Commercial folding workbenches such as the Work-Mate offer portability plus clamping power. Even sawhorses and a sheet of plywood can provide portable, temporary work space.

Unless you have an unlimited budget and an understanding spouse, recycling found fixtures can help you get organized. An old portable dishwasher, for example, can not only provide shelves, but with the heating element plugged in, can also give you a place to warm materials.

You can find used wooden cabinets at garage sales that will work well. And don't overlook those metal kitchen cabinets, the kind popular in the '50s. They provide great storage for materials such as glue, paint, nails and small tools. You can also consider plastic pans used with a slide-in rack and other kitchen organizers. Even items such as plastic milk crates can provide convenient, floor-to-ceiling, cubbyhole storage.

Fold-up workbenches can help solve space problems. This bench, originally designed by Shopsmith, is low-cost, simple to build and easily flips up out of the way.

OUTLETS AND LIGHTS

A modern workshop depends on power, but your electrical system shouldn't be haphazard. In addition to being unsafe, stumbling over cords, using extensions to get to hard-to-reach outlets and dealing with tangled cords slow efficiency and boost frustration levels. If you group power tools in the center of a work area, consider installing overhead outlets – it eliminates running cords through walkways. Install plenty of outlets near workbenches, about one every three feet. Outlets directly over workbenches, cord reels, multiple outlets and continuous outlet strips also help beat cord problems. (Overhead outlets and switches also reduce the chances of little tykes getting into trouble. They can't plug in a tool if they can't reach the outlet. I even put my shop light switch on the ceiling to discourage little kids from going into the shop alone.)

You have to see well to enjoy working on projects. Poor lighting, a common shop problem, is easily corrected with hanging fluorescent fixtures, shaded incandescent lamps and even small portable task lights. If you want to see what you're doing, be generous with lights. You could even line the perimeter of your shop with fluorescent fixtures.

The goal is to avoid all shadows, especially over workbench areas. A good way to monitor light levels: place a small object, such as a pencil, on end to check for shadows. Don't forget to make the best use of any natural light. Consider setting up main work areas near any available windows. Light-colored walls also can brighten up a shop.

ADAPTING YOUR SHOP

If a modification to your shop increases its efficiency, don't hesitate to make one. If you need "port holes" in your garage shop to feed lumber to power tools, cut them out and install hinged trap doors. If you don't have room for lumber, consider a bump-out on one side or use overhead storage boxes attached to the ceiling. Garage workshop additions can range from adding a lean-to for a workbench to doubling its width or length. For example, you could double the length of your garage. Your cars still could go in the new front, while you use the rear part to house shop equipment. By hanging canvas or plastic between the two parts, you can keep sawdust off the cars and easily heat the shop during winter.

If you live in cramped quarters, don't give up. Even if you live in an apartment, you can devise a portable work surface made of plywood to use over a kitchen counter or wet bar. A simple bench such as this can be outfitted as elaborately as you want with tool holders, even a small vise. Another option: the great outdoors. I know some woodworkers who get lots of projects done using a canvas-covered workbench during good weather.

A specially built plywood top for a wet bar or kitchen counter can provide an excellent temporary work surface for home projects.

SHOP COMFORTS

Up to 80 percent of the work you do in your shop can be thinking and planning, and that's why it's a good idea to have a drafting table to work at. I like to keep plenty of paper, drawing tools, tape and other planning aids in the shop for just this reason. Other essentials are a calculator, desk lamp and comfortable stool.

I like to take time to provide myself a few other creature comforts, such as mats for standing on the concrete floor, a small radio and a clock. If you have kids who like to be in the shop, set up a place for them so they'll be out of the way of power tools, yet feel included.

Don't be chintzy with small tools. Small hand tools such as pliers, screwdrivers and open-end wrenches have a habit of either disappearing or being in the wrong place when you need them. A solution is to buy a few more of each. I got tired of running after screwdrivers and the like for small projects around the house, so now I have several sets of varying degrees of sophistication. I keep one in the kitchen, one in the garage, one in each vehicle and one in the shop. The time I save running around hunting them down has more than paid for the extra tools.

One of my workshop pet peeves is not being able to find one of the hundreds of small parts I need for a project. So I try to make sure they are visible, accessible and organized. Small-parts cabinets are one answer. I'd suggest trying to stick with clear plastic drawers. Then mount cabinets at eye level so you don't have to shuffle through all the drawers to find what you need. Small shelves between studs are also useful, and baby-food jars are almost indispensable. Old cake pans are good for storing odds and

If you don't have room for a drafting table, consider this idea. Hinge a section of hollow-core door under a wall cabinet and outfit it with screw-in legs.

ends; they're flat, so you can find items quickly.

Hardest of all is avoiding collecting junk. No matter if your shop is large or small, a pack-rat habit can lead to reduced efficiency and wasted space. If you are cramped on space, there's no way around it: you need to get in the habit of throwing things away. At the very least, regularly sort like-sized lumber into piles. But don't make the piles too big; you won't use what you can't see. If necessary, store materials such as big sheets in other places. Plywood and long lumber, for example, can be kept in the garage and cut to approximate length before being brought down to a basement workshop.

KEEPING IT SAFE

As I get older and have grandchildren, I find I'm more mindful of shop safety, including good eye protection. If you don't like goggles, or if they conflict with your glasses, try one of the full-face shields. Some other general safety tips:

- Use push sticks, instead of your fingers, when feeding wood into tools.
- Keep kids out of the shop when you are sawing, routing or turning wood.
- Keep the shop floor free of clutter that could trip you up at a bad time.
- Don't discard those safety shields that come with your equipment; they are supplied for good reasons.

CHAPTER 9

ROBERT TUPPER:

HOMEMADE SHOP SOLUTIONS

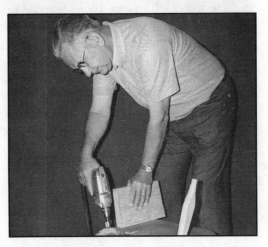

You might say Robert Tupper and his wife, Alice, had a "workshop romance." Alice started coming over to Robert's parents' workshop to finish projects when they were both still in high school. They discovered two things. One, they liked working on projects together. Two, they liked one another. Their time together over the workbench led to marriage and two children, Kathleen and Donald. It also led to a life of shared shop work.

After Robert returned from duty during World War II, he began teaching woodworking at the high school in Canton, South Dakota. Robert recently retired from his job as principal of the school, after nearly 40 years, to devote full time to shop work and occasional sojourns across the country in a Ford van he and Alice customized for comfortable camping.

Over the years, Robert has come across various ways to make his and Alice's shop jobs more efficient. "We don't claim to have all the answers for shop projects," Robert says, smiling. "We like to say there are three ways of getting a job done: the right way, the wrong way and the way we do it!"

Our basement workshop has a 40-year collection of tools. One thing that's helped me get organized is a special workbench Alice and I built years ago. The bench has solved the problem of how to keep the tools within reach, without having to stretch to get tools on a wall-mounted rack.

I think it's a good idea, when building benches, to think twice about their heights. Generally benches are about four inches below waist level. But another factor is the height of power tools in your shop. We built our main workbench to exactly match the height of our table saw. That way the bench can be used for extra support when sawing oversized material. It's something to keep in mind, even if you are deciding how to set up a power miter saw in your shop. For example, you could set it into a dropped section of your workbench. Then the saw's table height will match the bench surfaces on either side for support of long boards.

There are other things, too, that you can do to increase your efficiency on projects in your shop. One is to find adequate storage space.

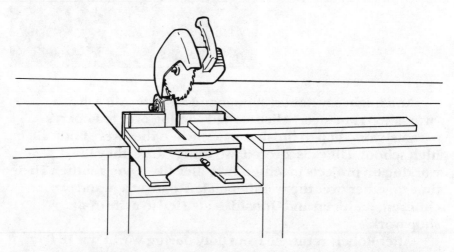

There are two ways miter saws can be positioned on a bench to facilitate cutting long material. One way is to build the surface up around the saw; another, shown here, is to drop the saw down from the bench surface.

CREATING STORAGE

It can be one thing to find a spot to store something, but quite another to find what you have stored. Two ways to beat the problem for tools is to use small rolling carts and special tool carriers, which are good alternatives to the classic carpenter's toolbox. For smaller parts, we like our special bank of small wooden drawers under our main workbench. A cutout in the top of the bench opens directly over two drawers. We can move a drawer with needed parts to the top level, then remove special covers over the cutout for instant access.

Our master workbench can also be easily moved anywhere around the shop. It has two straight three-inch casters under one end, two three-inch swivel casters under the other. Unless you have a bench like ours, you can try to keep as many tools on the walls as you can for easier organization and access. Or build yourself carts that roll out of the way or special carriers for the tools used only occasionally, such as chainsaw equipment.

Twenty-five long, divided drawers hold assorted nails, screws, short dowels, hinges, catches and electrical parts in this bench. Each drawer can be moved up to the top of the bank to line up under an opening in the bench top.

TOOL BOARDS

We've built what I call tool boards – sections of pegboard designed for slide-in storage under the workbench. Related tools go on separate boards; one for metalworking tools, one for upholstery tools, another for measuring tools and so forth. Each can be pulled out and set across the front of the bench, one at a time. If only one tool is needed, its board is pulled out just far enough to get it, then the board is pushed back in.

You can also build these tool boards in pairs. You could set them side by side when you store them on top of your workbench, then latch them together back-to-back to make a balanced tool carrier. Or you can hang smaller versions of these tool boards on the wall. It all depends on what

Tool boards like this one can be made of ½-inch pegboard and kept under a workbench. Keep related tools grouped on individual boards.

This movable rack holds plywood and dimensional lumber in the shop. It's eight feet long, 24 inches wide and 60 inches high. A caster centered on each end supports whichever end is the heavier.

kind of space you have available. For example, you could also use the space under your workbench for two-drawer file cabinets. You could put manuals, plans and drawings in some. Others could hold hand and power tools.

LUMBER RACKS

Space for materials is crucial. Our solution is a rack on casters, divided into sections for lumber of varying lengths and widths. The idea can be tailored to any size shop. You can also solve the problem with overhead racks of pipe that hang about 1½ feet down from the ceiling. You can use floor flanges screwed to the joists and ¾-inch pipe sections screwed to tees and elbows. Or you can reserve one side of your shop for storage. A narrow rack, about 6 feet high and 1 foot wide, can work well. You could even build another small bench to the inside of it, complete with vise and grinder.

ADAPTING TOOLS

Sawdust, wood chips and foul air drag down shop efficiency and can be unhealthy as well. A shop vacuum is a must. Because it makes cleanup easier, you're likely to do it more often. Shop vacuums can be hooked up directly to tools or to a permanent vacuum line.

We adapted our power miter saw to direct sawdust away from the wall in back by attaching a two-inch PVC elbow and tube to the saw's sawdust outlet. I wired a light coil spring to the saw to hold the loose-fitting elbow in place. The other end of the pipe rides in a large U-shaped support. The saw can swing to either side and the pipe stays in place.

WOOD LATHE EXTENSION

We keep an eye out for how we can adapt tools to make them work better for us. One example is our wood lathe. Most home shop wood lathes have a capacity of under 36 inches, yet occasionally longer turnings are needed. A solution we came up with was building an extension onto ours. I built it using ¼-by-2-by-2-inch angle iron for the bed and 2-by-2-inch square tubing for the legs. The tail stock slides right along the angle-iron bed. Crosspieces of 1-inch angle iron, welded to the flats of the 2-inch angle irons, support the bed. Additional supports of ⅜-inch rod, welded between the bed angles and cross angles, stiffen the bed.

This lathe bed extension was made up for turning six-foot-long posts. The lathe extension bed is of ¼-by-2-by-2-inch angle iron and the legs are 2-by-2-inch square stock.

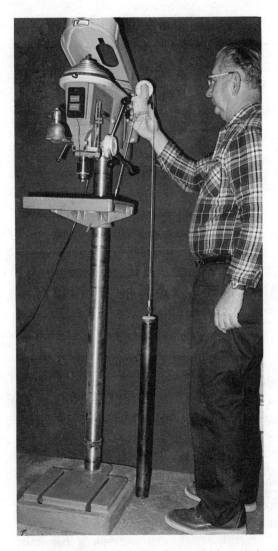

The components of the counterweight system include the pulley bracket that fits in the top of the column, the cable and the lead-filled pipe.

I used ⅜-inch bolts through the angle supports to hold the extension to the lathe table. For leveling, I made a ½-inch hole in the cross tube of the leg and welded a ⅜-inch nut over its center to accept a carriage bolt. Turning the bolt takes care of uneven floors and makes the lathe solid.

I originally made the extension to turn a half-dozen six-inch-diameter posts that were six feet long. When I'm not using it, I take the extension off and store it out of the way.

DRILL PRESS COUNTERWEIGHT

Another example of making a tool easier to work with is the counterweight I made for our drill press. The cast-iron table of our drill press,

Here you can see how the pulley bracket fits on top of the column. One end hooks to the lead weight inside the column; the other to the drill table.

like most all of them, was difficult to raise by hand. So we added a counterweight to balance the weight of the table. We hooked a $\frac{3}{32}$-inch steel cable to a $\frac{1}{8}$-inch-thick strip of iron that fits over the clamp bolt on the table. The cable passes between the motor frame and drill press head to a pulley mounted above the drill press column.

I made the pulley frame out of wood turned with a shoulder and stub for a close fit in the top of the column. A notch in the top of the plug holds the wooden V pulley. The 2½-inch pulley has a ¼-inch-deep round-bottomed V in the edge. A force-fitted piece of ⅜-inch copper tube in the pulley turns on a $\frac{5}{16}$-inch bolt axle. A ½-inch hole in the plug under the edge of the pulley lets the cable through to the counterweight inside the column.

I adjusted the length of the cable to pull the table within 2 inches of the chuck when the weight rests on the floor. We made the counter-weight at a local service station. First we capped the bottom end of a 31-inch length of 2¼-inch exhaust tailpipe, then filled it with discarded lead wheel-balance weights. Then we heated the pipe with a gas torch to melt the lead. (We made sure we had good ventilation.) The metal clamps on the weights floated to the top as the lead melted.

We then welded a metal cap with an eyebolt to the top of the lead-filled pipe. The weight and attached cable were installed by laying the drill press on its side and slipping the weight in the top of the column and threading the cable through the pulley plug, pulley and motor frame to the table strap iron. The table was lowered on the column to take up the cable slack before the drill press was tipped back upright.

The counterweight weighs 50 pounds, or 1.6 pounds per inch. We sometimes add an auxiliary table to the drill press for special jobs, and the combined weight is just over 50 pounds. The counterweight makes it easy to adjust the tables.

PROJECT HELPERS

If there's a way to come up with something to make things easier on ourselves, we do it. For example, we fashioned a special metalworking corner for our main workbench. If you tend to do a lot of bending and pounding in your shop, you will find one useful. Here's how we made it.

First we found a short section of large angle iron (about ⅜ by 6 by 6 inches) and fastened it to one corner of our workbench. Then we drilled assorted holes in the plate for bending round metal. We even added lips to the holes to give us a fast way to punch glue grooves in dowels. We welded a large-diameter shaft stub to the outside edge, level with the top, to make easy work of those rounding jobs. We really use it a lot.

Sometimes the better solutions are the simple ones. For example, if you've ever tried recaning a chair, you know that getting the spline loose from the old seat can be quite a job. We thought about this and came up with a special, handy little fulcrum to use in conjunction with a ⅛-inch chisel.

To make the fulcrum we just drilled a ½-inch hole in the side of a 2-inch length of 1-inch-diameter dowel. By placing the chisel through the dowel we could pry up and down on the chisel handle to get the spline out. We'd just keep working the dowel forward to lift the old spline out in long strips. (We find that it's best to soak the old glue around the spline with brown vinegar for a couple of hours before starting to peel it out.)

Or, let's say you need to make those hundreds of holes for shelf supports. We needed to do this once, so we thought about it and came up with a special hole-drilling guide made of flat iron. We drilled ¹⁷⁄₆₄-inch holes, staggered at 1-inch intervals on alternate sides of a centerline of a ⅛-by-1-inch flat-iron strip. Then we drilled a ¹⁄₁₆-inch hole on the centerline near each end of the strip so we could tack in ¾-inch brads to keep the strip in place on the side of a cabinet.

A special guide made of strips of flat iron can make drilling shelf support holes much easier. When drilling, you can make a depth gauge for your drill from a section of dowel.

We used tape to indicate where the top and bottom holes were to be drilled. To make holes the right depth, we made a depth gauge by drilling a $^{17}/_{64}$-inch hole the full length of our drill bit through a section of $^5/_8$-inch dowel. Then we cut the dowel off to allow the bit to come through by $^5/_8$ inch. This bit stop helped us drill holes to the $^1/_2$-inch depth for the $^1/_4$-inch shank used for typical shelf supports.

You can also come up with ways to help improve the accuracy of hand tools. Once I was faced with converting five conventional chairs to captain's chairs and I was finding it difficult to drill the holes for the spindles at the right angle and depth. So I made myself a guide from a short piece of 2×8, with one edge beveled to give the correct angle. I cut the end of the piece at the angle that the spindles leaned. By holding the guide next to the hole position, I could line up the spade bit with the end of the guide to drill the hole. I used a piece of tape on the drill bit to help maintain the correct depth as I drilled the hole.

MORE SOLUTIONS

We like to keep our eyes open for homemade solutions whenever we work in the shop. For example, once we were making up a large quantity of picture frames and faced the problem of how to clamp the frame parts together. So we made some clamps out of sections of a heavy upholstery coil spring. (Most upholstery shops have new replacement springs or might even save a broken spring for you if you ask.) I ground through the spring with a grinder to form semicircles with sharp points on the ends of the curves. (You have to be careful when grinding so the springy material won't slip and get caught in the wheel.) Then we clamped the curved, pointed spring in a vise and used Vise-Grip pliers to bend the point at nearly right angles. (Again, you have to be careful because the points are sharp!)

We made the bending easier by heating the bend spot red-hot with a torch. (You have to cool it at once so the point and curve won't lose its temper.) One coil spring will yield two or more sets of clamps. To use them, put glue on your picture-frame parts, grasp the spring clamp at the bends and put one point against one side of the corner. Then pull the other bend open while holding the clamp so it doesn't move the frame. Put the second point against the frame and release the tension. There won't be much movement but you can see the joints tighten up. After the corners have been clamped it's easier to go back and repull the first clamps. The frame will stay together. We always double-check the cor-

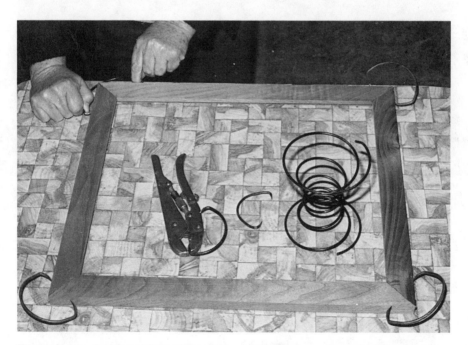

These picture-frame holding clamps are made from discarded upholstery springs. You need to be careful when making and positioning these—the ends are very sharp.

ners with a square, and if needed, the corners can be squared up by pushing opposite corners toward each other.

Another solution we came up with is the system we use to mark the furniture we work on for other people. We made up a small logo with a little "idea" light bulb, hammer and the words "Wood Projects Since 1936" and had it made into a rubber stamp. We use the stamp, plus two others, on all the projects that go through the shop. A second stamp has the date and whether it was a repair, remodeling or refinishing job. A third stamp has our name and address on it. Our stamps serve several purposes. They indicate what was done and when. And because we agree to take care of any problems that might develop, the stamping keeps everyone honest.

CHAPTER 10

RUSS BARNARD:

ADVICE FROM A SHOP BOSS

Russ Barnard wouldn't trade jobs with anyone. He's one of those guys who, after putting in a full day in the shop, will go home, grab a bite to eat, and head back to the shop "just to mess around."

Russ is shop foreman at the Kuempel Chime Clock Works, a 70-year-old company that was one of the first in the country to offer clock kits to the home builder. The shop is set back in the woods, off a little blacktop road that winds through the many back bays of Lake Minnetonka, Minnesota. Outside, in front, is a sign that reads, "Visitors Welcome!"

Thousands of past and potential clock-kit builders have found their way here, taking advantage of the opportunity to actually visit the factory. The front showroom is a clock-builder's paradise: glimmering, finished hardwood; shining glass; hundreds of precision clock movements ticking away and chiming in unison on the hour, half-hour and quarter-hour.

But the action is out back in the shop where the hundreds of intricate parts from walnut, cherry and oak are worked. Russ Barnard has been at the helm of the clock-parts shop for nearly a decade now, supervising the use of a shop full of equipment all hooked up to an elaborate sawdust collection system. On a rather hot, Friday summer afternoon, after the week's work has wound down, Russ sits down and offers some tips that could help any beginner, and probably a few woodworking professionals, as well.

I'm 58 now, and the first 25 years of my working life I was a floor layer and cabinetmaker. So when Audrey McGregor, the owner of this place, asked me to replace the former shop boss who retired in his 70s, I already had a pretty good working knowledge of using tools and getting jobs done.

But one thing's for sure, shop savvy doesn't come all at once. A shop professional's total know-how builds up over the years, bits and pieces at

You can duplicate patterns easily, without a pencil or other marker. Just use a plain sheet of paper and press around the outline of the object.

a time – a tip here, an idea there, experimenting and failing, improvising and succeeding. Many good shop techniques are not original ideas, but adaptations of knowledge that have been passed down through the generations.

USING SOME SLICK SHOP TRICKS

What's the best way to make a pattern from an existing piece that you want to duplicate? Well, there's a slick procedure that makes you wonder why you never thought of it yourself. Let's say you want to duplicate the shape of a small part, say a push stick. With this method you don't need a pencil, carbon paper or even a rule; just a sheet of white paper and an awl.

To duplicate the shape, simply lay the paper on top of the piece, then rub around the edges with your fingers. The outline of the piece takes form on the paper. Then you have some choices. To duplicate the pattern, lay the paper with the outline on top of the wood you plan to use. Get out the awl and punch little holes through the paper and into the wood. If you are working with straight lines, holes at each end of the line are enough.

For curves, punch the holes closer together. Take the pattern off, "fill in the dots," and you're ready to cut. I usually make the holes to the outside of the pattern line, then I cut directly through the holes. You can even use this trick to copy patterns fast and accurately from existing pieces of large furniture.

EASY MEASURING

There's also a trick to sharpen up your measuring. It's tough to make precise measurements smaller than, say, $\frac{1}{16}$ inch. So, if you need a bunch of similar parts, how do you make sure they measure precisely the same down to $\frac{1}{16}$ inch? The trick is to measure a number of pieces at once, say four or eight at a time.

Measuring a number of pieces at a time will multiply any error, making it easy to see how much the group of boards is off without dealing with ultrasmall fractions. Say I'm measuring eight pieces, all of the same intended width, and find all eight are $\frac{1}{8}$ inch wider than they should be. By dividing $\frac{1}{8}$ by eight, I know I have to shave $\frac{1}{64}$ inch from each one. This is a good way to double-check your setup.

To get even more precise with a tape measure, I never use the end, but start at the one-inch mark. I try to make sure this mark is at the exact edge of an outside board. Then I'll measure across and subtract the one inch from the reading.

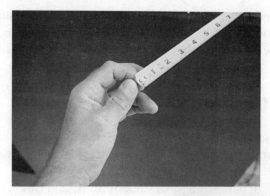

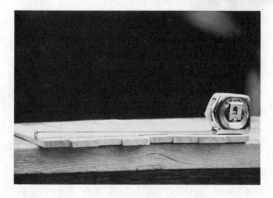

The key to making super-accurate measurements of small pieces is to measure a number of them at once. Then just divide the error by the number of pieces measured.

CLEAN MARKING

Another thing I discovered when I came here is that a good marking system is essential in a production shop such as this one. Other than for occasional measuring, you won't see carpenter pencils or even lead pencils used to mark wood here. What we use instead is common white blackboard chalk, the kind you can buy at the store. The main advantage is that chalk wipes off easily without a visible mark. We use special marks to indicate whether the edges and ends of wood parts have been cut to size. For example, I'll make a mark similar to a backwards L to indicate that an edge has been run through the jointer and is square to the end.

THE BEST PUSH STICKS

We make ourselves a lot of smaller items we need right here in the shop, things such as push sticks for sawing and jointing. Whether you buy or make your own push sticks, there's more to them than meets the eye. Two things are important: having a shape that allows you to get a good, firm grip and having a shape that extends far enough over the board you cut so you can easily keep it firmly against the table and fence.

Push sticks don't have to be fancy. You can make them quickly on a band saw. Just remember that it's the shape at each end that's important. If you decide to buy push sticks of metal, avoid those with short stubby ends. You can't keep enough pressure on the board with them.

SETTING UP EQUIPMENT

In a woodworking shop where expensive hardwoods are handled, you'd expect to find a multitude of special woodworking bench vises. We have some of those, but our crew also uses conventional machinist's vises. They're converted for working with wood by using simple, specially built wood inserts that ride the shank of the vise and provide "soft jaws" for holding wood. They're quick and easy to make, keep jaw marks off your project and stay in place surprisingly well. The wood inserts need to be specially built for your vise. Those used on a typical vise are about eight by eight inches, cut out to set over the vise shank and fitted on the back side to fit the vise jaws. In some cases you can get by with one insert.

We're also careful about how we position a vise on the bench. You can save yourself a lot of hassle if you take the time to position the vise to work with you instead of against you. If it's set up right it can be used in conjunction with a spacer made of a common 2 × 4. We have one vise positioned so that, with the spacer set against the back jaw, work can be set in front of the bench and reach all the way to the floor for added stability.

But what happens when you want your work to be set on the bench? Simple. Just slip the 2 × 4 spacer against the front jaw, and the work lines up so the bench can be used for support. It's such a simple thing, but can really make your bench work much easier. To position the vise, all you have to do is set your spacer up against the back jaw and line up the front of the spacer with the edge of the bench. You're in business.

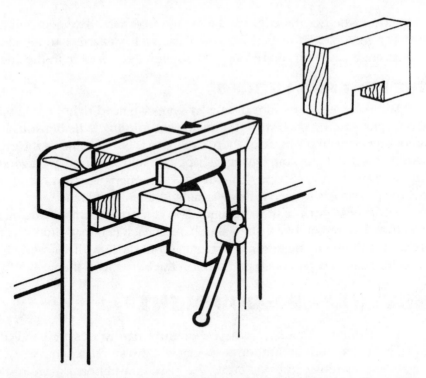

A vise, positioned like this, can be used with a spacer to hold projects that reach the floor. Or, with the spacer against the front jaw, the vise can hold projects on the top edge of the bench.

THE WORKBENCH

Another thing you'll notice in our shop is that there's not a store-bought workbench in the place. Instead, most of our benches are built of 1 × 8s and 2 × 4s. The 1 × 8s are cut 32 inches long, then run through a table saw at an angle to make up the corner legs. The side of one leg is cut ¾ inch narrower than the other. This is done to allow for the ¾-inch thickness of the stock so when butted against each other, both corner legs will be the same width.

Once the corner legs are cut, we simply build two rectangular frames of 2 × 4s and, using drywall screws, fasten the legs to the frames. One frame is flush with the top; the other about 12 inches above the floor. Then we use ¾-inch plywood over the top and fit ½-inch plywood or flakeboard over the bottom 2 × 4 frame to make a shelf. If we plan to use the bench for gluing, we'll lay a piece of Masonite on top of the bench. We make the benches fast; in fact, we have a tapering jig made up to cut the legs on a table saw. The benches are super sturdy, look good and are cheap to make.

We also came up with a solution for working on tall projects, such as the hoods of grandfather-clock cabinets that reach more than seven feet in the air: a sliding "box" step built into the end of one of our low-cost workbenches. Now when working on the top of a clock frame, we just pull out the step and jump on top. Not only does the step eliminate sore muscles, but it lets us do a better job because we can see what we are doing.

The step is a simple wooden box of ¾-inch stock with a cover that overhangs the box by 1½ to 2 inches. Slots are cut into the workbench legs to accommodate the cover overhang. A simple oval hole at the front side of the box provides a pull handle.

Another time-saver is our permanently mounted router jig. If you have a routing jig that you find yourself dragging out and mounting on a bench time and again, you might consider our solution. We had the same problem with a large jig used to edge-finish the doors of grandfather clocks. So we took the jig and mounted it to one side of the bench with double-action hinges. When the jig is not being used, it just hangs down

Hinging larger jigs for routing can save time. This jig, for clock doors, hangs down alongside the workbench when not in use.

and is latched to the side of the bench. When we want to use it, we simply unlatch it and flip it up and over. When used, it lays flat and solid on the bench.

CONTROLLING WOOD MOISTURE

It's a fact that 99 percent of the problems in fitting matching wood parts together in the shop are the result of improper humidity levels. We try to keep our wood at 8 percent moisture content. To do that, we need to keep watch over the humidity levels in our shop. You can easily do the same by making a hygrometer like the one I use.

All you need are two inexpensive thermometers, an old plastic medicine bottle and less than half a foot of wicking (you can buy wicking at a drugstore). Mount the thermometers side by side on a board, with the medicine bottle in the center, below the thermometers. Put water in the medicine bottle, then cut a hole in the cap of the bottle and run the wicking from the bottom of the bottle out and up to one of the thermometers. Slip the wicking over the base of the glass.

Now you will be able to make your own "wet-bulb" readings. To do this, make yourself a paddle to fan the thermometers. After a minute of fanning, the thermometer with the wick (the wet-bulb thermometer) will have a lower reading than the dry-bulb thermometer because of evaporation. By using the readings on both thermometers, in conjunction with the conversion chart on pages 92 and 93, you can determine the relative humidity and the percent moisture equilibrium (the moisture content you can expect in the wood over time at current conditions).

I have a target of 68°F and 42 percent relative humidity, which results in an 8 to 10 percent equilibrium moisture content.

You can make your own shop hygrometer with two thermometers, a plastic bottle and some wicking. Fan the thermometers for a minute, then take the readings. See Table 10-1 to convert your readings.

This little device, adapted from a key-ring holder, fits on your shoe and grounds out static electricity.

STATIC ELECTRICITY

Although you want to control the humidity in your shop, keep in mind that too little moisture in the air during winter can cause a minor, but irritating, problem: static electricity generated while using equipment such as a band saw or sander. It isn't so much that the electric charges hurt – they just come so unexpectedly that it is easy to lose control of your work. One day I got an idea to solve the problem: rig up a small clip, such as the kind used to clip key rings on a belt, with a short

(continued on page 94)

USING THE HYGROMETER CONVERSION CHART

To use the conversion chart on pages 92 and 93 to determine the relative humidity and equilibrium moisture content (EMC) of your workshop, first take the readings on your thermometers. Let's say the dry-bulb temperature is 70°F and the wet-bulb temperature is 55°F. The wet-bulb depression (the difference between the two temperatures) is 15°. To find the EMC, locate the 15°F wet-bulb depression column, across the top of the table, and follow it downward until it intersects the 70°F dry-bulb temperature line, which runs down the left-hand side of the table. The relative humidity is 36 percent and the EMC at the intersection (in italic type) is 7.2 percent.

(continued)

TABLE 10-1

Dry-bulb temperature (°F)	Wet-bulb depression (°F)													
	1	2	3	4	5	6	7	8	9	10	11	12	13	14
30	89	78	67	57	46	36	27	17	6	-----	-----	-----	-----	-----
	15.9	*12.9*	*10.8*	*9.0*	*7.4*	*5.7*	*3.9*	*1.6*	-----	-----	-----	-----	-----	-----
35	90	81	72	63	54	45	37	28	19	11	3	-----	-----	-----
	16.8	*13.9*	*11.9*	*10.3*	*8.8*	*7.4*	*6.0*	*4.5*	*2.9*	*0.8*	-----	-----	-----	-----
40	92	83	75	68	60	52	45	37	29	22	15	8	-----	-----
	17.6	*14.8*	*12.9*	*11.2*	*9.9*	*8.6*	*7.4*	*6.2*	*5.0*	*3.5*	*1.9*	-----	-----	-----
45	93	85	78	72	64	58	51	44	37	31	25	19	12	6
	18.3	*15.6*	*13.7*	*12.0*	*10.7*	*9.5*	*8.5*	*7.5*	*6.5*	*5.3*	*4.2*	*2.9*	*1.5*	
50	93	86	80	74	68	62	56	50	44	38	32	27	21	16
	19.0	*16.3*	*14.4*	*12.7*	*11.5*	*10.3*	*9.4*	*8.5*	*7.6*	*6.7*	*5.7*	*4.8*	*3.9*	
55	94	88	82	76	70	65	60	54	49	44	39	34	28	24
	19.5	*16.9*	*15.1*	*13.4*	*12.2*	*11.0*	*10.1*	*9.3*	*8.4*	*7.6*	*6.8*	*6.0*	*5.3*	
60	94	89	83	78	73	68	63	58	53	48	43	39	34	30
	19.9	*17.4*	*15.6*	*13.9*	*12.7*	*11.6*	*10.7*	*9.9*	*9.1*	*8.3*	*7.6*	*6.9*	*6.3*	
65	95	90	84	80	75	70	66	61	56	52	48	44	39	36
	20.3	*17.8*	*16.1*	*14.4*	*13.3*	*12.1*	*11.2*	*10.4*	*9.7*	*8.9*	*8.3*	*7.7*	*7.1*	
70	95	90	86	81	77	72	68	64	59	55	51	48	44	40
	20.6	*18.2*	*16.5*	*14.9*	*13.7*	*12.5*	*11.6*	*10.9*	*10.1*	*9.4*	*8.8*	*8.3*	*7.7*	
75	95	91	86	82	78	74	70	66	62	58	54	51	47	44
	20.9	*18.5*	*16.8*	*15.2*	*14.0*	*12.9*	*12.0*	*11.2*	*10.5*	*9.8*	*9.3*	*8.7*	*8.2*	
80	96	91	87	83	79	75	72	68	64	61	57	54	50	47
	-----	*21.0*	*18.7*	*17.0*	*15.5*	*14.3*	*13.2*	*12.3*	*11.5*	*10.9*	*10.1*	*9.7*	*9.1*	*8.6*
85	96	92	88	84	80	76	73	70	66	63	59	56	53	50
	-----	*21.2*	*18.8*	*17.2*	*15.7*	*14.5*	*13.5*	*12.5*	*11.8*	*11.2*	*10.5*	*10.0*	*9.5*	*9.0*
90	96	92	89	85	81	78	74	71	68	65	61	58	55	52
	-----	*21.3*	*18.9*	*17.3*	*15.9*	*14.7*	*13.7*	*12.8*	*12.0*	*11.4*	*10.7*	*10.2*	*9.7*	*9.3*
95	96	92	89	85	82	79	75	72	69	66	63	60	57	55
	-----	*21.3*	*19.0*	*17.4*	*16.1*	*14.9*	*13.9*	*12.9*	*12.2*	*11.6*	*11.0*	*10.5*	*10.0*	*9.5*
100	96	93	89	86	83	80	77	73	70	68	65	62	59	56
	-----	*21.3*	*19.0*	*17.5*	*16.1*	*15.0*	*13.9*	*13.1*	*12.4*	*11.8*	*11.2*	*10.6*	*10.1*	*9.6*
105	96	93	90	87	83	80	77	74	71	69	66	63	60	58
	-----	*21.4*	*19.0*	*17.5*	*16.2*	*15.1*	*14.0*	*13.2*	*12.6*	*11.9*	*11.3*	*10.8*	*10.3*	*9.8*
110	97	93	90	87	84	81	78	75	73	70	67	65	62	60
	-----	*21.4*	*19.0*	*17.5*	*16.2*	*15.1*	*14.1*	*13.3*	*12.6*	*12.0*	*11.4*	*10.8*	*10.4*	*9.9*
115	97	93	90	88	85	82	79	76	74	71	68	66	63	61
	-----	*21.4*	*19.0*	*17.5*	*16.2*	*15.1*	*14.1*	*13.4*	*12.7*	*12.1*	*11.5*	*10.9*	*10.4*	*10.0*
120	97	94	91	88	85	82	80	77	74	72	69	67	65	62
	-----	*21.3*	*19.0*	*17.4*	*16.2*	*15.1*	*14.1*	*13.4*	*12.7*	*12.1*	*11.5*	*11.0*	*10.5*	*10.0*
125	97	94	91	88	86	83	80	77	75	73	70	68	65	63
	-----	*21.2*	*18.9*	*17.3*	*16.1*	*15.0*	*14.0*	*13.4*	*12.7*	*12.1*	*11.5*	*11.0*	*10.5*	*10.0*
130	97	94	91	89	86	83	81	78	76	73	71	69	67	64
	-----	*21.0*	*18.8*	*17.2*	*16.0*	*14.9*	*14.0*	*13.4*	*12.7*	*12.1*	*11.5*	*11.0*	*10.5*	*10.0*
140	97	95	92	89	87	84	82	79	77	75	73	70	68	66
	-----	*20.7*	*18.6*	*16.9*	*15.8*	*14.8*	*13.8*	*13.2*	*12.5*	*11.9*	*11.4*	*10.9*	*10.4*	*10.0*
150	98	95	92	90	87	85	82	80	78	76	74	72	70	68
	-----	*20.2*	*18.4*	*16.6*	*15.4*	*14.5*	*13.7*	*13.0*	*12.4*	*11.8*	*11.2*	*10.8*	*10.3*	*9.9*
160	98	95	93	90	88	86	83	81	79	77	75	73	71	69
	-----	*19.8*	*18.1*	*16.2*	*15.2*	*14.2*	*13.4*	*12.7*	*12.1*	*11.5*	*11.0*	*10.6*	*10.1*	*9.7*
170	98	95	93	91	89	86	84	82	80	78	76	74	72	70
	-----	*19.4*	*17.7*	*15.8*	*14.8*	*13.9*	*13.2*	*12.4*	*11.8*	*11.3*	*10.8*	*10.4*	*9.9*	*9.6*
180	98	96	94	91	89	87	85	83	81	79	77	75	73	72
	-----	*18.9*	*17.3*	*15.5*	*14.5*	*13.7*	*12.9*	*12.2*	*11.6*	*11.1*	*10.6*	*10.1*	*9.7*	*9.4*
190	98	96	94	92	90	88	85	84	82	80	78	76	75	73
	-----	*18.5*	*16.9*	*15.2*	*14.2*	*13.4*	*12.7*	*12.0*	*11.4*	*10.9*	*10.5*	*10.0*	*9.6*	*9.2*
200	98	96	94	92	90	88	86	84	82	80	79	77	75	74
	-----	*18.1*	*16.4*	*14.9*	*14.0*	*13.2*	*12.4*	*11.8*	*11.2*	*10.8*	*10.3*	*9.8*	*9.4*	*9.1*
210	98	96	94	92	90	88	86	85	83	81	79	78	76	75
	-----	*17.7*	*16.0*	*14.6*	*13.8*	*13.0*	*12.2*	*11.7*	*11.1*	*10.6*	*10.0*	*9.7*	*9.2*	*9.0*

SOURCE: *Forest Products Laboratory, Forest Service, USDA.*
NOTE: *Relative humidity values in roman type. Equilibrium moisture content values in italic type.*

Wet-bulb depression (°F)

15	16	17	18	19	20	21	22	23	24	25	26	27	28	29	30	32	34	36	38	40	45	50
------	------	------	------	------	------	------	------	------	------	------	------	------	------	------	------	------	------	------	------	------	------	------
------	------	------	------	------	------	------	------	------	------	------	------	------	------	------	------	------	------	------	------	------	------	------
------	------	------	------	------	------	------	------	------	------	------	------	------	------	------	------	------	------	------	------	------	------	------
------	------	------	------	------	------	------	------	------	------	------	------	------	------	------	------	------	------	------	------	------	------	------
------	------	------	------	------	------	------	------	------	------	------	------	------	------	------	------	------	------	------	------	------	------	------
------	------	------	------	------	------	------	------	------	------	------	------	------	------	------	------	------	------	------	------	------	------	------
------	------	------	------	------	------	------	------	------	------	------	------	------	------	------	------	------	------	------	------	------	------	------
10	5	------																				
2.8	*1.5*																					
19	14	9	5	------																		
4.5	*3.6*	*2.5*	*1.3*																			
26	21	17	13	9	5	1	------															
5.6	*4.9*	*4.1*	*3.2*	*2.3*	*1.3*	*0.2*																
32	27	24	20	16	13	8	6	2	------													
6.5	*5.8*	*5.2*	*4.5*	*3.8*	*3.0*	*2.3*	*1.4*	*0.4*														
36	33	29	25	22	19	15	12	9	6	3	------											
7.2	*6.6*	*6.0*	*5.5*	*4.9*	*4.3*	*3.7*	*2.9*	*2.3*	*1.5*	*0.7*												
41	37	34	31	28	24	21	18	15	12	10	7	4	1	------								
7.7	*7.2*	*6.7*	*6.2*	*5.6*	*5.1*	*4.7*	*4.1*	*3.5*	*2.9*	*2.3*	*1.7*	*0.9*	*0.2*									
44	41	38	35	32	29	26	23	20	18	15	12	10	7	5	3	------						
8.1	*7.7*	*7.2*	*6.8*	*6.3*	*5.8*	*5.4*	*5.0*	*4.5*	*4.0*	*3.5*	*3.0*	*2.4*	*1.8*	*1.1*	*0.3*							
47	44	41	38	36	33	30	28	25	23	20	18	15	13	11	9	4	------					
8.5	*8.1*	*7.6*	*7.2*	*6.7*	*6.3*	*6.0*	*5.6*	*5.2*	*4.8*	*4.3*	*3.9*	*3.4*	*3.0*	*2.4*	*1.7*	*0.9*						
49	47	44	41	39	36	34	31	29	26	24	22	19	17	15	13	9	5	1	------			
8.8	*8.4*	*8.0*	*7.6*	*7.2*	*6.8*	*6.5*	*6.1*	*5.7*	*5.3*	*4.9*	*4.6*	*4.2*	*3.8*	*3.3*	*2.8*	*2.1*	*1.3*	*0.4*				
52	49	46	44	42	39	37	34	32	30	28	26	23	22	20	17	14	10	6	2	------		
9.1	*8.7*	*8.2*	*7.9*	*7.5*	*7.1*	*6.8*	*6.4*	*6.1*	*5.7*	*5.3*	*5.1*	*4.8*	*4.4*	*4.0*	*3.6*	*3.0*	*2.3*	*1.5*	*0.6*			
54	51	49	46	44	41	39	37	35	33	30	28	26	24	22	21	17	13	10	7	4	------	
9.2	*8.9*	*8.5*	*8.1*	*7.8*	*7.4*	*7.0*	*6.7*	*6.4*	*6.1*	*5.7*	*5.4*	*5.2*	*4.9*	*4.6*	*4.2*	*3.6*	*3.1*	*2.4*	*1.6*	*0.7*		
55	53	50	48	46	44	42	40	37	35	34	31	29	28	26	24	20	17	14	11	8	------	
9.4	*9.0*	*8.7*	*8.3*	*7.9*	*7.6*	*7.3*	*6.9*	*6.7*	*6.4*	*6.1*	*5.7*	*5.4*	*5.2*	*4.8*	*4.6*	*4.2*	*3.6*	*3.1*	*2.4*	*1.8*		
57	55	52	50	48	46	44	42	40	38	36	34	32	30	28	26	23	20	17	14	11	4	------
9.5	*9.2*	*8.8*	*8.4*	*8.1*	*7.7*	*7.5*	*7.2*	*6.8*	*6.6*	*6.3*	*6.0*	*5.7*	*5.4*	*5.2*	*4.8*	*4.5*	*4.0*	*3.5*	*3.0*	*2.5*	*1.1*	
58	56	54	52	50	48	45	43	41	40	38	36	34	32	31	29	26	23	20	17	14	8	2
9.6	*9.3*	*8.9*	*8.6*	*8.2*	*7.8*	*7.6*	*7.3*	*7.0*	*6.7*	*6.5*	*6.2*	*5.9*	*5.6*	*5.4*	*5.2*	*4.7*	*4.3*	*3.9*	*3.4*	*2.9*	*1.7*	*0.4*
60	58	55	53	51	49	47	45	43	41	40	38	36	34	33	31	28	25	22	19	17	10	5
9.7	*9.4*	*9.0*	*8.7*	*8.3*	*7.9*	*7.7*	*7.4*	*7.2*	*6.8*	*6.6*	*6.3*	*6.1*	*5.8*	*5.6*	*5.4*	*5.0*	*4.6*	*4.2*	*3.7*	*3.3*	*2.3*	*1.1*
61	59	57	55	53	51	48	47	45	43	41	39	38	36	35	33	30	27	24	22	19	13	8
9.7	*9.4*	*9.0*	*8.7*	*8.3*	*8.0*	*7.7*	*7.5*	*7.2*	*7.0*	*6.7*	*6.5*	*6.2*	*6.0*	*5.8*	*5.5*	*5.2*	*4.8*	*4.4*	*4.0*	*3.6*	*2.7*	*1.6*
62	60	58	56	54	52	50	48	47	45	43	41	40	38	37	35	32	29	26	24	21	15	10
9.7	*9.4*	*9.0*	*8.7*	*8.3*	*8.0*	*7.8*	*7.6*	*7.3*	*7.0*	*6.8*	*6.6*	*6.4*	*6.1*	*5.9*	*5.6*	*5.3*	*4.9*	*4.6*	*4.2*	*3.8*	*3.0*	*2.0*
64	62	60	58	56	54	53	51	49	47	46	44	43	41	40	38	35	32	30	27	25	19	14
9.6	*9.4*	*9.0*	*8.7*	*8.4*	*8.0*	*7.8*	*7.6*	*7.3*	*7.1*	*6.9*	*6.6*	*6.4*	*6.2*	*6.0*	*5.8*	*5.4*	*5.1*	*4.8*	*4.4*	*4.1*	*3.4*	*2.6*
66	64	62	60	58	57	55	53	51	49	48	46	45	43	42	41	38	36	33	30	28	23	8
9.5	*9.2*	*8.9*	*8.6*	*8.3*	*8.0*	*7.8*	*7.5*	*7.3*	*7.1*	*6.9*	*6.7*	*6.4*	*6.2*	*6.0*	*5.8*	*5.4*	*5.2*	*4.9*	*4.5*	*4.2*	*3.6*	*2.9*
67	65	64	62	60	58	57	55	53	52	50	49	47	46	44	43	41	38	35	33	31	25	21
9.4	*9.1*	*8.8*	*8.5*	*8.2*	*7.9*	*7.7*	*7.4*	*7.2*	*7.0*	*6.8*	*6.7*	*6.4*	*6.2*	*6.0*	*5.8*	*5.5*	*5.2*	*4.9*	*4.6*	*4.3*	*3.7*	*3.2*
69	67	65	63	62	60	59	57	55	53	52	51	49	48	47	45	43	40	38	35	33	28	24
9.2	*9.0*	*8.6*	*8.4*	*8.0*	*7.8*	*7.6*	*7.3*	*7.2*	*6.9*	*6.7*	*6.6*	*6.4*	*6.2*	*6.0*	*5.7*	*5.5*	*5.2*	*4.9*	*4.6*	*4.3*	*3.7*	*3.2*
70	68	67	65	63	62	60	58	57	55	54	52	51	50	48	47	45	42	40	38	35	30	26
9.0	*8.8*	*8.4*	*8.1*	*7.8*	*7.6*	*7.4*	*7.2*	*7.0*	*6.8*	*6.5*	*6.4*	*6.2*	*6.0*	*5.8*	*5.7*	*5.4*	*5.2*	*4.8*	*4.6*	*4.4*	*3.8*	*3.3*
71	69	68	66	65	63	62	60	59	57	56	54	53	51	50	49	46	44	42	39	37	32	28
8.9	*8.6*	*8.2*	*7.9*	*7.7*	*7.4*	*7.2*	*7.0*	*6.8*	*6.6*	*6.4*	*6.2*	*6.0*	*5.9*	*5.7*	*5.5*	*5.3*	*5.0*	*4.8*	*4.5*	*4.4*	*3.8*	*3.3*
72	70	69	67	66	64	63	61	60	58	57	55	54	53	52	51	48	46	43	41	39	34	30
8.8	*8.4*	*8.1*	*7.7*	*7.5*	*7.2*	*7.0*	*6.9*	*6.6*	*6.4*	*6.2*	*6.0*	*5.9*	*5.7*	*5.6*	*5.4*	*5.2*	*4.9*	*4.7*	*4.5*	*4.3*	*3.8*	*3.3*
73	71	70	68	67	65	64	63	61	60	59	57	56	54	53	52	50	47	45	43	41	36	32
8.7	*8.3*	*8.0*	*7.6*	*7.4*	*7.1*	*6.9*	*6.8*	*6.5*	*6.3*	*6.1*	*5.9*	*5.8*	*5.5*	*5.4*	*5.3*	*5.1*	*4.8*	*4.6*	*4.4*	*4.2*	*3.7*	*3.2*

section of small chain. Then put the clip on your shoe, so the chain just touches the floor to "ground out" errant electrical charges.

I tried one and it worked; no more sparks snapping at my head or chest. It's best to put the clip directly under the ankle on loafer-high work shoes and put it to the outside of the shoe. I first tried it on the inside of a shoe, but found myself tripping on it.

USING SHOP TOOLS

There are quite a few things you pick up if you work in a shop every day. You find out that "going by the book" isn't always the best or fastest way. For example, chances are your owner's manual tells you to use a square next to a table saw blade to check it for true 90° squareness. I won't argue that this doesn't work, but I have a better way to check blade squareness.

First I make a single cut through a piece of flat scrap to end up with two blocks. Then I lay the blocks end to end as they were in the original board, and check the fit. Next, I turn one of the blocks bottom-up, and check the fit again. Then I return it to the original position, turn the other block bottom-up and check the fit. If I get a tight fit in all positions, I know the saw is at 90°. If there's a gap, I make adjustments. You can do the same thing to adjust the fence on a jointer. Some guys say, "Well, on a jointer it doesn't make any difference because the boards will still fit together since the edges will all be at the same angle." That's true, but if you have a square edge, you'll be able to turn boards end for end to adjust grain patterns, plus the boards won't tend to slip when you put the clamps to them.

We are always on the lookout for ways to eliminate errors when working with equipment. For example, when I first started at this shop, I noticed that often the first piece of work run through the machines in the morning ended up as scrap. The reason? The person who had used the machine at quitting time the day before didn't bother to return the machine to a "quit" position. Now we have established the habit of returning saws, jointers and other equipment to a standard 45° or 90° setting when we knock off work for the day. This way, in the morning, we know what the setting is. This helps even if the same person is using the equipment again, because it's hard to remember what the last setting was the day before.

BLADE INSERTS

You'll find, if you work with shop equipment every day, you get to know the precise number of crank turns for numerous settings on a half-dozen machines. But you are always looking for ways to modify the machines to make them more efficient or safer. For example, almost all table saws come with a metal or plastic insert that fits in a recess in the area around the blade. You can take it out for removing or installing blades or other cutting tools. Saw makers warn that you should never operate the saw without the proper insert in place, either a saw blade insert when sawing or a combination dado-molding insert when dadoing or molding. The insert helps keep small pieces of wood from getting wedged in beside the blade. To further cut down the chances of this happening, I make up my own special inserts of wood, one for each common setting such as 90°, 45° and 22½°. Doing this gives added insurance, and they're easy to make. Cut the shape on a band saw, then position, clamp down and raise the blade (set at a chosen angle) on up and through the wood insert.

I have four different blade inserts that allow just enough room for the blade, instead of just one that allows gaps at the sides of the blade.

Making your own table-saw blade inserts for common saw settings is easy and keeps wood from wedging in alongside the blade.

PATTERN BLOCKS

You should not only look to make your machines more efficient, but yourself more efficient, as well. When I started here, repetitive work was still done the hard way, with saws and other equipment set up from scratch for specific operations. After I got familiar with the work being done, I instituted what I call my "numerical control system." Much of the shop's work is cutting smaller pieces of hardwoods to specific lengths, either at 90°, beveled or mitered. The key to my system is using small blocks of wood inside a sliding table on a table saw. For example, one block set on the table is used to make one specific cut by butting the stock to be cut against the block. That same block plus another one or more are used as spacers to make other cuts.

I have four drawers full of my pattern blocks, which are really little story poles – pieces of wood with useful measurements marked on them. On each block, I've written out not only the cut it's used for, but also what other blocks are used with it and other information pertinent to the cutting procedure. The only thing I need to watch is that during winters the blocks sometimes will lose moisture and shrink enough to throw the measurements off. So every so often I double-check the cut with a rule and, if the block needs it, I'll use layers of tape to build it back to the right length.

This sliding table is used with various-sized spacer blocks to duplicate specific cuts. Notations are made on each block to indicate a particular cut and whether it's used with other spacer blocks.

FASTENING AND CLAMPING

The Kuempel clock kits we make are easy to assemble because they're designed to be built using what we call Jiffy Nails. The metal fasteners have curved edges which, when driven into slots that have been precut in two pieces of wood, draw the two pieces together. The advantage is that you can just tap the fastener into place and it draws preglued pieces into a tight, perfect fit without clamps. Using the little fasteners can free you from having to use clamps on joints that slip and slide, and they're worth experimenting with if you need to glue a bunch of joints that are mitered or beveled.

We cut the slots on small, older table saws set up with narrow-kerf blades and angled fences. But you can easily do the slot cutting with a backsaw. Most of our Jiffy Nails require matching 22-gauge saw kerfs across the face of each piece of material to be joined. The most popular Jiffy Nail sizes are ⅝ inch wide and ½ or ¾ inch long, and one that's ⅜ inch wide and 1 inch long. They run about $4 a pound.

When it comes to clamping, most folks have a problem with regular store-bought C-clamps. These clamps have the annoying habit, during any kind of use, of the lower jaw's ball-joint socket coming loose, even falling off. I got tired of putting up with loose or missing jaws, so one day I reached over and grabbed a circular turning that was left over from clock making. It already had a ¼-inch hole through the center, so I positioned

(continued on page 102)

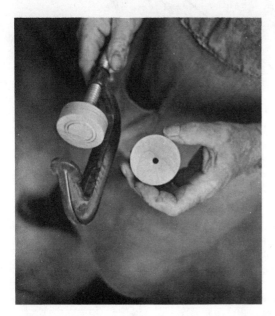

One easy way to overhaul a C-clamp is to make up a new lower jaw out of a hardwood turning, drilled to fit over the ball at the end of the threaded section.

MAKING AND USING JIGS

It's intriguing to watch any professional tradesman with some experience under his belt because of the tricks and shortcuts he employs to get the project done faster and better. One fellow who maintains a deep admiration for these tricks of the trade is Bob Beckstrom. A licensed general contractor from Albany, California, he specializes in residential remodeling in the San Francisco Bay area. He also teaches remodeling at the Owner Builder Center in Berkeley. Because of his teaching and writing—he's written a number of articles and several books, including *Ortho's Home Improvement Encyclopedia* (Ortho, 1985)—Bob is able to maintain a beginner's outlook.

He remembers what it's like to be just starting out on the learning curve and remembers the tricks that can make a difference. As an example, he points out some of the handy little jigs that you can build to guide your tools when performing repetitive carpentry jobs.

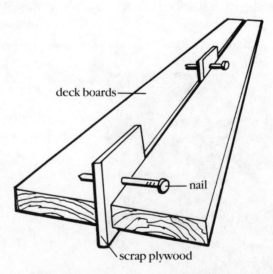

deck boards

nail

scrap plywood

Using a piece of ¼-inch scrap plywood punched with a nail can work well as a spacer when installing deck boards, and you don't pinch your fingers.

You might think that making a jig will complicate your work. It's an extra step you have to fool with before getting to the business at hand. But in fact, jigs can be easy to make, and using them can save you huge chunks of time. Better yet, jigs can actually improve the quality of your work.

Among the simplest jigs to make is one that you can use when making a deck, when you need to maintain uniform spacing between the deck boards. A lot of people advocate using nails for spacers, but nails can drop between the boards, and you lose them and you pinch your fingers. Instead, I recommend taking pieces of ¼-inch scrap plywood and driving nails through them. The nails keep the plywood from dropping between the boards, so you can just lift the jigs up and use them over again.

Another extremely simple jig consists of nothing more than a block of wood with a hole drilled through it. You can use this as a depth gauge for drilling holes; it helps you make sure that your drill bit won't penetrate all the way through the wood you're drilling into. You might use this jig when drilling hinge holes for cabinet doors, for example. You want the holes to be deep enough

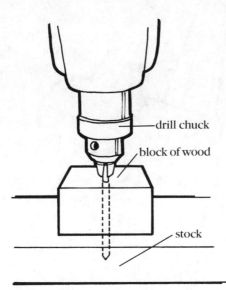

A rough depth gauge for drilling holes can simply be a block of wood of the right size. Just drill through it and leave it on the bit.

(continued)

MAKING AND USING JIGS – *Continued*

for the screws, but you don't want them to extend all the way through the wood, marring the surface on the other side.

Some jigs are useful in finish work, when you're striving for great precision. Others come in handy even in the roughest jobs. There's a jig that can help you with a particularly heavy-duty task – creating a poured concrete foundation. You need to have anchor bolts spaced out along each section of your sill plate, and you can use this jig to place the bolts precisely where you want them, long before pouring the concrete. There's nothing to it, really. The jig is just a piece of scrap 2 × 4 that you spike to the top of the forms with duplex nails. In the middle of the 2 × 4, drill a hole, insert the anchor and secure it with an anchor nut. The real benefit of this jig is that it gives you peace of mind on the day of the pour, because it's one less thing to worry about. You can put all the anchors in place a week ahead of time and forget about them.

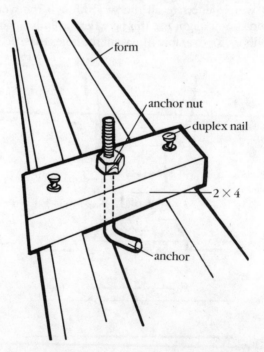

To position anchor bolts in a poured foundation, spike scrap 2 × 4s to the top of the forms, drill holes and secure the bolt with a nut.

After the concrete has cured, just pull out the duplex nails, unscrew the anchor nut and slide the 2 × 4 up and off of the anchor.

All of these jigs can be fabricated in a couple of minutes. There's another jig, one that takes longer to build, but can prove to be extremely useful for such tasks as cutting treads for a staircase, or for fitting shelves in a bookcase. Glen Kitzenberger, a super carpenter who teaches here, showed me this one. Imagine a staircase with walls running up both sides. The treads should be cut perfectly, so no cracks are left exposed on either side. It's difficult to measure each dimension and angle accurately. Glen's jig handles the job. It consists of two pieces of plywood with an arm placed between them. The arm has slots, allowing you to attach the arm to the plywood with wing nuts. You can move the plywood pieces in and out, swiveling them to get the angles just right. Position the plywood pieces, tighten the wing nuts, then lift the jig and use it as a pattern for cutting the tread. If you try it, you'll find it works like a charm.

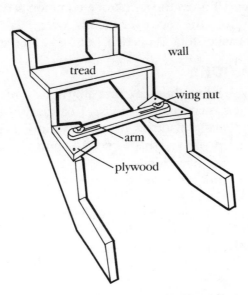

A jig that's helpful when cutting stair treads can be made of two plywood sections spanned by an arm that's attached with bolts and wing nuts.

the hole over the ball and cranked the clamp closed so the ball was seated inside the hole. It's the best darn modification yet. The turning stays on, is softer than metal and provides a larger surface for clamping. We now have four or five clamps modified this way.

FINISHING PROJECTS

From gluing to sanding to oiling, there are plenty of tricks you can use to make finishing your projects go more smoothly.

GLUE MARKS

It's really discouraging to finish a beautiful piece of wood only to find ugly glue marks that seem to shout "Amateur!" The tool we use most often to prevent this problem might surprise you – it's a small paint scraper with a 1½-inch blade. Though we have a boxful of traditional wood scrapers of different sizes and shapes, we keep coming back to this little tool. If the blade is kept sharp, it takes off glue in ultrathin shavings so you can easily tell when to stop without marring the wood. The trick in using the scraper is keeping it sharp and knowing how to sharpen it. I use a fine metal file, running it across both front and back edges, then (and here's the trick) press the shank of a common screwdriver across the front edge to "roll" the edge over slightly toward the handle end. No grinding wheel or whetstone is needed, just a good file and screwdriver.

SANDING BLOCKS

Most folks with home shops are probably not aware of the possibilities of making their own sanding blocks. I have a whole drawerful of sanding blocks specially made to dress up various configurations of wood. They're of every size and shape I need – convex, concave, square – and all are about a foot or so long.

These blocks work great and they're easy to make. I use scraps of sanding belt material and just glue them on with carpenter's glue. You can make them up as the need arises. If you have a problem getting into a place, just figure out what shape will work and make up a block. They're especially helpful when dressing up stock such as cove molding.

FINISHES

When putting a finish on a project, we have our tried-and-true methods. Although you might think that a production shop faced with a wide choice of finishes would be using the absolute latest in high-tech finishes, it's not so here. Our continued favorite finish, especially for oak, is one that's been on the market for years. It's called Velvit Oil. It's applied after staining and a quick wet sanding, and results in a finish as smooth to the hand as butter. On walnut, I don't use any stain, just the Velvit Oil. For oak and cherry, I use two different stains of our own formulation, then apply the Velvit Oil. Velvit Oil is available from us for about $5 a pint. (Write to Kuempel, 21195 Minnetonka Blvd., Excelsior, MN 55331.)

SCRAPS

If you ever make up a number of the same project, when you get done, take a look at your scraps – your leftovers might be valuable. With some imagination, you might be surprised by what you can make from them. For example, I found myself with boxfuls of one certain odd-shaped scrap. The problem of storing them got me to thinking. Then one day I took one over to the band saw and in 20 seconds turned it into a duck. Now, what can you do with a little duck of expensive walnut? Plenty. I found they could be used as decorations on top of a wood sign; outfitted with crosspieces for spice racks, made into towel racks or paper-towel holders; drilled for candle holders and other uses. If you're the kind that can't throw out scraps, look at what you've got. You might find a good way to both get rid of the scraps and make money to boot.

PART 3

Measure Twice
And Cut Once

CHAPTER 11

KIM RASMUSSEN:

THOUGHTS ON MEASURING

There's a sign in Kim Rasmussen's construction office that says, "The faster I work, the behinder I get!" It's a good reminder, says the owner of Northern Sun Construction, a Minnesota firm that specializes in quality energy-efficient housing. He says it's a tribute to precision that begins with the first step of construction — measuring.

Kim talks about measuring basics as he works on a new superinsulated house in a suburb of the Twin Cities. The building schedule has been delayed again and again, so now it is mid-January and what might have been pleasant work is a chore that requires gloves, plenty of hot coffee and a sense of humor. But some of his observations about measuring can help anyone about to tackle a building project.

The obvious problem with inaccurate measurements is wasting material. But that's not the big problem, which is the pure frustration of having to do something twice. Let's say you're putting up siding and, because of sloppy measuring, most boards have to be cut twice. You can see it will take you much longer to finish the job compared to another carpenter who appears to be working at a snail's pace, but cuts every board perfectly.

If you do a poor job of measuring, it will affect your work, no matter what you're building. You are only as good as your measurements. There's an old adage: Measure twice and cut once. Take time to make sure you are getting an accurate measurement and double-check it before you do any cutting.

On the job we don't actually measure twice. But we do read the measurement twice as a matter of course – usually to $\frac{1}{32}$ inch. We mark our line, then cut so the saw kerf is just on the outside of the line. If you don't watch this, you can be off because of the saw kerf.

USING MEASURING TOOLS

There are lots of tools available to help you do a good job of measuring. These include the framing (or rafter) square, try square, combination square, straightedges, T-bevel, measuring (or long) tape,

If you need to take an inch or so off a board, try this. Set your combination square to the right length, then hold your pencil at its end and run down the length of the board.

carpenter's metal tape, folding rule, calipers, dividers (or compass) and depth gauge. And you can include the level, line level, marking gauge, chalk line and plumb bob.

For most of our measuring we use a framing square and a 25-foot metal tape. The square has one 16-inch leg and one 24-inch leg. These lengths make it easy to mark for studs either 16 inches on center or two feet on center. We rarely use a folding rule. But one thing I learned about folding rules is that it's best to lay it on edge to take measurements, otherwise the thickness of the rule leads to inaccuracies.

Though we still depend on our framing squares, an innovation becoming quite popular is the Speed Square. It's triangular and each leg is about six inches long. A number of manufacturers make similar squares and they work great, especially for measuring angles. Of course, framing squares and folding rules can be used to measure angles, too, and the T-bevel is built for that specific purpose.

TAPES

The 25-foot tape is a must for a serious carpenter, not only because of the length, but because these tapes are one inch wide and rigid enough to make measuring easy for one person without any help. One thing about tapes is that you'll notice they have a special hook on the end that moves a little and appears to be defective. But there's a reason for this. If you are measuring a length of board, for example, and you hook the end over the edge of the board and pull it toward you, then the hook slides to the proper position. If you are taking an inside measurement and are pushing the tape, the hook slides toward the case slightly to compensate for its own thickness. So don't think a tape is defective if the end slides a little. Tapes do wear out, though. If you check your tape and it's off, then your best bet is to simply get a replacement tape.

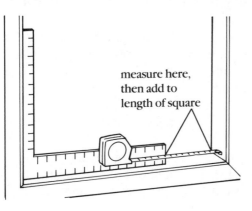

measure here, then add to length of square

When taking inside measurements, try using both your combination square and tape as shown here.

When taking inside measurements with a tape, you can read the measurement that shows and simply add on the length of the case (usually two or three inches). But another – and more accurate – way to do it is to also use a combination square. Position the square upside down in one corner. Then draw the steel tape to the blade of the square and add the length of the square's blade. It's fast and precise.

Measuring tapes don't lie, or do they? Let's say you are working with a crew and someone is doing the actual measuring and someone else is doing the cutting. If the pieces are off, take a minute and draw out all the tapes you are using on a board to see that they measure the same. In other words, *synchronize* your tapes. I almost got fired once, working for a finish carpenter. He called out the measurements, I did the cutting. But all my cuts were $1/16$ inch short. After about an hour we checked the tapes and mine was reading short because the end was slightly bent.

STORY POLES

One thing about measuring is that you always do it in order to do something else. And in some cases, such as during remodeling where you are working with existing rooms instead of a blueprint, you don't really care what the measurement is – you just need to duplicate the actual length or width. This is where story poles or marking patterns are useful.

Story poles are basically lengths of lumber, either one piece or two pieces nailed or clamped together, which allow you to quickly transfer specific distances. For example, you can use a story pole cut off at a desired ceiling height for furring out a ceiling to make it level. You can use it to level out a basement floor for concrete. You can also use a story pole, marked off in specific increments, to mark off the sides of a house for siding.

Carpenters also make story poles to help them frame up walls. They mark them with the height of the horizontal members and the length of the vertical members. That way they can mark lumber fast without always having to go back to the plans.

Story poles are really master marking patterns that eliminate the need to pull out the tape or square repeatedly. (They don't have to be fancy, but should be accurate.) For example, let's say you are putting up 10-inch cedar siding with a 2-inch overlap. Instead of snapping chalk lines for every course, you can cut out a pattern on a scrap piece of 2×4. By butting it up against the siding you can find where to position the next board precisely.

We use a version of a story pole to cut studs. If we are framing in a basement with eight-foot studs, for example, we cut off one stud to the exact length and nail a scrap of plywood on the end. Then we can use it as

A simple story pole made from a piece of 2 × 4 can save incredible amounts of time on such jobs as putting up wood siding. Snapping chalk lines occasionally will help make sure you're on target.

a master pattern, sliding it over uncut 2 × 4s to quickly mark a cutting line.

When making duplicate, repetitious cuts, it's important to avoid what I call the growing pattern syndrome. This occurs when someone will cut one stud to length, then use that cut stud to mark the next stud, then use that newly cut stud to mark the next one, and so on. After two or three cuts you can be off quite a bit. If each stud is off $\frac{1}{16}$ inch, for example, by the time you cut four studs you will be off $\frac{1}{4}$ inch. It's best to use just one pattern and use it for marking every cut.

SHORTCUTS

There are measuring shortcuts you can use to divide up a board or sheet of material. For example, say you want to divide a board exactly in half. You can use a compass, put the pivot at the end and draw an arc; do the same at the other end. The middle of the board will be where the two arcs cross. You can do the same thing with a straightedge or square by drawing an X diagonally from opposite corners. The middle is where the lines cross.

If you want to divide a board into three equal pieces, you can use your square. Lay it on the board, with the start of the scale against one edge. Then angle the rule so that you get to a number that is easily divided by three (9, for example). Then simply mark the board at three inches and six inches. By making those two cuts you have three equal pieces. Likewise, if you want four equal pieces, angle the rule to numbers

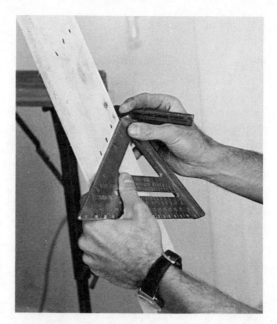

If you need to divide a board into equal parts, you can use the old carpenter's trick of angling your square so it falls on a number divisible by the number of parts you need.

such as 8, 12 or 16. If you want five pieces, you would use 10, 15, 20 and so on.

Many times you need a level or plumb bob to measure out vertical and horizontal lines. Though the common levels you see are the basic two-foot-long levels, we generally use the four-foot-long levels. And we prefer those made of wood; they seem to keep a true edge longer than the metal levels. Combination squares have a built-in level; they're also handy for marking out lines parallel to the edges of material.

A long straightedge, either one you make up out of lumber or one you buy, is helpful when measuring out cutting lines on long sheets or boards. So is the chalk line. By using these you only need to make two measurements, one on each end, then either clamp your straightedge to the piece or snap a chalk line to use as a cutting guide. We use chalk lines a lot when sheathing, framing up walls and hanging drywall.

In some cases, especially in finish carpentry, special tools are needed to do your measuring that would otherwise be nearly impossible. For example, let's say you are installing a fancy piece of ceiling molding and have to cut the end of a new piece of molding to fit exactly over the piece meeting it in a corner. You can buy a contour pattern tool that consists of numerous wires that slide to match the contour of the existing molding. Push it up against the molding and you have an exact pattern you can transfer.

TRICKS AND TECHNIQUES

Sometimes, no matter how careful you are in measuring, you must "cheat" a little to get things done right. For example, we have a trick we use in cutting trim molding to get a good, tight fit. After we transfer the measurement, we lay the material onto the miter saw. But before we make the cut, we slip a carpenter's pencil under the molding (about an inch away from the blade, on the side of the board we want to keep), then make the cut. The front of the molding ends up just slightly wider than the back. This keeps the back of the molding (the part next to the wall) from touching first and causing a gap at the front of the joint.

Sometimes it's how you do the measuring that counts. When we use a compass it's mostly to mark out ceiling boxes when hanging drywall or paneling. But to avoid intricate measuring for fixtures, outlets, furnace ducts and so forth, we use hard carpenter's chalk. Instead of measuring, we simply rub chalk around the edge of the protrusion. Then we push the sheet into position and hit it with our hands. The chalk transfers to the back of the sheet and we have a perfect cutting guide.

Kim, like most professional carpenters, is good at close-enough measuring. This is how he uses his finger to guide the pencil for approximate, rough-cut marking.

Let's say you have a chair that has a tendency to rock because one leg is short. To solve the problem, you can measure from the seat to the bottom of each leg, finding the shortest leg and cutting the other three the same length. But doing this allows room for error. So, take a shortcut. Put that chair on a surface you know is level. Then take a piece of scrap wood ¼ or ⅛ inch thick, hold it against each leg and make a pencil mark. Cut the legs all at that line and, presto, you have a chair that's good and solid to sit on.

Measuring inside diameters of pipe can be tricky, and here's where calipers are handy. When measuring the outside of piping, you can wrap a string around it and then measure the string. But a better way is to use your metal tape, but wrap it around the pipe so that it overlaps. For example, wrap it so that you have several extra inches on the end. This way you can keep both sections of tape flat on the pipe, read the measurement edge-to-edge, then subtract the amount of the extra tape.

One cardinal rule of measuring: don't take anything for granted. It's a big mistake to assume any room in your home is square and plumb, even if it was built last summer. Many homeowners, when they start measuring out a room, are often surprised to find that walls are not exactly plumb and corners are not exactly square. Sometimes a stud wall can be built true and square, but one or two studs may be bowed out enough to make a corner crooked after drywall or paneling is installed. The careful carpenter will measure the tops and bottoms of walls, all along the wall, and will check to see if all corners meet at right angles. You can use a framing square to do this, but you can also make yourself a large try square from scrap wood to do the job.

CHAPTER 12

BRIAN RINGHAM:

KEEPING IT ON THE LEVEL

"Ever hear of the Norwegian level?" Brian Ringham asks with a smile. He says he's not joking. Where he grew up, back in the old days the Norwegian farmers who couldn't afford a level would use a pan of water. When the water was the same distance from the rim all the way around, the board it was sitting on was level. It worked!

Brian has his own construction firm now and is close to celebrating his tenth year of business. One thing he's learned, he says, is that taking the time to keep things square and level in the beginning stages of any project will pay off many times over before it's done. He says it's something that's easy to overlook or fudge on, especially if you're in a hurry. But if you take shortcuts to start out with, Brian will bet that you'll be paying for it throughout your project in the extra time it will take to make adjustments.

Things have changed a lot since the days of the Norwegian pan levels. There's hardly anyone who can't afford an all-purpose two-foot level today. You can find them for less than $5 and they're good enough for the occasional project around the home. And the choice of levels can be almost overwhelming. If you have some extra money to spend, and the inclination, you can buy levels 18, 24, 28, 30, 42, 48, 72, even 78 inches long.

You can buy torpedo levels, line levels, combination squares with leveling vials, even stick-on vials to make your own leveling tools. It used to be that levels were only available with wooden frames with vials held in place with plaster. But today you can buy levels with frames made of cast-aluminum, magnesium and even high-impact structural foam and with vials that are easily replaced and/or adjustable.

The 24-inch level is the most common, and in the trade it's a primary tool for the rough-work carpenter. The 18-inch level is used mainly by plumbers, steamfitters and pipe fitters; it fits nicely into a 19-inch tool-box. The 28-inch level was originally popular with finish carpenters

Brian uses these levels on the job as a finish carpenter. He bought the 78-inch level to help him install large energy-conserving curtains.

back in the early 1900s. Window casings were 30 inches wide, and this level would cover maximum surface and still fit into the casing. The 42-inch level was originally sold mainly for tile setters because older bathrooms were usually tiled and were a little more than 42 inches wide.

The 48-inch level is the classic mason's length. At one time concrete blocks were 15 inches long, so this level would span three blocks at once. The 72-inch level is the original level for the 6-foot-by-8-inch door jamb.

Today you can even buy magnetic levels to use with steel framing. And you can buy leveling devices that use a laser beam to establish a level. Then there's the transit – a more expensive, precision leveling tool.

One thing to remember when using levels is that the bubble should be centered exactly within the vial. A lot of folks think that if the bubble is touching one line or the other, they've got it level; this will be close, but not precise. Another thing to remember is that levels can get out of whack, especially if they've been dropped, nicked or tossed around. You should check the accuracy of your levels, then either adjust the vial or replace it if need be.

CHECKING A LEVEL

With the level on its working edge, lay it on a flat surface and check the position of the bubble. Then turn the level 180° (swap end for end), and check the bubble again. It should be in the same position. That's the first test.

The second test is to do the same thing, but this time turn the level over on its opposite working edge (swap top for bottom). Again the bubble should stay in the same position. You can also check for plumb by holding the level against a flat surface perpendicular to the floor. Check

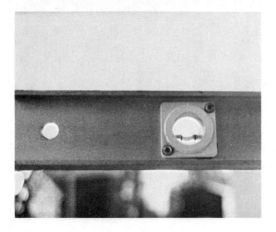

The key to precision is to make sure the bubble in the vial is exactly centered, not just touching the lines.

the bubble in the plumb vial, then turn the level over so the opposite working edge is against the wall. The bubble should be in the same position.

Stores that sell expensive levels to tradesmen often have a special jig to test the accuracy of a level before you take it home. If you're paying $50 for a level, you want it to be accurate. But one thing to keep in mind when using a level is that its accuracy is directly related to the amount of surface it covers. For example, the vial in a combination square is useful, but the level is measuring a surface of only about four inches. The longer the surface, the more accuracy you will have. I use a six-foot level when I need real precision, or, for example, when I'm hanging an insulation curtain that will span 20 feet or so.

Sometimes you need extra length for accuracy; other times you need the length just to reach to where you want to make a mark. But there are ways to extend the reach of a level in rough carpentry. For example, you can set your two-foot level on top of a carpenter's square or straightedge to get level marks for a header. You can even use a 2 × 4 that's four feet long or so. Eyeball it to see that it's straight and true, and set the level on top of it.

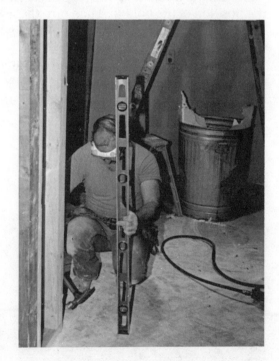

The longer the level, the more accurate. If you need to, you can set it on top of a square, straightedge or piece of lumber you know is straight and true.

USING LEVELS

The line level is handy for leveling over long distances. The key to using a line level is to keep the line (or string) you use as tight as possible and keep the level centered on the string. Most professionals use nylon line instead of cotton. I pull that line as tight as possible, then try to give it an extra pull to get it extra-taut. Even so, over 20 feet, the line level will still depress the line slightly. You need to adjust for this slight depression.

Clear plastic hose works great to extend a level line over distances. Hold one end vertically next to the mark you want to transfer and fill with liquid until it's level with your mark. The level of the liquid at the other end will be exactly the same height. This works well for leveling posts, for example, or for getting a level line around a room to help you put in a floor or ceiling. Keep in mind that sun shining on one end of the hose can change the liquid level.

Levels can also be used to help you find pitch or slope; in fact, some torpedo levels have markings to indicate ⅛ or ¼ pitch. These make it simple to position plumbing pipes that need to drain. But you can use a level on top of a 2 × 4 to determine slope. For example, let's say you want a brick patio to slope ¼ inch per foot. With your level on top of an eight-foot 2 × 4, you should have a 2-inch drop at one end when the bubble reads level.

(continued on page 123)

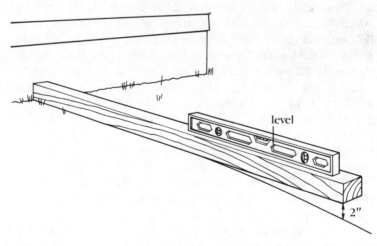

Setting a level on top of a straight eight-foot-long 2 × 4 can help you check slope. For predetermined slope, you can tack a 2-inch block on one end, for example, to get a slope of ¼ inch per foot.

USING A WATER LEVEL

Sometimes you need to check levels of objects that are at a distance from each other. One simple way to do this is to use a water level. Two men who devised their own easy-to-make water levels tell why and how.

WILL BEEMER

Batter boards are used to help set up building lines. They're set about four feet or more away from the corner layout stakes, with 2 × 4s used for stakes and 1 × 6s for ledgers. The ledger boards should be level and the batter boards should be level with each other. An ideal build-it-yourself tool to have for this operation, says Will Beemer of the Heartwood Owner-Builder School in Washington, Massachusetts, is a water level. According to Will, it's cheap and simple to make.

This water level is simply a clear plastic tube and a plastic jug. To make one, first measure the diameter of the tube, then cut a hole of the same size in the jug lid. Fill the jug with water, screw the lid on, and push one end of the tube far enough into the hole so that it extends well below the surface of the water.

Now, suck on the other end of the tube to create a siphon effect. The water will flow into the tube. When water starts to flow out the free end, lift the end of the tube a little higher than the top of the jug. The water in the tube's free end will stabilize at the same level as the water in the jug. If you put the jug next to an object and hold the end of the tube next to another object, you'll be able to tell if the two objects are level with each other.

For example, if you want to use it to help level batter boards, put the jug on a milk crate or some lumber so the water in the jug is slightly lower than the top of your first set of batter boards. Next, tie the end of the tube to the second set of batter boards.

Then suck on the tube. When the siphoning action stops, pour more water into the jug. The water will rise in both the jug and the tube, because water always seeks its own level. Keep pouring water into the jug until the surface of the water in the jug is even with the top of the first set of batter boards. At this point, you'll have three things level with each other: the top of the first

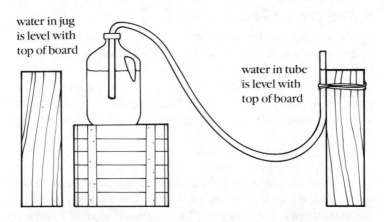

water in jug
is level with
top of board

water in tube
is level with
top of board

A jug level can help with jobs such as setting up batter boards. It can be used with plastic tubing; clear is best.

set of boards, the surface of the water in the jug, and the surface of the water in the tube.

Now all you have to do is compare the surface of the water in the tube with the top of the second set of batter boards. If they are level with each other, then you know that the second set of boards is level with the first set.

Some tips for using a water level:

• Put food coloring or some other dye in the water to make it easier to see.

• Don't get any air bubbles in the tube; they can cause inaccurate readings. (If bubbles get in, remove them by letting all the water drain out of the tube, then start over.)

• Use a clear tube so you can inspect for bubbles. The best is ¼-inch vinyl tubing from a plumbing supply store. Don't get kinks in it or your readings may be off.

• When using the setup outside, be sure it is either completely in the sun or completely shaded to avoid inaccurate readings due to solar gain on half of it.

• Read the bottom of the cup-shaped surface inside the tube. The cup shape is called the meniscus; sight along the bottom of it.

(continued)

ROBERT TUPPER

When Robert Tupper wanted to establish a slope away from his house, he relied on the old principle that water will seek its own level in an open hose.

I added 18 inches of clear plastic tubing to each end of my garden hose, using hose couplings. Then I taped one plastic end to a four-foot stake pounded in the ground. I taped the other plastic end to a portable four-foot stake with a yardstick attached. (This stake was *not* set in the ground.)

To use the device, I first put the two tubes side by side and marked the water level on the yardstick. By standing the portable stake at various places in the yard and checking the reading, I could figure out how much dirt I had to move to get the slope I wanted. As the ground level dropped, the water level in the tube came up.

Water seeks its own level in an open hose, so Robert Tupper came up with a way to use that principle to help him establish a slope away from his house.

Likewise, you can use the same technique to estimate how far walls are out of plumb. Let's say you hold your level with one end on the floor along a wall and read the plumb vial. You see that there's a ¼-inch gap between the level and the wall. If you are using a two-foot level and the wall is eight feet high, you'll know the top of the wall is 1 inch out of whack if the stud is straight. And don't forget that the plumb bob is also a leveling device; it gives you a perfectly vertical line.

TIPS ON CARE

Levels deserve good care, not so much because they cost money, but because you want them to be accurate. If your level gets a nick in it, take time to smooth it out. I take my six-foot wooden level in the house every night during the winter to avoid having it go through freeze and thaw cycles that could affect its accuracy.

Take care when transporting your levels, too. One good way to transport levels is to use the cardboard core of carpet rolls. Saw off a proper length, then cut out wooden ends with your saber saw. If you should drop your level, it has a better chance for survival if it is inside one of these protectors.

CHAPTER 13

JIM YOUNG:

SAWING THE STRAIGHT AND NARROW

If you watch any construction crew at work framing up a house you can quickly figure out that most of the work boils down to measuring, cutting, positioning and fastening. Mistakes anywhere in the building process can be critical. Learning a few tricks of the trade can reduce "do-overs," boost efficiency on the job and make the end result more satisfactory. Sawing is no exception, says Jim Young, formerly the director of Cornerstones owner-builder school in Brunswick, Maine.

Jim, now working as a freelance designer, takes a break from building his own house to reflect on some things that have helped him do a better job of sawing lumber.

A while back, I saw a carpenter doing something that made so much sense, I thought it should be in the first chapter of every how-to carpentry book. He was cutting a bunch of floor joists to the same length. And to start the job, he carefully stacked up his boards on the ground so that the pieces were all flush and square at one end. Then he measured the top piece and marked the cut line. Next, he set his circular saw so that the blade cut about ⅛ inch deeper than the thickness of one board. When he made the cut, the blade cut into the piece below, leaving a nice mark that showed where he should cut the next board. He was able to go right down the stack that way, without having to measure each piece separately.

Actually, if you don't do this sort of thing for a living, make sure the saw is cutting true 90° and remeasure after every three or four pieces, just to be sure you haven't wandered a bit. And you can use a framing square to check that the other ends stay flush and square. This basic technique makes perfect sense; it's a real time-saver.

USING A SAWHORSE

A common problem for beginners is cutting a piece of wood between two sawhorses. It may look easy, but if you try it you can see there's a

Professional carpenters become proficient at cutting boards on one sawhorse.

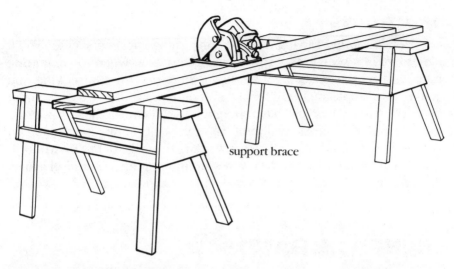

Cutting boards between two sawhorses is easier if you use a couple of 2 × 8s or 2 × 10s for support. Set your blade to cut just a fraction deeper than the board you are cutting.

problem – the two halves of the wood will tend to buckle, and your saw may bind or even kick upward. But you often need to make the cut in the middle of a board, not near an end. Here's what you can do. To prevent binding, you can put one or two 2 × 8s or 2 × 10s on the sawhorses as a work surface. Put the cutting piece on these supports, and set your saw so the blade cuts just a fraction deeper than the thickness of the piece. The support pieces will get marked slightly, but their strength won't be impaired, and you can still use them.

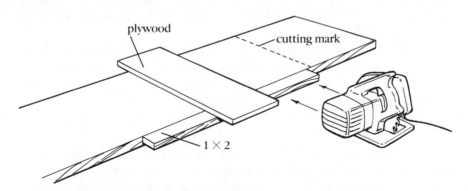

To cut a number of pieces of lumber at the same angle, you can make yourself a simple angle guide from plywood and a 1 × 2.

ANGLE CUTS

Here's another sawing tip, one concerning angle cuts. Often you'll have to make several cuts at the same angle, such as when you're cutting rafters. To get the angles right without a lot of repetitive measuring, you can make a simple angle guide. Use a straight piece of 1 × 2 and a scrap piece of plywood that also has a straight edge. Then nail the 1 × 2 across the plywood at the angle you want. You can position this angle guide on the rafter and push your circular saw along the edge of the plywood to get your angle cut. You can put away your framing square or level gauge. With this tool you get both an angle and a cutting guide.

USING THE HANDSAW

Sometimes the simplest tools are the hardest to master,
observes Charlie Huddleston, instructor at the Owner Builder
Center in Berkeley, California. As an example, he admits that
even though you can figure out how to use a handsaw within a
few minutes, learning to use one well can be a different matter.

Beginners heave and strain on the saw and end up with ragged cuts. By contrast, experienced carpenters seem to slice through wood without effort, and each cut they make is even and precise. But the most difficult thing is cutting straight. Even if you start with a good clean line scribed on the surface of the wood, it's common to wind up with an uneven, wobbly cut. Saws just don't seem to want to go in a straight line. But there's a fairly easy solution. Instead of looking at the blade or at the wood you're cutting into, look down the line, just ahead of the blade. It's like keeping your eye on the road. If you look at the place you're going instead of where you are, your body and brain tend to automatically head there in a straight line.

There's a complicating factor, though. You don't want your cut to be straight just on the top surface of the wood; you also want it to be straight vertically. You're operating in three dimensions, not two. What I often do is draw a vertical line on the cut end of the piece of wood, as well as a horizontal line on the top. Then – here's the critical part – I begin the cut with the saw held smack on the vertical line.

As the cut progresses, I gradually work the saw back into the normal angle for cutting. The start is all-important. If you begin with a good vertical cut, you should be able to maintain it. Try to keep your shoulder

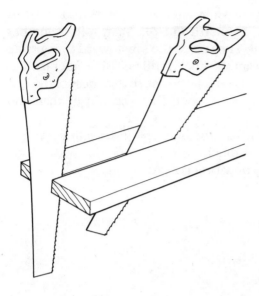

Drawing a vertical line on the end of a board, as well as on top, can help you begin to cut straight with a handsaw. Gradually work the saw back to the normal angle.

and elbow in the same plane with the saw blade and edge of cut. This will help keep the cut square and straight.

Another factor in making precise cuts is learning to be consistent. Get into a natural flow. Make each stroke as much like all the others as possible. Most novices try to force the saw through the wood. Instead, just get into a comfortable position, lock yourself into it and ride the saw. It should be a steady, rhythmic flow. Apply a slight pressure when you push the saw, then relax when you pull it back. Your cuts will be straighter, and you won't exhaust yourself by constantly fighting the tool.

A couple of other tips have to do with the thickness of the line you draw, and the thickness of the saw blade. People tend to forget that a pencil line has a certain dimension. This can be critical in finish work, when you're trying to make absolutely precise cuts. You can sharpen a pencil to a fine point, but even then the line may be too thick for real precision.

What I do is draw the line with a razor knife. The knife gives about the thinnest possible line. The only thing you have to be careful about is to put the line where you want it. You can erase a pencil line, but not a knife line.

People also tend to forget that the saw blade itself has thickness. It's far thicker than the line you draw. If you saw straight down the middle of the line, the blade will overlap it on both sides, and you'll wind up with a slightly shorter piece of wood than you wanted. Carpenters deal with this problem by following the rule: *Leave the line on.* Many follow another maxim: Cut *to* it, not *through* it. They place the saw toward the outside edge of the line because they want the line to still be visible after the cut is made, but not the whole line. If you left the entire thickness of the line on the wood, you'd have a piece of wood that was bigger than you wanted.

The ideal is to leave exactly half the line. That takes a fine eye, and you don't have to worry about it much for most work. But with a little practice, you'll be surprised by how precise you can get.

CHAPTER 14

CHARLIE HUDDLESTON AND DALE McCORMICK:

WHEN BOARDS AREN'T PERFECT

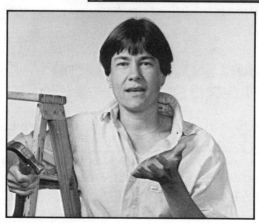

Lumber is almost never straight. Old-timers usually proceed on the cynical assumption that every piece of wood is guilty until proven innocent. They suggest you eyeball every piece of lumber you use, looking for the odd twists and deceitful curves that can sabotage your construction project.

The best time to inspect your wood, of course, is before buying it. Charlie Huddleston, an instructor at the Owner Builder Center in Berkeley, California, starts off this chapter with some other solid thoughts about lumber. He's seen plenty of it in the 22 years he worked as a general contractor and builder, and the last 13 years he's assisted owner-builders with their projects.

Dale McCormick was an instructor at Cornerstones, an owner-builder school in Brunswick, Maine. She has some useful tips on how to buy lumber and what you can do if you find yourself with less-than-perfect specimens.

By Charlie Huddleston

Be especially wary when you order a load of lumber to be delivered. The sad truth is that the folks at the lumberyard may not treat a home-owner nearly as well as they'll treat a contractor who is a frequent customer. They know the homeowner isn't going to order another large load next month, or maybe ever again. So there's a strong temptation to unload some inferior merchandise on him or her.

Be very critical when the truck arrives. Before allowing the driver to unload, look the wood over as carefully as you can. You won't be able to see it all, but inspect as much as is visible. If the wood is obviously flawed, refuse to accept it. And later on, if you find that some bad wood was stuck in the middle of the load, toss it into a pickup truck and take it back. Usually, if the wood is really in sorry shape, you can exchange it for good lumber.

CHECKING FOR COMMON LUMBER PROBLEMS

Lumber is heir to many misfortunes. In extreme cases, you may discover you've been sold wood that is badly splintered, rotted or even infested (wood-eating bugs can ride into your home deep inside new lumber the same way tropical spiders try to sneak into the country inside banana crates). A less serious problem occurs when lumber is festooned with large knots (driving a nail into a rock-hard knot at the base of a stud is no fun). The most common problem, though, is simple lack of straightness.

The best time to get rid of bad lumber problems is when you buy the lumber, or at the time of delivery. Be picky; you're the customer.

Some pieces of lumber have crowns, meaning that they're curved on their narrow side. Others are bowed – they are curved on their broad sides. And some are warped or twisted. You can't escape it. The best you can do is to know where to use each type of lumber and where to avoid using it.

Take 2 × 4 studs, for instance. Twisted 2 × 4s are the worst. The only thing to do with one is to cut it up into short sections and use it for blocking. It's no good for anything else.

If I had to choose between a bowed stud and one with a crown, I'd take the one with the bow. A bowed stud is not as strong as a perfectly straight stud, but at least it stays inside the plane of the wall, whereas a crowned stud pushes out of the plane, causing all sorts of headaches when you try to put on the drywall or paneling.

SORTING 2 × 4s

It's a good idea to divide your studs into three categories: the straight ones, the slightly curved ones and everything else. Then select from these three categories when building various parts of a wall. The basic rule is this: If you're going to do anything with the stud besides nailing finish wall material to it, it should be straight. Consequently, try to use your straightest studs around the doors and windows. Trying to install a straight window frame in a crooked opening can be a real headache.

Wall intersections are less critical than doors and windows. You can use slightly curved studs there. For one thing, you may be able to pull them more or less straight by toenailing one stud into another. But beyond that, even if a corner stud stays slightly curved, finishing the wall won't be overly difficult. It's fairly easy to cut a piece of paneling to fit such a curve.

As for the studs in the "everything else" category, try to use these deep inside the walls, between the corners and the door and window openings. Tuck them away where you can forget them.

ESTIMATING LUMBER NEEDS
By Dale McCormick

There are fairly easy formulas you can use to help you determine how many studs you'll need for walls, floor joists and ceiling joists and rafters. There are also some simple calculations for estimating the number of plywood sheets you'll need for subflooring and wall sheathing as well as roof sheathing.

WALL STUDS

Estimating the number of studs you'll need for walls is fairly easy. If the studs will be spaced 16 inches on center (the normal distance), use this guide: *Buy 1½ studs for each linear foot of wall.* For example, order 30 studs for a 20-foot wall. This number will give you enough lumber for regular studs plus the double studs in the corners and around walls, and for the short studs under windows.

FLOOR JOISTS

Figuring out how many floor joists you need is a bit more complicated. There are two ways joists can be laid out. In one, each joist extends from one side of the foundation to the other. Normally, the joists are 16 inches on center. For this situation, use this formula: *Number of joists equals the length of the wall, multiplied by .75, plus 1.* For example, if the wall is 24 feet long, you would multiply 24 by .75 to get 18. Add 1, and you end up with a grand total of 19 joists.

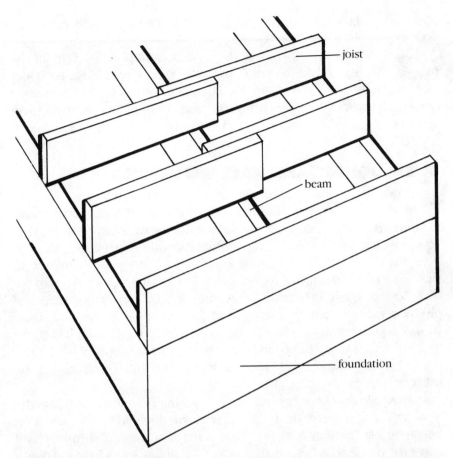

To determine the number of joists needed, multiply the length of the wall by .75, then add 1. If you have double joists meeting in the middle, as shown here, double the wall length in the equation.

The other way to lay out joists is to have one joist extend from one side of the foundation and another joist extend from the other side. Each pair meets in the middle of the span, where it is supported by a beam. In this case, you use exactly the same formula, but you double the length of the foundation wall. For example, if the wall is 24 feet long, you double this to 48. Then you multiply 48 by .75 to get 36, and you add 1 to get a total of 37 joists. If there will be stair openings in your floor, add an extra three joists per opening.

CEILING JOISTS AND RAFTERS

Virtually no figuring is needed to determine how many ceiling joists you'll need. In most situations, the total will be exactly equal to the number of floor joists. The only exception occurs if you have a different number of stairways leading into the attic than you have leading into the basement. Adjust the total by using the rule of thumb that each stair opening requires three extra joists.

To decide how many rafters you'll need, multiply the length of the ridge by .75, add 1, and then multiply by 2. Thus, if your ridge is 60 feet long, multiply 60 by .75 to get 45. Then add 1 for a total of 46 rafters spaced 16 inches on center. This is the number of rafters that will go on one side of the ridge. Double it, and you get 92, the number for the entire roof.

SUBFLOORING AND WALL SHEATHING

To calculate the number of plywood sheets you'll need for your subflooring, you first need to calculate the total floor area. If your house measures 30 by 60 feet, for example, the floor area is 1,800 square feet. From this, subtract the size of any stairwells or other openings. If you will have a single stairwell with an opening of 4 feet by 9 feet, subtract 36 square feet (4 × 9) from 1,800 to get 1,764 square feet.

Next, assuming that you'll be using regular 4-by-8-foot sheets of plywood for the subfloor, use this formula: *Number of plywood sheets equals floor area divided by 32.* So, you would divide 1,764 by 32 to get 55.13. Round this up to 56, and that's how many sheets of plywood you need. If your house is an odd measurement, say 51 feet, you'll have some waste and will need more sheets.

The technique for figuring wall sheathing is similar. Calculate the total wall area, subtract the total area of all windows and doors, and then divide by 32. The only trick is to remember that the wall sheathing will cover the headers and sills at the ends of the floors, so include the depth of the headers when calculating wall area.

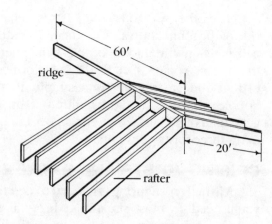

To determine the number of rafters needed, multiply the length of the ridge by .75, add 1, then multiply by 2.

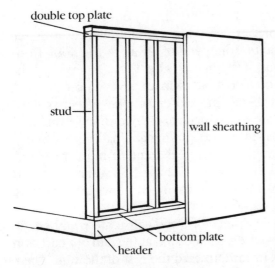

To estimate the number of 4 × 8-foot sheets of wall sheathing needed, figure the total wall area (including headers), subtract the areas of the windows and doors and divide by 32.

ROOF SHEATHING

To determine how many sheets of plywood you'll need for roof sheathing, you can use this formula: *Multiply the length of the ridge by the length of the rafter, and divide by 32*. Thus, if your ridge is 60 feet long and your rafters are 20 feet long, you multiply 60 by 20 to get 1,200. Then divide by 32 to get 37.5. Round up, and you have 38 sheets of plywood. This is the number of sheets you'll need to cover one pitch of the roof.

To get the number of sheets for both pitches, double the length of the rafters, then multiply by the length of the ridge. Thus, multiply 40 (double the 20-foot rafters) by 60 (the length of the ridge) to get 2,400. Divide this number by 32 and you get 75.

I think it's wise to follow the old saying: Too much is better than too little. There will always be some waste and some things you overlook. So when in doubt, buy a little more wood than you think you may need, particularly if you're using plywood, which has a waste factor of 5 percent. You can almost always take any excess back to the lumberyard at the end of the project.

WORKING WITH IMPERFECT LUMBER

You have to inspect each piece of wood you use so you can choose one that isn't bent too badly for the job you have in mind, and then figure out how to unbend it.

Typically, a long piece of wood will be slightly bowed or C-shaped. Let's say you want to nail a piece of wood to a straight line, as in porch decking, or you're nailing the bottom plate of a wall to the floor. Don't start by nailing it at both ends. If the board is bent, you'll never get the bend out of the middle – or you'll do it only with excessive force. Instead, nail down one end of the board, then move over a couple of feet, pull the board in the direction opposite to its curve, and drive your second nail. Work your way down the board this way, pulling and nailing as you go.

Be careful, though. Sometimes wood is bent in more than one direction. It might be more S-shaped than C-shaped. So you have to start by pulling it in one direction. Then, after driving in a few nails, you have to pull it back in the other direction.

In some cases, the curve in a piece of wood can act to your benefit. For example, it's a good idea to use a curved stud at the end of a partition wall. Be sure the stud curves inward, toward the rest of the wall. Then, when you nail this stud to an adjoining wall, the curve will tend to pull the two walls together.

For the most part, though, curves are a curse. And even if you try to straighten each piece of lumber as you go along, you're almost sure to run into situations where you have to correct an unwanted curve after you've already nailed the wood in place.

UNLEVEL JOISTS

One day my class was working on a deck where the ends of some joists extended a couple of feet beyond a beam. We wanted to put a

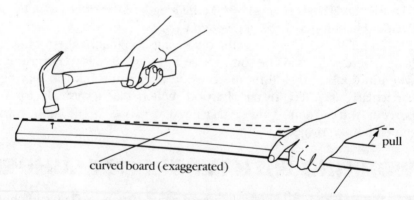

curved board (exaggerated)

pull

Sometimes you can salvage C-shaped and S-shaped bowed boards that are nailed flat by alternately driving nails and pulling the board back into a straighter position.

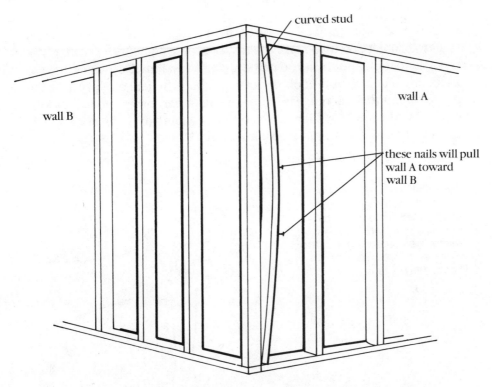

A bowed board can be used at the end of a stud wall, with the curve bending away from the adjoining wall. Nailing the stud will help pull the two walls together.

header on the joists. The beam held the joists firmly, of course, and the joists were basically level. But the very ends of the joists, which were hanging out there in the air, were slightly unlevel. A few of them had risen a fraction of an inch, and others had fallen a bit. Nailing the header on directly would leave some up and some down; it would have looked terrible.

Several student-builders wanted to plane the joists, but my rule is never to plane off more than $1/32$ inch. Instead, what we did was to nail the header to the first joist, then pull it down to nail it to the next joist (which was lower than the first joist), then pull it up to reach the third joist (which was higher) and so forth, pulling it up and down, as each joist required. The result was that the header served to pull the ends of all the joists into line.

Here's another great trick to straighten bad lumber. Let's say you've got two pieces of wood next to each other, such as two joists running along the side of a stairwell. If one of them is higher than the other, you'll want to bring it down, to make the two boards level with each other. The way I do that is to pound a 16d nail straight down into the lower joist, and I take my hammer and hook the claw around the nail and pry as if I'm going to pull the nail out. The top of my hammer forces the higher joist down. While I hold it there, someone else can drive nails horizontally through both joists, to pin them flush.

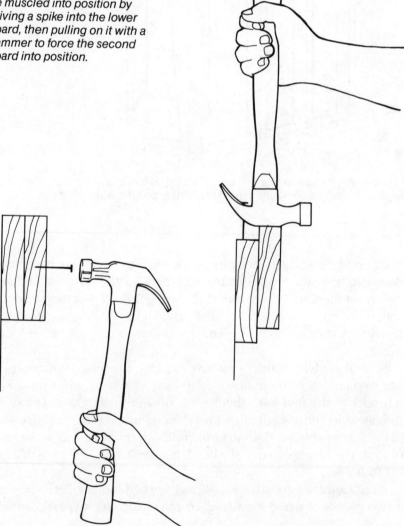

Two parallel boards that are not level with each other can often be muscled into position by driving a spike into the lower board, then pulling on it with a hammer to force the second board into position.

WORKING WITH GREEN WOOD

For your next building project, you might want to consider using green wood. That's a suggestion made by Elias Velonis, founder of the Heartwood Owner-Builder School in Washington, Massachusetts.

Green wood is lumber that has not dried; it still has sap in it. Using green wood can actually offer several advantages: it's frequently cheaper than kiln-dried, store-bought lumber; using it can be emotionally gratifying, especially if it has been cut from

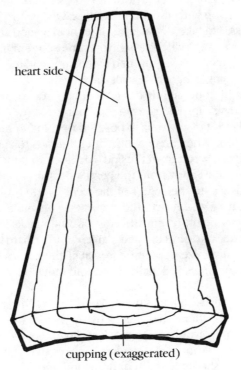

heart side

cupping (exaggerated)

As it dries, green wood tends to become cupped (curved when laying flat and viewed from the end). By using it heart-side up–on a deck, for example–you can help keep the edges from curling.

(continued)

WORKING WITH GREEN WOOD — *Continued*

trees on your own land and it can actually work better than dry wood in post-and-beam framing.

Green wood is going to twist slightly when it dries, and that's good for post-and-beam construction. The tenons and mortises will be pressed tightly together as the wood twists, so the structure will be that much more solid.

There are some tricks to working with green wood. The lumber is cut in local sawmills and it often emerges in a variety of irregular sizes. Your 2 × 10s, for example, may range anywhere from 9½ to 10¼ inches in width. If you use these for floor joists, you can wind up with a very uneven floor. One way to prevent this unevenness is to take all the joists, line them up and arrange them from narrowest to widest. Then you can use them in that order, with the 9½-inch joists at one end of the floor, and the depth of the joists increasing progressively all the way over to the other end. The floor will slope slightly, but not enough that you notice it, and you won't have dips and rises in the floor.

Another bit of advice is to position the lumber *heart side up, heart side out.* When green wood dries, it tends to cup. That is, if you look at the wood from the end, you'll see that the edges have curled. They curl away from the heart side, the side of the wood that was closest to the center of the tree.

By putting the heart side up when you build a deck, for example, you help prevent the edges of the planks from curling upward (a deck made of cupped planks could be hard to walk on). You'll also minimize cupping if you nail the planks down with screw nails or ring-shank nails. They hold much better than regular nails.

Despite the advantages green wood has in some applications, there are times when you shouldn't use it. Use dry wood anywhere that you want to avoid gaps. It won't shrink or cup nearly as much as green wood. Trim and any other surfaces that you want to be weather tight should be built of dry wood, too.

There are two primary ways to get dry wood. You can buy it from a lumberyard, or you can save money by drying out a load of inexpensive green wood. If you have green softwood, such as pine, try to dry it for about one year per inch of thickness. For hardwood, such as oak, make it two years per inch of thickness.

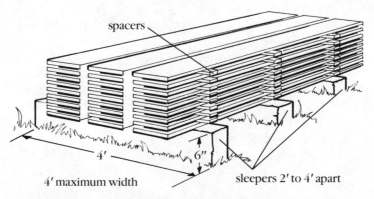

spacers

4'

6"

4' maximum width

sleepers 2' to 4' apart

Stacking green wood correctly is important. Stack level, with spacers of dry wood set directly over sleepers positioned from two to four feet apart.

Ideally, the wood should be kept in a well-ventilated shed or garage or under a tarpaulin during the drying process. But you can keep the wood outdoors as long as you bring it into a dry, heated area four to six weeks before using it. This will help remove water that may have soaked into the wood.

Wherever you put the wood, try to stack it carefully. Be sure the sleepers form a level plane for the wood to rest on. If a stack is made up of 1× lumber, the spacers should be no more than two feet apart. For heavier lumber, the spacers can be up to four feet apart. Put the stacks in a well-drained area, and keep the bottom layers of wood at least six inches off the ground. Cover the stacks to ward off rain, but allow air to circulate around the wood.

Try to use spacers of dry wood, positioned directly over the sleepers. The maximum width of each stack should be four feet, so you will have the greatest possible air movement through the stack. And remember to stack the wood in such a way that you can unstack it conveniently. It's generally a good idea to have separate stacks for large and small pieces of wood. Try to put the pieces you'll use last on the bottom, and the pieces you'll use first on the top.

CHAPTER 15

DUANE CLARKE:
LESSONS ON NAILING

One old-timer says he got a lesson in nailing his first day on the job. After lunch, he came back to find half of the handle on his brand-new hammer sawed off. He told the foreman, who smiled and explained that because the end of the handle wasn't being used anyway, he had taken the liberty of removing it. The foreman was making a simple point: A hammer works better if you grab it by the end of the handle. But there's more to the art of hammering nails and nailing procedures.

Eight years on home construction crews and several years of teaching others to build homes, decks and garages have kept Duane Clarke thinking about the basics of using a hammer. Duane is an instructor in home building for Knox, a major home center chain in Burnsville, Minnesota. He says it's worthwhile to work on good nailing techniques.

145

The holding power of a nail will mostly depend on how big a nail you use, the kind of nail you use, where you position that nail and what kind of wood you're nailing into. Nail suppliers have big charts on what nail to use where. But in rough construction only a few nails are used for a majority of the work:

- 16d cement-coated sinkers for rough framing
- 8d cement-coated sinkers for flooring and roof sheathing
- 16d galvanized casing nails for hanging windows and doors
- 4d, 6d or 8d finish nails for interior trim work

I like to use cement-coated nails rather than common nails because their coating actually allows them to be driven easier, plus the resin helps seal the holes. But if you start driving a cement-coated nail and stop, it grabs and is easy to bend. So once you start, keep driving it until it's in.

CHOOSING AND USING NAILS

When selecting nails for length, one thing to keep in mind is the thickness of the lumber. Generally nails are driven first through the thinner board into the thicker board. The nail should penetrate two-thirds of the way into the second board. This is true unless you are nailing hardwood, where you don't want that nail to go much farther than halfway into the second board.

If you ever get into situations where nails penetrate the second board, you can increase their strength by clinching. Use two hammers, with one hammer held against the head of the driven nail. Use the other to bend over the point of the nail with the grain. It's possible to get a good clinch using only one hammer if you approach it correctly. First, hit the nail at the side of the point with the edge of the hammer face. This will bend the nail without backing it out. Continue to bend the nail over by hitting it under the point to complete the clinch.

How many nails you use depends on what you're nailing into. I generally use two nails at the ends of 2 × 4s, three nails for 2 × 6s and 2 × 8s and four nails for 2 × 10s and 2 × 12s. I like to position the nails 1 to 1½ inches in from the edges of the board. Some carpenters like to nail as far as possible from the ends of boards. They'll move back on the board and angle the nail into the second board. The angled nail will have more holding power than one nailed straight into the end grain. The farther from the end of the board that you nail, the less likely it will be that the board will split.

Some nail-driving techniques may come as a surprise. If you watch a professional carpenter closely, you'll see that he positions that nail to match the arc of the hammer. In other words, he will angle that nail toward him slightly so that when the hammer strikes it hits the nail squarely on the head. In rough framing, nails are usually driven at an angle toward the center of the board. This increases nail holding-power.

People have different ways of toenailing. When I started construction work, I had problems until an old carpenter took me by the hand and showed me a good way. Instead of big spikes, I use 8d nails and use two on each side. If I'm nailing a stud into a plate, for example, I first position the

(continued on page 150)

TOENAILING BASICS

On a spring day, taking a break from stacking huge piles of lumber, Charlie Bates gets to talking about using the hammer, a tool that's used in virtually every house that's ever been built. Charlie, an instructor at Yestermorrow, an owner-builder school in Warren, Vermont, observes that our world would look a whole lot different today if it weren't for the hammer, probably one of man's earliest tool inventions.

Good hammering basically boils down to good nailing, and good nailing means good construction. It starts with selecting good lumber and choosing the right nail for the job. But there are ways to make sure the nailing you accomplish with your hammer is adequate for the job. Take toenailing, for example. People think of toenailing as a very rough nailing procedure, and sometimes it is. You can use toenailing to pull a warped plank into line, for example. Let's say you're putting down subfloor planks, and one of them is slightly warped. You can drive a nail into the edge of the plank at a very shallow angle and then just pound the daylights out of it. Eventually, if the plank doesn't split, the nail will pull the plank over. But that's not what toenailing is really all about. When done correctly, toenailing is a very flexible, useful technique. It's not something you turn to as a last resort; it's often the right solution for a particular problem.

The primary purpose of toenailing is to pin together two pieces of lumber that butt against each other – a floor joist and a

(continued)

TOENAILING BASICS — *Continued*

header, for example. The secret is to drive your nails at the proper angle. What you want to do is take advantage of the grain in the pieces of wood. If a nail goes into a piece of wood from the end so that it is parallel to the grain, it will be easy to pull out. Toenailing prevents this.

Generally aim to drive your nails in at a 30° angle. This way, the shaft of the nail comes into the header almost at right angles to the grain. The grain grips it and holds it firmly in place by compression. Meanwhile, the head of the nail grabs the joist, so even though the shaft is pretty close to being parallel to the grain of the joist, you can't pull the joist from the header. If you use three or four nails, toenailed from both sides of the joist, the structure is going to be really strong.

Precision toenailing also pays off when you have two pieces of wood running side by side. You might have two joists next to each other, and one of them might be warped so that it is higher than it should be in the middle. The brute force approach would be to drive a nail downward through the warped joist, trying to

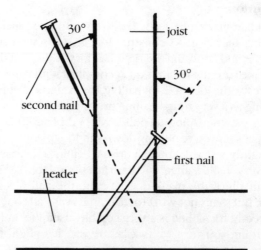

Toenailing techniques can vary. Charlie likes to drive three or four nails, toenailed from both sides at about a 30° angle.

force it into line with the other joist. This might work, the same way that you forced the plank to straighten it out.

But brute force isn't always the best approach. For one thing, if you hit the nail too hard, most of the force will be taken by the nail itself, not by the joist. So the nail will go in, but the joist might not move much. For another thing, you can go at the problem from the other direction. You can drive a nail upward, going through the straight joist into the warped joist. You don't have to whack away at the nail, because the nail will literally pull the warped joist downward. It seems unbelievable, but it works. The nail sort of claws its way upward, pulling the joist down as a result.

Toenailing can also be used to simplify the process of raising a wall. When you start to move a wall into position, for example, it's not hard for the bottom of the wall to slip across the floor surface and maybe even fall off the edge of the floor. But some well-placed nails can keep the wall from slipping. Drive duplex nails through the bottom plate of the wall into the floor to pin the bottom of the wall where you want it. Now you can lift the top of the wall and the duplex nails will bend as you raise the wall. When you get the wall all the way up, the nails will pull out of the floor just as you get the wall vertical. All you have to do is pull the double-headed duplex nails out of the wall and you're home free.

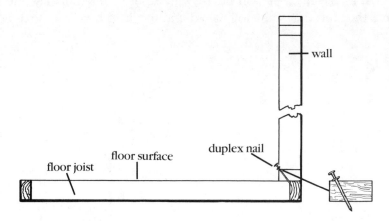

To keep walls from sliding, you can tack the bottom with duplex nails. They'll bend as you raise the wall. After the wall is up, pull them out.

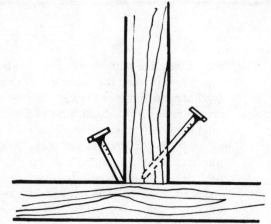

Toenailing can be easier if you first drive a holding nail on one side to keep the stud in place. After driving two nails into the opposite side, remove the holding nail and toenail that side of the stud.

stud next to my line, then move it back ⅛ or ¼ inch and tap a nail straight in to hold the stud as I nail from the opposite side. I drive the two nails in, then come around and drive in the opposite two. Then I pull out the holding nail. The idea is to have the nails come through the center of the stud into the plate.

Another toenailing trick is to use spacer blocks. After I get one stud in, I cut myself a spacer of 2 × 4, even 2 × 2. If the studs are 16 inches on center, the spacer block will be 14½ inches long. I simply lay one end against the stud that's already nailed and use it to hold the next stud I nail in.

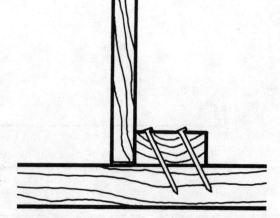

Nail position can affect holding power. This is a good way to drive nails bearing a heavy load. The load force will drive the nails in deeper.

In other nailing, the basic idea is to position the nail so that the load will fall across the nail, rather than with the length of the nail. You want the strain to be crosswise to the nail. This takes advantage of the nail's shear strength. You can pull a nail out easily, but it's tough to shear it off. Another basic rule of thumb is to try to position nails so any weight will tend to push the nail deeper.

I use a 22-ounce framing hammer for rough carpentry. This hammer is exactly 16 inches from the end of the handle to the top of the head, and can be used to mark off 16-inch centers. I often see new carpenters lay that hammer down and pull out their tape, not realizing they could use the hammer itself. For finish work I use a 16-ounce hammer. On both I prefer the straight claw over the curved claw; I don't have to reach over as far when pulling out nails.

To do any serious hammering, get yourself a leather nail pouch. I prefer a belt with side pouches because the pouches stay out of the way when I'm kneeling down to nail or when I'm climbing ladders.

REDUCING BOARD SPLITTING

One thing that plagues any carpenter is board splitting. If you find that the boards you are nailing are splitting, one trick you can use is to blunt the end of the nail before driving it. There are also other ways to help reduce splitting. For example, if you are nailing close to the edge of a board and you know it will split, you can nail the board first, then cut it to length after the nails are in. You can also predrill holes for the nail. One way is to cut the head off of a nail, chuck it in your drill and use it to make the hole. Another slick way is to invest in what's called a nail spinner. This is a device you set in your drill, then insert the nail and drill it into position. The nail will go in within ¼ inch or so, then you drive it home with a hammer and nail set.

It's also good to know that nail sets, used to drive nails below the surface of wood, come in different sizes. I use three sizes. When you try to use a nail set that's too big, you can end up making the nail hole larger than it needs to be. A nail set, with its concave head, can also be used to drive nails back out of boards.

NAIL HELPERS

There are some nail strength helpers, such as mastic and clips and brackets. Metal clips for joists and posts can save time on projects such as decks and increase the strength of the joints significantly over nails alone. Mastic works great to increase the holding power of furring strips on

(continued on page 154)

NAILING FOR STRENGTH

Nailing is actually a precision art, observes Patrick Foster, an instructor at Cornerstones owner-builder school in Brunswick, Maine. He notes that there's much more to it than just slapping nails into the wood as quickly as possible.

Even when framing a house, the goal is to achieve tolerances of as little as $1/16$ inch. If you do sloppy work, little errors will start adding up on you. And, before you know it, the floor plan will be

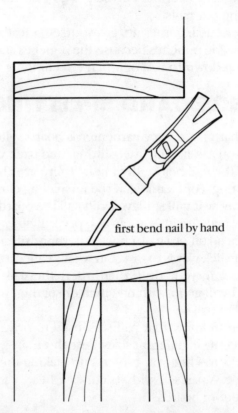

first bend nail by hand

If you're in a situation where there's not enough room to swing a hammer, one solution is to first bend the nail by hand so you can hit the head more squarely.

off slightly, your kitchen cabinets won't fit right and you've got headaches.

INCREASING YOUR PRECISION

There are tricks you can use to increase hammering precision. Once in a while you need to drive nails in a confined space where you can't really reach. To give yourself sufficient room for your swing, you can literally bend the nail by hand before hitting it. Then, in effect, you can drive the nail around a corner. Sounds crazy, but it works.

Another trick is to use a nail to draw two pieces of wood together. For example, if you're nailing partition walls to exterior walls, the top plates will overlap. The obvious way to nail the plates together is to drive a nail downward through the plates. But if you nail upward at an angle, the nail actually pulls the two walls together. It's action and reaction: the nail goes in one direction, the top plate goes in the other.

If you're nailing into brittle wood, you can use the old carpenter's trick of blunting the point of the nail. A sharp nail acts as a wedge, driving wood apart. This can cause brittle wood to split. But a blunt nail punches through the wood directly in front of the nail while leaving the surrounding wood intact.

To blunt the nail, what I do is to find a nail that's already in the wood. I turn the new nail around, placing it head-to-head with the first nail. Then I can simultaneously hit the point of the new nail while driving the first nail a little deeper into the wood.

A special brittle-wood situation is installing clapboard siding, such as cedar. Hitting a nail into the clapboard can make it split, and nothing looks worse than split ends on new clapboard. So I carry a small push drill with me, and I quickly make a small hole for each nail before driving it in.

Probably the main thing people need to work on when nailing is their attitude. When I find that I've missed on a few swings, I try to remind myself of a couple of things: first, to keep my eye on the nail like a batter keeping his eye on the ball and second, to slow down my swing. You really don't have to swing fast to hit with sufficient force. A slow, deliberate swing will do, and it's much easier to control.

masonry walls. It can help prevent squeaks when you're installing ½-inch CDX plywood over joists for subflooring. If I'm putting up an interior wall on a basement slab, and I know that the wall is going to be permanent, I'll use both cut nails and mastic under the bottom plate. Generally I put either a cut nail or a masonry nail between every other stud.

NAILING PATTERNS

In some situations nailing patterns can be critical. These include nailing in windows and doors, and nailing finish flooring, roof sheathing and drywall. Each of these situations requires caution. Generally nails should not be driven through window jambs. When installing sheathing, try to follow the instructions of the manufacturer. Plywood sheets, for example, will call for a different nailing pattern than waferboard.

Nailing patterns for drywall can vary, too. My rule of thumb is to select nails to get 1- to 1¼-inch penetration into the wood. I use two sets of two for putting drywall on walls and three sets of two for drywall on ceilings. This simply means using nails in pairs, spaced evenly between the edge nails. I drive the first nail of the pair in, then the second. Then I go back and give the first nail another tap.

PULLING NAILS

My hunch is that there's a stigma attached to the subject of pulling nails, which stems from when each of us were beginners learning to pound nails. Pulling a nail on the job was a sign of failure and inefficiency. Another reason could be that pulling nails is more or less a personal thing. There are no hard and fast rules. How you do it depends not only on the tools you have and use, but also on techniques you pick up by watching others and trying different ways yourself.

There are basically two kinds of nail-pulling operations. First there is pulling nails that are bent in the process of hammering or mistakenly driven into the wrong place. Any time you watch a crew frame up a house, you'll see your fair share of nail pulling. Knots, slippery hammer faces, defective nails, weak-shanked nails such as aluminum, and awkward nailing positions can all mean bent nails.

Then there's pulling nails in order to either dismantle or recycle lumber. Here nail pulling is a secondary job; the first order of business is to get that lumber apart, then to take care of the nails if that lumber is to be reused.

How difficult it is to get nails out depends on the nail itself, how and where it was driven and the size and type of lumber. Cement-coated sinkers used today have made nail pulling somewhat tougher. The resin on the nail "sets" once it has been driven. As a result, these nails are harder to get moving. Other hard-to-pull nails, besides bigger spikes, include ring-shanked nails because of their tremendous gripping power.

The easiest nail to pull is probably the duplex nail, which is made to be pulled. Used for temporary fastening of such things as scaffolding, wall bracing and so on, the double head allows instant access for pulling tools.

NAIL-PULLING HELPERS

Over the years hand-tool manufacturers have assembled a wide variety of nail-pulling helpers. Basically, they fall into the categories of the *claws,* which include the hammer and the common gooseneck wrecking bar; the *prybars,* which include the ripping bar and stripping bar; and the *chisels,* which include the clapboard and electrician chisels. Of course, many tools are hybrids with claws on one end, prybars on the other. Chisels, like other tools such as sledge hammers, help you pull nails indirectly.

Regardless of the tool, almost all nail pulling uses the basic types of leverage, what physics teachers call first- and second-class levers. With the first-class lever, the fulcrum (or pivot point) is between you and the load, or the nail you are pulling. This is the leverage you get with hammers and other clawed tools that are 90° to the handle. With the

There are probably more tools than you realize that are available for pulling nails. At the back of this photo, from left to right: three cat's-paws, two wrecking bars (often mistakenly called crowbars), two double-headed wrecking bars, two prybars and a ripping bar (on the floor). In front, counterclockwise from left: a sliding-handle nail puller, three small prybars, a splitting wedge, a framing hammer and a hand-drilling hammer.

second-class lever, the load is between you and the fulcrum. You use this kind of leverage when using tools with nail slots in the handle.

Unless we're tearing down a building, carpenters such as myself will depend on a few basic tools to pull nails: a hammer, a cat's-paw, a couple of flat prybars and a medium-sized gooseneck bar. And we will use them in that order, with the bulk of normal nail pulling falling to the hammer.

USING HAMMER CLAWS

Now, most people think of a hammer as a nail-driving tool and don't give as much thought to its nail-pulling function. I depend on 22-ounce and 16-ounce framing hammers, but I prefer the straight claws instead of curved claws for a couple of reasons (1) the straight claws are easier to get between two pieces of lumber and (2) with the straight claws I don't have to bend over as far to get the claws under the head of a nail. That's my preference, but many old-timers like curved claws; they say they get better leverage with them.

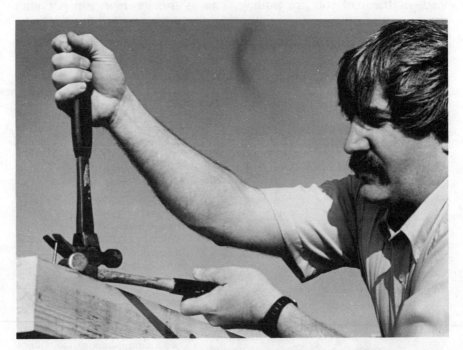

To get more leverage, some people use a second hammer. Whenever you pull nails, use a steady, smooth pulling motion and avoid forcing and jerking as much as possible.

Although much controversy exists about the merits of various types of hammer, there is general agreement that the strongest is a one-piece, solid-steel forged hammer. With head and handle in one piece it will take a super amount of punishment. Still, if you're a guy who was a star lineman on your school's football team, you won't have too much trouble putting that hammer out of commission.

Regardless of the hammer, when pulling nails, the idea is to use a steady, smooth pulling motion and avoid a lot of force, and especially jerking, as much as possible. So when you buy a hammer, look at it from the standpoint of pulling, as well as driving, nails. The claws should be heat-treated and well tempered. The V between the claws should be clean and sharp to let you get a good grip on a nail as big as 10d. Be aware that the weakest part of the hammer is just behind the head where it's the thinnest, in part to absorb shock when pounding nails.

Many carpenters use a block of wood as a fulcrum for better leverage. This works well on deeply imbedded nails as well as on those just started.

To reduce stress on this part of the handle and redistribute the load, you'll see many carpenters use a scrap block of wood as a fulcrum to give better leverage. It can even be a length of ¾-inch-thick board or a short piece of 2 × 4. You might think that using scrap wood as a fulcrum is more important when pulling nails that are deeply imbedded or nails that are driven into hardwood such as oak. This is true, but it's equally useful when pulling a nail that's just started an inch or so; the block gives the hammer added height for easier pulling.

Using wood blocks can help you gain leverage with other claw-type nail-pulling tools as well. I've even seen people weld a short stub of rod crosswise to the front of a hammer head to gain instant leverage.

NAIL-PULLER'S TRICKS

Of course, wherever the point of the nail protrudes, the easy way to pull the nail is to drive it back out, at least so the head is accessible. Clinched or bent-over nails can be restraightened using the claws of a hammer upside down. Or use the hammer claws, or another tool, to pry two boards apart, then hammer the top board back to expose the nail head.

Often the head of the nail will break off during pulling. If this happens, one way to gain purchase on the nail is to push the nail as far into the V notch of the hammer claws as possible, then twist the hammer a quarter turn to each side. The sharp inside edges will groove the nail to provide grip as you pull it. Or use a pliers or nippers, along with a piece of scrap wood if necessary, to inch the nail up and out.

What about nails that are already driven home? If you don't have anything else, you can use a wood chisel to carefully chip out the wood around a nail head. But the ideal tool is the cat's-paw. Cat's-paws dig right into the wood and get under the nail head so you can pull it out enough to grab it with a hammer or crowbar. In rough framing, many carpenters get around the problem by using a second hammer to drive the claws of the first hammer, either to get the claws under the nail head, or to help the claws get a good grip on a nail without a head. This works, but is frowned upon by safety experts who point out that this practice can lead to dangerous bits of metal flying from the hammers. Carpenters in a hurry, who consider time as money, often dismiss the advice. Still, it only takes one piece of metal in your retina to make you a believer. I'm one now, but it took a close call before I became a convert. A chip from a cross-hatched hammer face hit me in the eyelid, a fraction of an inch from disaster. I didn't feel it right away but noticed my eyelid bleeding. The metal is still in there as a reminder. (Tool manufacturers, tired of lawsuits, have put the onus on the user by affixing warning labels on hammers that advise wearing safety goggles at all times. The folks who follow tool-related court cases say that now the first question you will hear when you sue a tool company will be "Were you wearing safety goggles?" If not, they say you might as well forget about any big settlement.)

Ways to get around the danger involved in striking another tool, either a hammer, cat's-paw or other tool, is to use a nonmetal mallet or a hand-drilling hammer or light sledge. The best bet, in any case, is to wear safety goggles. In some cases you can use a diagonal cutting nippers to pry the nail up. Or, if the end of the nail just barely penetrates through the lumber, you can use a nail set to back the nail out enough to get your hammer claws under it. The concave head of a $\frac{2}{32}$ or $\frac{3}{32}$ nail set will fit over the nail's point to keep it from slipping off.

How big a nail can you pull with a hammer? At times in soft wood you can pull 16d spikes without a problem. But the general rule of thumb is that if the nail is bigger than 8d or 10d, put the hammer down and grab something bigger such as a gooseneck crowbar or wrecking bar. (The purists define the "crowbar" as a hefty five- or six-foot-long straight bar and the gooseneck types that resemble a cane as "wrecking bars." But both carpenters and the people selling them often call the goosenecks, crowbars.)

Other than pulling nails in the process of fastening lumber together, nail-pulling may take place during either *salvaging* (dismantle and recover operations) or *wrecking* (destroy maneuvers). The most common is salvaging.

SALVAGING OPERATIONS

One special problem in salvaging is pulling nails from trim or molding that you want to reuse. Sometimes you want to reuse the millwork to save money. Other times, you may need to save and reuse it because it would be too hard to replace with new material.

I carry two small, flat prybars on the order of the Wonderbar or Superbar for this kind of work. One is a cheap one (about $3), which I grind down quite thin on the end; the other is a more expensive version (about $6 to $8). I use the pair of prybars in a "buddy system." When I start removing trim, for example, I slip the thin end of the cheaper bar behind the molding first. The thin edge helps prevent making a notch at the back of the trim. Then I insert the second bar and use both to inch the trim off.

An alternate way of taking off trim is to use a nail set to punch the nail completely through the wood. The disadvantage is that you can end up with a bigger nail hole. Still another way to remove trim, especially

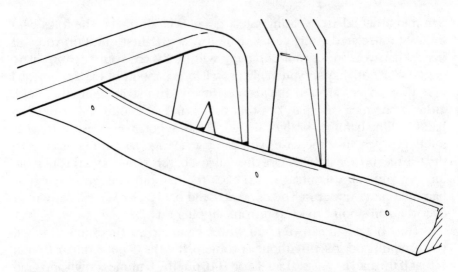

When removing delicate trim, two prybars work well, especially if one is ground down thin on one end. Drive the thin end in first, pull the trim out toward you and insert the second bar.

trim with flat-headed nails (such as you might find in multistage baseboard molding), is to first pry the molding out, then push it back so the nail heads are exposed. Then using nippers, cut the heads off.

At this point you can use the nail set to drive the shank of the nail through. Or you can pull off the molding, drive the nail shank in slightly so it can be covered with putty, then nip off the end of the nail that protrudes on the back side.

In cases where you pull trim off and have thin finish nails protruding from the back, it's often easier to pull them all the way through, rather than to try to back them out with a hammer. For this job, a Channellock (or tongue-and-groove) pliers works great. The rounded edge over the upper jaw acts as a perfect "rolling" fulcrum.

When removing doors and windows installed with casing nails, what works well for me is either a Sawzall or some sort of hacksaw to cut the nails off between the frame and rough opening. After taking off the trim and wall materials, cut the nails. Then, after pulling the unit out, you can easily either back out the nails, or leave them in place and trim off what's left on the back side.

What about nails in concrete? If you are removing walls and prying up a bottom plate, cut nails will generally pull right through the lumber.

So you end up with nails sticking up out of the concrete. The solution is not to try to pull them out, but to simply break them off. Cut nails are brittle and a couple of whacks with a sledge does the job. Wear your goggles. If the plate was glued, as well as nailed down, your only answer may be a sledge and ripping bar, though this approach leaves you with a pile of splinters.

WRECKING MANEUVERS

You might shudder at the thought of tearing down a building such as a garage or house. But, if it's 2× construction (2 × 4s, 2 × 6s, 2 × 8s and so on), you will be surprised at how nicely it comes down if you work at it step by step. Taking apart such buildings is actually "backwards building." Work at it in steps and, most importantly, pay as much attention to cleanup as you do to tearing things apart.

A good part of the cleanup operation is taking care of nails, pulling them if at all possible (it saves saw blades later). If you don't have time to pull them, at least back them out. If you don't back them out, bend them over. You'll not only avoid trips to the doctor, but you'll make your worksite a lot more comfortable to walk around in.

There's plenty to choose from when it comes to nail-pulling tools. On the racks of a well-stocked hardware store today you'll see, for example, some newer variations of the crowbar. One has a double head shaped somewhat like a horseshoe, with claws on each point. The handle is angled at about 45°. This tool can work well for prying up flooring, siding, sheathing and roof boards. You set the tool on the joist or rafter and slip its two-pronged head under the board and push down on the handle to get the job done fast.

Another version of the wrecking bar has a rockerlike head, with claws on each end. This tool lets you use either a forward or backward motion to pull nails out. The double head lets you move fast over boards with backed-out nails or on roof boards, for example, that are riddled with leftover shingle nails.

The commercial nail puller is the most expensive nail-pulling tool you can buy. It costs about $35, and for general construction you won't get that much use out of it. But it can be worthwhile buying if you do a lot of salvage work, especially if you have a considerable amount of plywood sheathing to remove and save. The tool has a sliding handle that acts as a pile driver to push one of its jaws under the nail head. Then you simply push the tool forward and the second jaw grabs under the nail head. As you continue in a forward motion the tool pulls the nail out.

Wood-splitting wedges can also come in handy in wrecking work. Wedges are especially helpful when you need to separate large nailed-together beams or headers. Instead of trying to pull nails out individually, put the lumber on edge and use prybars or crowbars in tandem to start splitting it apart. When you get the two pieces separated enough, insert a wedge. Then keep moving down toward the other end of the lumber. Keep adding wedges as the split opens up while you work from one end to the other.

Pulling staples is another matter. For smaller staples, the kind you shoot with a staple gun, you can buy a staple-pulling tool that looks like a screwdriver with a little claw on the end. But a regular screwdriver works, too; you can use a small, flat piece of wood held between your thumb and the top of the staple to help pull it out evenly. Ranchers use what's called a fencing tool for pulling out big fence-post-type staples; it has a special pointed head to dig out staples evenly. If you don't have such a tool, one trick you can use is to insert a nail through the opening in the staple and slip the claws of your hammer under the nail.

In heavy-duty wrecking operations, there are a few more tools you can add to your arsenal, including the sledge hammer and sledge maul. These are weapons of last resort, but often necessary, for example, when removing stud walls that have been end-nailed through the plates instead of toenailed. A couple of whacks on one side of a stud generally drives the spikes through the 2×4 sideways. If you are somewhat careful, however, you will be able to salvage most studs despite the splintering.

BUYING NAIL-PULLING TOOLS

Unfortunately, there are no obvious guidelines to follow when buying nail-pulling tools, including hammers. But a number of features can add up to higher quality, including size, weight, balance, the material used and how it's processed and finished.

Gooseneck wrecking bars are usually made of heat-treated, high-carbon steel with designations such as 10-78 to 10-80. The 10 stands for a straight carbon series steel and the second set of numbers indicates the percent of carbon. Many flat prybars are made of 10-95 spring steel, heat-treated for hardness.

Nail-pulling tools that are forged in one piece generally will be stronger than those with welded parts. If you are buying a tool that has been welded, take time to examine the welded bead closely. Avoid buying a tool that looks like it might have a defective bead. Breaking such a tool under heavy pressure can be dangerous, especially if you're working on a roof or in any other precarious position.

Generally the best clue for quality is price; because of the competitiveness of the tool market, most of the time a higher price translates into higher quality. Nail-pulling tools should last you a long time if you take care of them. Those tools that get returned to manufacturers have, in most cases, been misused. Many are muscled with extensions and others have been overheated during grinding.

PART 4

MAKING ROUGH CARPENTRY GO SMOOTHER

CHAPTER 16

JOHN CONNELL:

ADVICE FOR WALL RAISERS

There is nothing as exciting for even old-time builders as seeing the stud walls go up. It conjures up images of old-fashioned barn raisings, when everyone and his brother in a whole township would gather to turn a pile of lumber into a real structure, one that would be put to good and useful purposes.

Whereas a bona fide barn raising involved timber framing, post-and-beam construction or balloon framing (where studs go from foundation all the way to the rafters), modern-day builders most often deal with platform framing (eight-foot stud walls) and new-fangled lumber such as plywood.

But there are tricks of the trade, even with factory-produced plywood, explains John Connell, president of a progressive owner-builder school called Yestermorrow in Warren, Vermont. A licensed architect, John has a pedigree pages long that describes his design and building accomplishments. He reflects on the problems and advantages of using plywood for modern-day construction.

I don't often see plywood used properly. It's an excellent material but you have to know what you're doing. One point that's often overlooked is that, just like other types of lumber, plywood has a grain. Plywood is made of several layers of wood, with the grains running at right angles to each other. But the overall grain of a sheet of plywood runs along the length of the sheet from top to bottom. This fact has practical consequences that you shouldn't ignore.

INSTALLING PLYWOOD

Most people seem to think that if you put plywood sheathing on the corners of a house, you'll make the house sturdy enough so that a strong wind won't be able to knock the walls out of alignment. Well, the theory is correct; that's why you brace the corners of the house. But people often install the plywood *vertically* with its grain running parallel to the grain of the studs. But it's weaker this way than if you install it *horizontally*. You want the plywood to extend horizontally across the studs so that the strength of the plywood's grain will truly help to brace the studs.

There are a few other factors to bear in mind if you want to get maximum strength from plywood. One is that plywood sheets will be rigid only if they are nailed down on all four sides. This generally means you'll have to install blocking. Also, you should not skimp on nails. Space them four inches apart, maximum, to really anchor the plywood. In fact, it's best to glue the sheet in addition to nailing it. What you're aiming for is to secure the plywood to the framing as solidly as possible.

CUTTING PLYWOOD

There are some common problems anyone working with plywood can encounter. One is splintering. Sheets of plywood really do tend to splinter, especially when you cut them with a hand-held power saw. The reason is that the teeth of the saw are moving upward when they cut through a sheet. It's similar to a whale surfacing, coming almost straight up and carrying everything with it. This can be a real nuisance in finish work – if you're cutting plywood siding, for instance, and you want the surface to be free of flaws.

There are several ways to combat splintering. One way is to adjust the saw so that the blade extends only about one tooth's length below

Splintering can be a plywood-cutting nightmare. Adjusting the saw blade depth and learning to cut plywood backside up are two ways to get better-looking results.

the bottom of the sheet. This way, the teeth come up through the wood at a shallower angle, so there's less splintering.

Another approach is to turn the plywood over and cut along the back surface instead of the front. You'll still get splintering, but it will be on the back, where it won't be visible. There's a drawback to this technique, though. You have to reverse all your cuts. For example, if you want to take three inches off the right-hand side of the sheet, you have to remember to make the cut on the left-hand side, because you're cutting on the back. This method can get confusing if you're cutting out a complicated shape. So here's an alternative: go ahead and cut on the front surface, but do it with a piece of scrap wood lying on top of the plywood. You'll cut through the scrap wood, and because the scrap wood presses against the plywood, the scrap will prevent splinters from pushing up.

GETTING THE WALLS PLUMB AND STRAIGHT

If there's any part of a new home that you want to get exactly right, it's the load-bearing walls. They provide the valuable service of keeping the roof from crashing down on your head. Patricia Fels, an instructor at the Northwest Owner-Builder Center in Seattle, offers tips on getting walls up the right way.

measure from corner A to D and from corner C to B

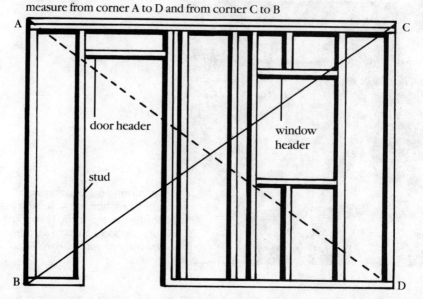

Squaring up a wall before raising it can be done by measuring the wall diagonally from corner to corner. When the measurements are equal, walls should be square.

The best time to square a wall is while it's still lying flat on the deck, before you tilt it up into position. Don't assume that it's going to be square just because you cut all the lumber carefully and nail it together firmly. The frame will be quite flexible, as you'll see if you push hard on one of its corners.

So what you do is measure the wall diagonally. Assuming that the top plate is as long as the bottom plate and that the ends of the wall are equal to each other, the wall will be square if the diagonal measurements are equal. Adjust the wall so these measurements check out the same. Don't tilt it up until they are right.

But be careful. The wall will deform if you tilt it without first locking it into its square configuration. So attach the plywood sheathing to the wall while the wall is still on the deck. If that will make it too heavy to lift, an alternative is to attach diagonal braces as a temporary measure until you raise the wall and put the sheathing on.

To be sure you position the wall exactly where you want it, snap a chalk line on the platform before lifting the wall. The line should show where the inner edge of the bottom plate will go. Stand the wall up, get it to toe the line and nail down the bottom plate. Then secure the wall with wall-to-platform braces. The braces will hold the wall until you have all the walls in position and you've put on the second floor or the roof – until the walls are firmly anchored at both the bottom and top.

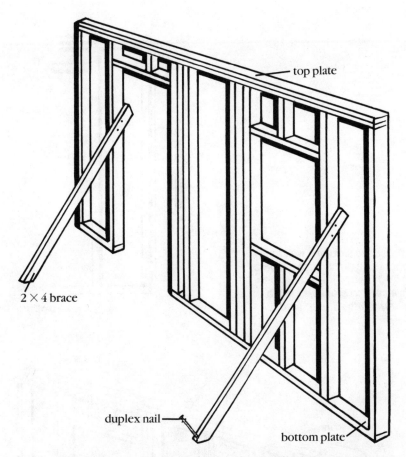

top plate

2 × 4 brace

duplex nail

bottom plate

If you don't want to attach sheathing before raising because of the weight, you can steady a wall temporarily with diagonal braces and duplex nails.

The braces will be there for a while. But here's a tip. To make it easier to remove the braces when you need to, use duplex nails on the braces. Because of their double heads, duplex nails are easy to pull out.

Another tip is to extend some of the braces to the ground instead of to the platform, if possible. Otherwise, the interior of the house is going to get awfully crowded with braces and you'll have trouble moving around in there.

Getting the wall to stand straight takes some doing. You can check for plumbness with a plumb line, or use a carpenter's level together with a long, very straight piece of wood that has identical blocks attached at its ends. The blocks will hold the wood away from the stud you're checking, so you'll get an accurate reading even if the stud is slightly warped. Work your way down the wall, checking for level both on the fronts and sides of the studs, and adjust the wall as necessary by repositioning the braces.

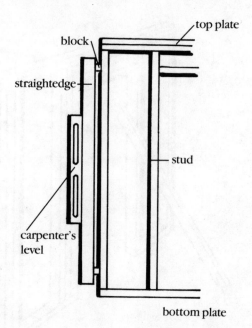

To check the side of a wall for plumbness, you can use a plumb line or, as shown here, a carpenter's level and blocks, to avoid problems with warped studs.

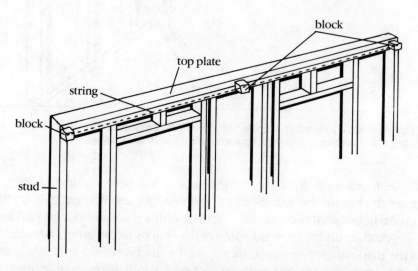

To check if the top of a wall is straight, attach a string to blocks on the ends of the top plate. Then move another block between the string and the plate. It should fit evenly along the length of the string.

There's still one more factor to bear in mind. Besides getting the wall plumb, you need to get it straight, too. Making sure the bottom plate lies along the chalk line will keep the bottom of the wall straight. You can use the "eyeball" method: have another person eyeball the top plate while you push or pull with braces to get the top plate straight. Or, to be sure the top of the wall is straight, attach equal-sized blocks to the ends of the top plate, stretch a string between the blocks, then check all along the top plate with another block cut from the same stock. If this third block fits in snugly everywhere along the plate, you know the plate is straight.

It's not really complicated. In fact, making sure your walls are straight will actually simplify things for you. Besides making the home more structurally perfect, it will simplify all the other work you do on your walls – everything from hanging doors to putting up drywall to hanging wallpaper. If you've ever tried to cut wallpaper to fit the odd angle where two unstraight walls meet, you know the glorious virtues of straight and square walls.

KEEPING WATER OUT

Once the walls are up, ready for doors and windows, take this advice from Patrick Foster, an instructor at Cornerstones owner-builder school in Brunswick, Maine: Pay attention to drip caps and put them in correctly to keep out the water.

Drip caps rank among the unsung heroes of home construction. They are almost invisible, thin strips of sheet metal that perch above doors and windows. Most people probably don't even know they exist. But they serve the vital function of preventing rain or melting snow from leaking into walls, where it could soak insulation (lowering the R-value) and rot structural members.

The first thing to realize is that you may need to bend your drip caps before installing them. Although some caps come from the store with a built-in slope, other caps come without any slope; you need to bend them slightly before installing them, otherwise they'll catch and hold water instead of shedding it.

Sometimes the caps aren't long enough to go over a large window. In that case, you may need to use two or more sections of drip cap. The sections should overlap each other by two inches, and the overlap should be caulked and nailed.

It's also a good idea to fold the ends of a drip cap by cutting ¼-inch slits at each end of the cap and making the sections extend beyond both sides of the door or window frame by ¼ inch. Then fold down the ends of the cap so they hug the sides of the frame. It

(continued)

KEEPING WATER OUT— *Continued*

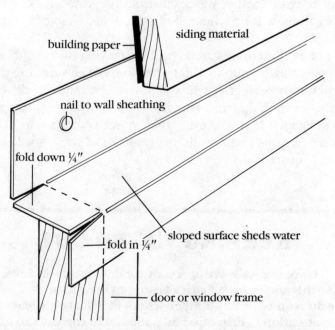

building paper

siding material

nail to wall sheathing

fold down ¼″

fold in ¼″

sloped surface sheds water

door or window frame

Some store-bought drip caps need to be bent slightly before installation. Fold sections of drip cap down around door or window frames and, if you use two or more sections, caulk between them.

looks neater, and it prevents water from blowing under the ends of the cap.

After the cap is installed, be sure to lap building paper over the top edge. Then, when installing wall shingles or siding, leave a space of about ¼ inch between the bottom of the shingles and the sloped surface of the cap. This space will prevent water from being drawn up under the shingles by capillary action.

CHAPTER 17

ELIAS VELONIS AND
BOB BECKSTROM:

FINESSING
THE FINISH
WORK

In the building trades there are what are known as rough carpenters and finish carpenters. Your status as either one can depend on the crew you are working with. On some crews it may be the rough carpenters, who wrestle rafters in place, who are the stars. On other crews, especially those whose members got their start by laying wood floors or building cabinets, it will be the finish carpenters who are held in highest esteem.

Yet either type of carpenter will agree that rough framing takes skill and, despite the term, often close-tolerance precision. Either type will also agree that finish work takes a good deal more time out of the building schedule than framing.

Elias Velonis, who's designed and worked on houses and other buildings for 20 years, has some strong feelings about the entire building process. A cofounder of the Heartwood Owner-Builder School in Washington, Massachusetts, he now operates his own environmental education design firm, Amidon-Roberts, out of Boston. In the first part of this chapter, he talks about getting involved in finish work, specifically, laying wood floors.

Next, Bob Beckstrom, a licensed general contractor and instructor at the Owner Builder Center in Berkeley, California, talks about a different type of finish work—installing leak-free skylights.

By Elias Velonis

Tongue-and-groove flooring is great stuff. The pieces interlock to provide a good, firm floor surface. There's a hitch, though. Unless you know what you're doing, installation can be a headache. People often buy the widest tongue-and-groove boards they can find. They reason that fewer boards mean less nailing, and they're right. But wide boards can be hard to work with.

DEALING WITH CROWNS

Almost inevitably, some of the boards will have crowns. That is, they will be bent instead of straight. You can push on the edge of a narrow board to straighten it out, but you'll have a much tougher time if the board is wide. I'd say six inches is the maximum width you should consider, and four inches or less is usually better, both aesthetically and for dealing with crowns.

One way to straighten tongue-and-groove boards is to use a power nailer. This tool, which you slug with a mallet, should pull most boards into line, provided they are not bowed too severely. Nailers are available from equipment-rental companies.

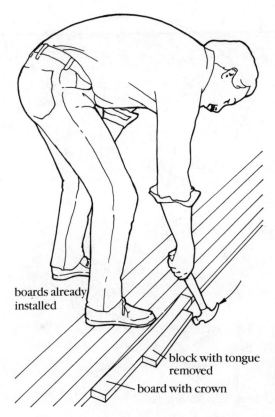

boards already installed

block with tongue removed

board with crown

Narrow tongue-and-groove boards are easier to wrestle into place than wide ones. To persuade boards with crowns, saw the tongue off a piece of scrap and use it between the board and your hammer.

If you want to use your trusty hammer instead of a nailer, remember a cardinal rule: *never hit a piece of tongue-and-groove with a hammer.* You may break off the tongue or mar the surface of the board. Use a block of scrap tongue-and-groove. Saw its tongue off, position it on the board you want to straighten and hit the block with your hammer.

For severely crowned boards, more drastic measures are called for. Here's what I suggest. Using duplex nails, nail a 2 × 4 at an angle on the subfloor. Drive the nails into the joists beneath the subfloor, so the 2 × 4 will be secure. Then drive a wedge of 2× wood (2 × 4, 2 × 6 or whatever) between this 2 × 4 and the tongue-and-groove block that you've positioned on the crown. The wedge will push the block, and the block will push the tongue-and-groove board into line. (Some carpenters use an auto jack with great success. The trick is to stand on the jack post to keep it from kicking up. A scissors jack works best.)

Besides dealing with crowns, you may have to cope with other imperfections in the tongue-and-groove material you buy. Unless you get the very best quality lumber, you may find that the boards are actually of

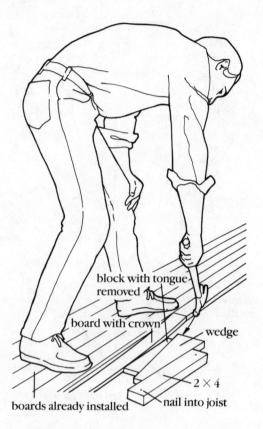

block with tongue removed

board with crown

wedge

2 × 4

nail into joist

boards already installed

For severely crowned boards, try a wedge. Nail a 2 × 4 to the subfloor and drive a wedge between it and a block with the tongue removed. This should get the crowned board back in line.

slightly different widths. Width is critical when you butt two pieces together. If one board is wider than the other, it will jut out farther, so you won't get a good fit when you try to install the next row of planks. I've found that I've had to measure each piece to be sure I select pieces of equal width to butt together. It's time-consuming, but the results are worth it.

INSTALLING WATERTIGHT SKYLIGHTS

By Bob Beckstrom

Nine times out of ten, if a skylight leaks, it's because not enough attention was given to the joints where the roofing material meets the skylight curb. A curb is the box that the skylight sits on, lifting it above the roof. It's possible to mount a skylight flush with the roof, but this causes all kinds of problems. You're much better off raising the skylight four inches, as called for in most model building codes.

(continued on page 182)

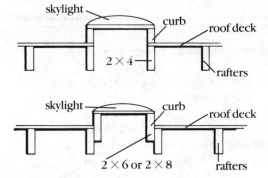

Skylight curbs can be made of 2 × 4s on top of the roof, or 2 × 6s or 2 × 8s positioned inside the opening cut between the rafters. Most codes call for skylights that are raised four inches.

TRICKS WITH BASEBOARDS

A basic reality for a finish carpenter is that corners, even in new construction, are hardly ever square. They may look square, but they're almost always off, at least a little. This obviously complicates things when you get down to the finish work.

Andy Inganni, instructor and cofounder of the Heartwood Owner-Builder School in Washington, Massachusetts, has ways to deal with perversity of corners when fitting baseboard moldings.

You can waste a lot of wood cutting and recutting pieces of molding, trying to get tight-fitting joints where the pieces meet in the corners. It really takes some forethought to eliminate this waste and do a good job. Here's what I suggest. Cut each piece very slightly longer than the bottom of the wall where it will go. This will help make sure you will get a snug fit with no gaps at the ends of any piece. For the first piece, cut both ends square. Then use a block plane to trim the ends so they fit the irregular angles you'll probably find in the corners.

Deciding exactly how long to make each piece of molding is a little tricky. Initially cut it long enough so that, after you've trimmed the ends, it will still be about $\frac{1}{32}$ inch longer than the wall. Be careful, though. If you wind up with a piece that's too long, and if you have drywall, the molding can tear the drywall tape in the corners. Then you'll have to remove the molding, put

(continued)

TRICKS WITH BASEBOARDS — *Continued*

joint compound on the torn corners again, and go do something else while you wait for the corners to dry.

When using square stock, you can go around the room cutting all the pieces the same way you cut the first one. But things get more complex if the molding has a decorative face.

You might assume that the best strategy is to cut the ends of decorative molding at 45° angles. This would work fine if the room's corners were exactly 90°. But because the corners are probably a few degrees off this ideal, your carefully cut moldings won't fit. You'll probably wind up with gaps. A better approach is to cut the pieces of molding so that they overlap in the corners.

You can install the first piece of decorative molding the same way as square stock, cutting each end square. But for the succeeding pieces, you'll have to get out your saws and do some mitering and coping.

Using a miter box, cut the end of the second piece of molding at a 45° angle. This will expose the profile of the molding's face. Now take a coping saw and follow the edge of the profile, undercutting about 3° from square. If the corners of the room were perfectly square, you would cut at a right angle. But by undercutting at about 3°, you'll create enough leeway so you can fit the piece into the corner, even if the corner is slightly more or slightly less than 90°. Because the pieces overlap, there won't be a visible gap.

You don't have to miter and cope both ends of the molding, just the end that will butt up against another piece of molding in the corner. Anytime an end will butt up against a wall surface, you can just square-cut it and plane it.

Proceed around the room, cutting and installing each piece of molding in succession. As for nailing the pieces in place, drive the nails into solid wood, not just into drywall or paneling. The top row of nails should go into the wall's bottom plate. If the molding is higher than the bottom plate, you'll have to find the studs to nail into.

If your floors are a bit uneven, you may wind up with some gaps between the bottom of the molding and the floor. You can cover these by installing toe molding: narrow, flexible strips of wood that go at the front edge of the molding. Have someone stand on the toe molding, so it bends down to be flush with the floor, then nail it directly to the floor.

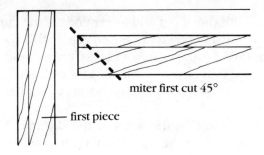

miter first cut 45°

first piece

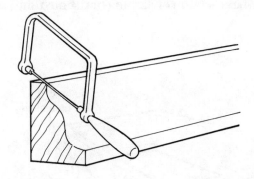

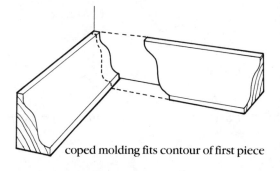

coped molding fits contour of first piece

One way to install baseboard molding is to install the first piece with a square, instead of mitered, end. To overlap the second piece, miter it at 45° to expose the molding face, then cope along the edge of the profile with a 3° undercut.

You can either construct the curb out of 2×4s and place it on top of the roof, or you can position 2×6s or 2×8s inside the opening you've cut between the rafters.

Install collar flashing at both the upper and lower ends of the curb. Collar flashing is an expense, but a necessary one. You can go to a sheet metal shop with the dimensions of your skylight and have them fabricate the collars for you. Most of the time, heavy galvanized metal flashing is probably adequate. But if you are prepared to pay extra, get copper. It will last far longer.

Do not use simple roll flashing on the sides of the skylight. The flashing along the sides should always be step flashing. It consists of short, rectangular pieces of sheet metal, bent into an L-shape and installed along the sides of the skylight so that they overlap each other. And then – this is critical – arrange the pieces so that they also overlap the roof shingles. (This way, if water gets under a shingle or under a section of flashing, it flows down the slope of the roof and is directed back out onto the roof surface by the next section of flashing or the next shingle it comes to.)

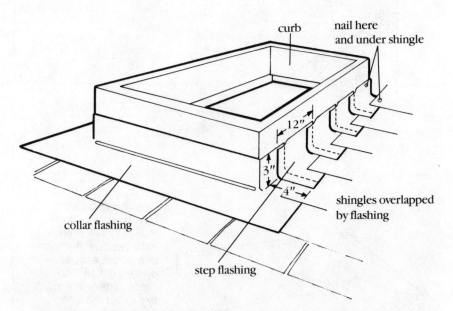

Install collar flashing top and bottom, and use step flashing, overlapping shingles along the sides.

If you're retrofitting a skylight onto an existing roof, it would be a matter of tucking each piece of flashing under each course of shingles, starting at the bottom and working up. The first piece of flashing to install is the bottom collar, overlapping each piece with the pieces above and below.

For the sake of aesthetics, you may want to paint the flashing. That will make it blend more harmoniously with the roof. To prepare galvanized flashing so it will hold a coat of paint well, you should etch it. Regular supermarket vinegar works just fine. You use it as an acid, lightly washing it over the surface of the flashing, then wiping it off. Next, apply a coat of primer and then spray paint the flashing whatever color you like.

PART 5

Your Homestead Plumbing And Power Company

CHAPTER 18

MILFORD ROUBIK:

COPING WITH PLUMBING REPAIRS

Milford Roubik, you might say, is a Thomas Magnum of home plumbing. Not that he drives a red Ferrari. This master plumber from West St. Paul, Minnesota, drives a Metro van, and inside it's a jungle of pipe, fittings and tools. But, Mel, as he's called, gets plenty of late-night calls for help that lead him into some interesting situations.

One night a woman called while Mel was watching the 10 o'clock news. She was frantic. Her neighbor had tried to fix a drip around the water meter in her house. But after he had cut the main pipe, he admitted he didn't know what to do next . . . and left with the basement slowly filling up with water.

Since Mel got his journeyman's license in 1976, he's had calls to fix just about everything that can go wrong with a

plumbing system. And he's seen enough to come up with some good advice on how you can avoid plumbing problems, even disasters, in your home.

Plumbing systems are pretty straightforward. There's no one big secret for working on them, but there are many techniques that are helpful. For the average homeowner, it's more of learning what *not* to do.

The first thing is not to let little problems grow into big ones. Second, if you're going to work on plumbing, don't start hacking away until you've figured out what you're going to do and how you're going to do it. Third, forget about the idea that you need to use big pipe wrenches and lots of muscle. In most cases, you'll do more harm than good.

A plumbing system is like anything else; it eventually wears out. Once or twice a year, visually check the whole system. If you have little problems such as drips, fix them right away. Let's say you have a two-handled faucet that starts to drip. If you don't fix it right away, you'll be turning down the handles harder to stop the water. In time, the screw holding the washer will gouge a hole into the faucet seat, wrecking the

The dripping hot-water faucet valve for this shower may only need new packing. (It helps to know the manufacturer's name when searching for older faucet parts.)

whole thing. Now, instead of a washer, you need to buy and install a complete faucet.

TACKLING YOUR OWN PLUMBING PROBLEMS

What plumbing projects are fair game for the homeowner? I say you can do anything if you take the time to figure it out. There's no hard-and-fast rule. It gets down to what's cheapest and the value of your time. If you tackle small repairs, certain approaches can help keep you out of trouble:

• Once you break into a plumbing system, try to have everything you'll need. Go over the job three or four times and write down what you have to buy. Then gather up all the supplies in one trip, even if you have to go to several stores. Before you start tearing things apart, lay the new parts next to the old parts so you know you have everything.

• Buy only two pipe wrenches, and make sure they're small ones, not more than 14 inches. (When I work on black gas pipe, I only use 12-inch pump pliers.) Try not to force anything. Sometimes homeowners shut off the water service to the house, but can't get it turned back on. Usually it's because they have turned the valve down so hard that when they try to open it up, the threads strip on the inside.

• If you're cutting out a section of old galvanized steel pipe, have a helper. While you cut, your helper can keep the pipe from shaking. Otherwise you'll break joints farther down the line and your small project will turn into a big job.

• If you're replacing steel pipe, measure the length between the fittings, then add ½ inch extra for threads on each end to go into the fittings. This is for supply pipe that's either ⅜ inch, ½ inch or ¾ inch in diameter. For 1-inch diameter pipe allow ⅝ inch for threads; for 2-inch pipe allow ¾ inch. Have someone else do the threading. You can use a union fitting to get the pipe back together.

• To get leak-free threaded joints, I use both Teflon tape and pipe compound. Put the tape on first, in a clockwise direction going with the threads. Then put compound over that. I do this except where small bits of tape could break loose and jam up delicate control mechanisms. I don't use the tape on gas lines, right next to a dishwasher or directly in front of a water pump with a pressure gauge.

• When soldering copper pipe, make sure fittings are clean inside and out. You can use emery cloth or sandpaper, but what also works well are those green Scotch-Brite pads. They don't shred if they get wet, as sandpaper will. And watch that you don't overheat a joint. Play the torch over it only until the

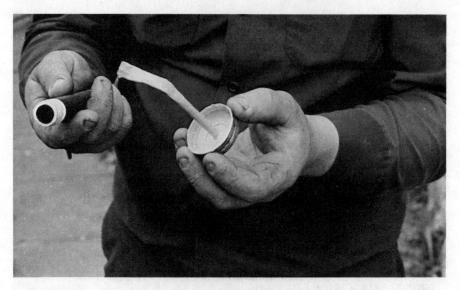

Using both Teflon tape and pipe compound on galvanized pipe joints will boost your chances of creating leak-free joints.

solder starts to run, then quit heating it. If the joint is too hot the flux burns and prevents the solder from sticking.

• It's hard to solder copper joints if there is moisture inside. You can use pieces of bread to hold back the moisture temporarily. Roll the bread up into little balls and stuff them into the pipe. But be ready with the torch; the bread will only dam up the water for a short time before it dissolves. For any soldering, wear gloves and long sleeves. Wear a cap and eye protection, as well, if you're soldering overhead.

• If you regularly have a problem with frozen pipes, the best solution is to cut a hole on the inside of the wall near the pipe and cover it with a louvered register. This way air from the house can keep the temperature of the pipe above freezing. There are different ways to thaw pipes; I use a regular small hair dryer.

• I don't do much work with plugged drains. For home use, I'd recommend only a small snake. If that doesn't do the job, I'd call a professional. My personal opinion is that liquid drain cleaners can be hard on pipes and traps. I try not to use them.

DECIDING WHEN TO REPLACE PLUMBING

Most of my work involves replacing plumbing. Often a homeowner could do the work, but a professional will be much faster. For example, it might take you a weekend to install a water heater, whereas I could do it in less than an hour. Here are some ideas on figuring out what needs to be replaced when.

WATER HEATERS

My rule of thumb is to replace a water heater if it's about 10 years old or older, especially if there is carpeting in the basement (which becomes a real mess after the flood). Some will plug along for 30 years. But I've also replaced many that were only 7 years old. When they die, 90 percent of the time it's because the tank starts leaking. The rest of the time the controls go out.

It's hard to tell how old a heater is by looking at it. But if a heater starts rumbling, beware. That's a sign there are deposits on the bottom that could pop the glass in the tank within a year. When you replace a heater, see that you don't get the hot and cold lines mixed up. It happens.

I use the thermocouple as a gauge on gas heaters. It's a small tube leading from the gas control to near the burner. It should last as long as

A "teenage" water heater is a candidate for replacement. This one's thermocouple has already been replaced (see the coil). The gas pipe feeding the heater also lacks a shutoff valve where it continues on to feed the clothes dryer (not shown).

The water supply lines leading to this bathroom faucet were connected without installing shut-off valves. The awkward instal-lation interferes with the drain pipe angle, resulting in slow drain action.

the tank. Sometimes it might go out on a heater that's only five years old if it was out of adjustment. But usually when a thermocouple goes bad it's a sign the heater should be replaced.

FAUCETS

If a faucet goes bad after about five years, I generally replace it. The reason is that often the faucet has dripped for months and the inside is probably damaged. But if it's a quality Kohler or Moen cartridge faucet, it could very well be worth fixing.

When getting new seats for faucets, it's best to know the name of the manufacturer. If you need a new faucet, my motto is to go for quality. A higher-priced faucet could last three times as long as a cheap one. With a good faucet you save the cost of a second and third faucet, plus the labor to install them.

Be cautious of starting to replace a faucet if you don't have stop valves underneath. If something goes wrong you won't be able to turn your home's water back on. Consider having a plumber install the valves, or do it yourself when you can get by without water for a while. With them, you can isolate a fixture from the house system and still have water.

TOILETS

Toilets rarely need to be replaced. Most of those that I replace are the older ones with a flush elbow connecting a tank on the wall to the bowl. Parts are hard to find for these, but fairly easy to find for the rest.

If you install a toilet, get that wax ring set straight under the base, otherwise it will leak. Don't forget that the parts inside a new toilet are loose and have to be tightened up before you turn on the water. And remember that you may be tampering with older pipes with a lot of junk in them. Flush out the supply pipe before installing new parts or you'll have problems.

SUPPLY PIPES

If the pipes in your house are 30 or so years old, corrosion can build up so the flow is only about half of what it could be. You can't tell just by looking at the pipes. I've opened up a pipe and haven't been able to get a pencil through it. Hot-water pipes will usually have more corrosion inside, though they might look better on the outside than cold-water pipes, which get discolored because of condensation. Look for the worst condition anywhere there is a galvanized-to-copper transition.

A simple test for corrosion is to open up the faucet on your laundry tub or utility sink, then turn on the faucet farthest away from the service line. If you don't get a stream the size of a pencil, consider replacing the pipes. I replace old galvanized steel pipes with copper. Unless you have the tools and a fair amount of experience, I don't recommend that you tackle pipe replacement yourself.

Though a newer model, this toilet's internal parts are corroded and are candidates for replacement. The ballcock is not the antisiphon type required today and can lead to pollution of the water supply.

HIRING A PLUMBER

How do you hire a good plumber? Unless you know of someone, or can get a recommendation, go by how long he's been in business. Those who've been around a while will be reputable. If you're hiring someone for a big project, try to get a written estimate. If it's a small job, you might have to settle for an estimate over the phone. I charge $32.50 an hour for replacement work. Bigger outfits will charge $40 to $60 an hour. That's because they keep a truck full of equipment and parts and have a higher overhead.

CHAPTER 19

RICHARD DAY:

PLUMBING
WITH PLASTICS

Probably only electrical work outranks plumbing as the project most dreaded by a homeowner. Plumbing seems complicated and appears to require a truckload of tools plus a head full of specialized know-how. It's a job that conjures up visions of water leaks, flooded floors, bruised knuckles and ultimate defeat.

If that sounds about right to you, you should have a talk with Richard Day. Rich makes his living writing about home technology from high up on Palomar Mountain in California. Where he lives, there's no electricity so he powers his computer with a diesel generator. Despite his isolated office, he is one of a handful of the top how-to writers in the country. He believes you shouldn't write about anything until you know 10 times more than you need to do the story.

One of Rich's main specialties is writing about using newer thermoplastic plumbing. "It's a lot easier to use," he says. "You don't need special tools and, best of all, if you make a mistake, it's real easy to correct."

In fact, he speculates that if you do your homework and have what you need on hand, you could plumb a water supply system for a typical house in one or two days using components of CPVC (chlorinated polyvinyl chloride) and PB (polybutylene). CPVC and PB are two of a handful of related materials—including PVC (polyvinyl chloride), ABS (acrylonitrile-butadiene-styrene), PP (polypropylene) and PE (polyethylene)—that are displacing traditional plumbing materials such as galvanized steel, cast iron and copper, and bringing on what could be called a revolution in the plumbing of the modern home. If you're on the verge of a plumbing project, Rich's advice can help get you on the right track.

The switch to plastics for plumbing systems has been coming on strong for a good half-dozen years. Plastics are ideal do-it-yourself materials; they cost less than metal, are immensely easier to install and promise longer service life than any of the older options.

Because plastics are so easy to work with, they've made almost any homeowner (with a little reading and planning) a potential plumber. In fact, some homeowners who've used the materials can't believe how easy they are to work with: to cut, to join, to install fittings and fixtures.

In fact, plastic components now are used in more than half of the plumbing projects being done, including those done by professional plumbers. Because there is no national plumbing code, it's impossible to pinpoint exactly where plastic plumbing can or cannot be legally used. However, plastics have been approved for use in plumbing by all six regional plumbing codes in the country. And only a few local codes do not follow a regional code. This means that chances are excellent that you may be able to use plastic plumbing in your home with the full blessing of city hall. But be sure to check with local officials before starting your project.

DOING THE WORK YOURSELF

Whether you are planning an addition, a repair or even a new installation, plastics are cheaper than metal. And with plumbers charging up to $50 or more an hour, you can save a bundle if you take advantage of the easy-to-install plastics and do the work yourself. By doing it yourself, you stand to save about three-fourths of the cost of hiring someone to do it. This is because the costs of plumbing are about 25 percent materials and 75 percent labor; the exact ratio depends on the quality of fixtures you select.

If you use plastic plumbing, you will be surprised at how easy it is to use. Besides being lightweight and easy to handle, it has many other advantages for the home plumber.

MINIMAL TOOLS

Because plastics join with either solvent welding or simple mechanical fittings, you don't need the traditional plumber's tools. And special adapters are available to tie in plastics with metal plumbing materials. You don't need, for example, expensive powered hacksaws, threading

Both CPVC and PB are available in copper tubing sizes and can be flared to fit standard flare fittings. This allows easy connections at faucets, other fixtures and appliances.

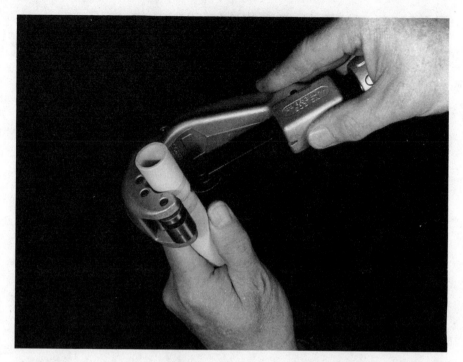

CPVC tubing can be cut squarely using a tubing cutter with an extra-large plastic cutting wheel, or it may be cut with a fine-toothed saw.

dies or even pipe wrenches. You don't need a torch for soldering, and you don't need solder or flux. With CPVC, for example, all you need is a hacksaw, a knife, a rag, cleaner/primer and solvent cement.

GOOF-PROOF CONNECTIONS

It only takes about five minutes to learn how to solvent weld. (Don't let the term scare you; it's only slightly more involved than using model airplane glue.) You simply cut the pipe to length and use a knife to remove any burrs. Next you wipe the outside of the pipe and inside of a fitting with a cleaner/primer, wipe off the primer and apply the solvent cement. You press the fitting in place, use a slight turn to spread the cement and in half a minute you have a leak-free fitting that will never come apart. It's that simple. With PB, it's even simpler. You just push the tube into the fitting full depth and hand-tighten. That's it!

If you do make a mistake, it's easy to simply cut out the error and, using inexpensive couplers, install a new section in just a minute or so. Plus, unlike threaded steel pipe, which requires straight-arrow alignment, with CPVC tube you can easily make slight bends to get to the next fitting. PB is flexible, so fitting it into place is never a problem.

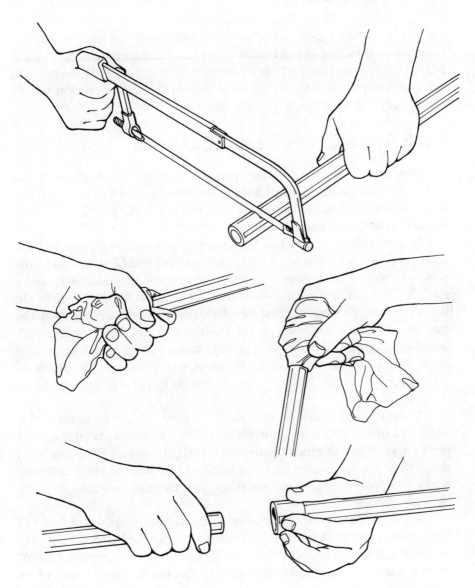

When joining CPVC by solvent welding, first cut the tube, then clean the mating parts using a cleaner/primer. Coat the tube end and fitting socket with solvent cement and join.

LONG-LASTING PIPING

These same plastics are used by industry to carry away some of the most caustic chemicals on earth. They are not susceptible to corrosion like metal components. This means years down the road you won't have to replace your water supply system because of corrosion built up inside the pipes. Other payoffs of plastic include more thermal resistance (eliminates sweating of cold water pipes) and reduced noise level from water hammer and water flow compared to metal pipe. However, you still need to plan out your plumbing system the same way you would when using any other piping materials.

LEARNING THE LANGUAGE

The biggest hurdle to using plastics is simply learning about the kinds of plastic available for plumbing and what's used where. Once you realize there are only about a half-dozen types used, plastic plumbing doesn't seem intimidating at all.

Any plumbing system can be broken down into two parts (1) the supply side, which brings in fresh, potable water and (2) the waste side, which carries wastes away to either your septic or municipal sewer system. CPVC and PB are the main plastics used on the supply side. On the waste side, or what's called the DWV (drain-waste-vent) system, the main plastics used are PVC (polyvinyl chloride) and ABS (acrylonitrile-butadiene-styrene). Before you use any plastic piping, check your local code. Not all municipal codes will allow you to use plastic piping in water supply systems. You may be limited to using it in just the DWV system.

If you can use plastic in your supply system, whether you use CPVC or PB is a matter of personal preference. They will cost about the same per foot; the big difference is that CPVC is rigid whereas PB is flexible. I think they are best used in combination, like hard-temper and soft-temper copper tubing. Used together, you can take advantage of the benefits of both.

If, for example, your installation requires you to go around a lot of corners and you don't have lots of fittings, you may be better off with PB. But if the system is mostly straight-line runs, you might favor CPVC because its solvent-welded fittings are cheaper to make than the mechanical fittings of PB.

CPVC presents a more workmanlike appearance where plumbing is exposed, and flexible PB works best when remodeling plumbing behind existing walls. Although PVC and PE can be used for cold-water pressure lines, only CPVC and PB can handle hot-water lines. PVC and PE are for outdoor uses only.

CPVC and PB both work well on water heaters and softeners with proper transition fittings. Occasionally you may still need good old-fashioned metal piping in situations that require firm mechanical support, such as when piping to a bathtub spout.

Both PVC and ABS in Schedule 40 DWV can replace cast iron or copper on the waste side. Where both are available, PVC is the material of choice. It's tougher and more chemical-resistant. ABS is used more on the West Coast, but nationwide PVC now accounts for about 90 percent of the plastic DWV systems currently being installed.

One thing to take advantage of is the fact that you can find PVC in two versions. Both have three-inch inside diameters, but one version has thinner walls. This thin-walled version, called Schedule 30 In-Wall, can be installed in a normal 2 × 4 plumbing wall instead of needing a 2 × 6 wall or furred-out 2 × 4 wall.

(continued on page 204)

INSTALLING A WATER HEATER

It's not that difficult to install your own water heater into a plumbing system made of plastic. Start by threading a pair of 8- to 11-inch galvanized steel nipples onto the water heater to protect the plastic pipes from conducted heat.

Thread two steel nipples onto the water heater.

(continued)

INSTALLING A WATER HEATER—*Continued*

Next thread a transition adapter onto the steel nipples, using a turn of Teflon tape for a watertight joint.

Then thread the transition adapter.

Install a line stop (with flow arrow pointing down) into the transition fitting. Then use pipe to connect the heater to the water main.

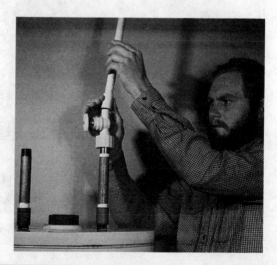

Install the line stop.

Some CPVC transition fittings may be connected directly to the heater's threaded tappings, as shown here.

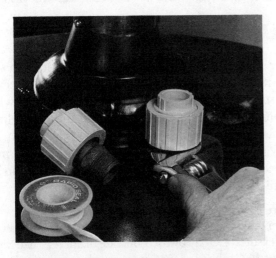

Connect CPVC transition fittings.

Here heat-resistant CPVC pipe is used for both hot- and cold-water lines. (Always check with your local codes before installing plastic plumbing.)

CPVC pipe is used here for both hot- and cold-water lines.

Sink traps are also available in plastic, and here is where PP (polypropylene) comes in handy. It's one of the toughest, most heat-resistant plastics available and a choice material for traps. You can also find traps of PVC. Some PVC traps have ABS slip-jaw nuts. Be aware that ABS is susceptible to stress cracking when in contact with animal fats or vegetable oils. Don't use plumber's putty or silicone rubber sealant on ABS nuts.

BUYING YOUR SUPPLIES

Before you decide to go ahead with a plastic system, or even make repairs to existing plumbing systems with plastic, a major consideration is finding a source of supply nearby. Try to find a parts supplier who is up-to-date on plastic plumbing, stocks a complete line and can help you plan out your project. A good dealer can save you hours of research, help you with any problems and also answer any nagging questions you might have about this new technology. There are a few guidelines that can help you in your installation:

• Water supply lines are generally ¾ inch for main lines and ½ inch for branch lines. Keep in mind that CPVC and PB used on the supply side are called tubes and are measured exactly by their outside diameters, like copper tubing. However, PVC pipe used on the waste side (and for irrigation and sprinkler pipes) is measured nominally by inside diameter, like iron pipes. A ½-inch pipe is therefore somewhat larger than a ½-inch tube.

• Make sure that the pipe, fittings, couplings or solvent cement you buy are compatible. Stick with one brand of materials if you can. By using one brand, all the fittings will fit and the solvent cements will be correctly matched. (Take time to read the directions the first time around. For example, one solvent cement may be needed for CPVC and another for PVC. Or you can use an all-purpose solvent cement; it works with all four solvent weldable plastics.)

• As with other items you buy, check the pipe and fittings to make sure a manufacturing defect hasn't slipped by the inspection process. The pipe and fittings should have an ASTM number, which means the product is up to the standards of the renowned American Society for Testing and Materials. Water supply tubing should also have "NSF-pw" stamped on it. This indicates the National Sanitation Foundation's approval that it may be used for potable water.

Studies show plastic plumbing to be safe from a health standpoint. (In fact, increased concern is surfacing with regard to the leaching of lead from metal plumbing systems.) But one precaution to take with plastic is to flush out any possibly toxic solvent vapors from the system after it is completed. This is easily done by flushing water through the system a half hour after the last joint is solvent-welded. The vapors actually dissolve in water and are carried away.

To flush out the system, open all faucets, then slightly open the main valve. When water comes out the lowest faucet, slow it to a trickle, then move on through the installation, closing other faucets the same way. Let the faucets trickle for about 10 minutes, wait for about a half hour, then repeat the procedure twice. After the third flushing, close all faucets, pressurize the system and open and close all faucets fully to get rid of any debris. Flush the toilet, too.

Don't be wary of working with plumbing officials in your area. Their job is to help you to make sure your installation is done correctly and in a safe manner. Show them your plans and take out a permit if required. If inspections are needed, consider them added insurance – they'll insure that your plumbing is done right.

CHAPTER 20

DAVE CHAPEAU:

BECOMING YOUR OWN ELECTRICIAN

Dave Chapeau says there are some popular misconceptions about home wiring. For one thing, he says, a lot of people think that electrical inspectors are "out to get" the homeowner who does his own wiring. Although it could happen in rare situations, he says it's nothing but a myth. "An inspector's job is not to drum up work for electricians, but to make sure home wiring is done so it won't be hazardous," Dave says.

However, unlike other home projects, wiring is one in which there's little guessing. In nearly all cases, there's a right way and a wrong way to do it. Dave, who's been an electrical contractor since 1972, has wired everything from hot tubs to smoke detectors in fire stations. He belongs to a special breed of professionals who must combine working with their hands with a lot of book learning. The bible for every electrician is the National Electrical Code (NEC) book, which is updated every three or four years.

As an electrical contractor, Dave is a one-man band and his business ebbs and flows with the economy and construction starts. He's been an electronics technician for both the U.S. Navy and Univac and a few years back also taught physical sciences at the University of Minnesota. He's a consultant to several architects on electrical system planning as well. Dave has probably had more than a thousand jobs approved by state electrical inspectors. On a rainy day between jobs, Dave talks about ways the budding home electrician can stay out of trouble.

To the beginner, working with electrical systems can be like playing Dungeons & Dragons: a dark, mysterious, unpredictable guessing game that can lead you down treacherous paths and into blind alleys. Truth is that it's almost exactly the opposite – it's a definite scientific, straightforward procedure.

If you've never done any wiring before and plan to tackle a fairly involved project, I'd suggest you first consult a few of the good do-it-yourself books and consider taking a night class on wiring for beginners. Then, try to line up a knowledgeable person you can go to if any questions come up.

AVOIDING PITFALLS

Before you start your wiring, call your local electrical code officials, tell them what you plan to do and ask if you need a permit. Although the NEC is very specific and extensive, there are some things to be aware of as you get going on your project.

CIRCUITS

In new homes, a kitchen must have two separate 20-amp circuits for receptacles. No lighting fixtures can be on these two circuits. Circuits for bathrooms, as well as outside and garage receptacles, must be protected by ground-fault circuit interrupter devices (often called GFCIs or GFIs). The code also requires at least one basement circuit to be GFI protected, as well as kitchen circuits with receptacles at countertop level that are within six feet of the sink. Generally ground-fault protection is provided by using a GFI receptacle device, though GFI circuit breakers can also be used.

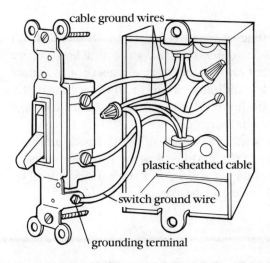

cable ground wires

plastic-sheathed cable

switch ground wire

grounding terminal

In most cases, only one wire can be installed under one screw, so what is known as a pigtail splice is used, as shown here.

GROUND WIRES

If you are using Romex wire with ground, you'll have a bare copper wire that must be connected to run continuously throughout the circuit. Let's say you are adding to a circuit with greenfield flexible conduit or EMT conduit and metal boxes. In this case you connect the ground wire to the metal box you are starting from. You can use either a green screw or metal grounding clip.

The ground wire always connects to the green screw on the receptacle using what's called a pigtail because you can never have more than one wire under a screw. If you have a number of ground wires coming into a box, they should all be connected together. In some cases you won't have anything to connect the ground wire to, such as with switches without ground screws used in a plastic box at the end of a run. In this case, just tuck the bare ground wire into the back of the box.

Let's say you have Romex wire coming into a metal box. In that case, don't just wrap the base ground wire under the screw for the receptacle cover. Use the green screw in the box, if there is one, or use a wire clip that attaches to the edge of the box, or drill and tap a hole for a new green grounding screw.

CONNECTIONS

It used to be that splice connections had to be twisted, soldered and covered with two kinds of tape. Now you can use electrical wire nuts and with some brands you don't have to twist the wires together unless you prefer to. But use the right size wire nuts; check the box or package for exactly how many wires you can get inside that nut, depending on the size of wire you are using.

BOXES

Generally boxes for receptacles are installed 12 to 18 inches from the finished floor. In new work, you need to have a receptacle for every 12 feet of wall. Keep in mind that railings for stairwells also count as part of the length of a wall. If you are adding a circuit in an older house, the receptacles needed can also be figured by the room's square footage. Consult the code book for the number required.

The code doesn't allow any splices outside of boxes inside a house. So if you need to make a splice in the middle of a run, you have to use a box. It's allowable to use a box with a solid cover on it inside a wall or ceiling, but you must keep all boxes accessible.

INSTALLING AN OUTLET

To install a new outlet, first cut the Romex cable sheathing with a cable ripper. Then use a wire stripper to remove the plastic cover of the cable and to strip insulation from the ends of the wire.

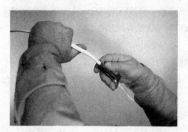

Cut the Romex cable sheathing.

Use a wire stripper to remove the plastic covering and strip insulation from the wire ends.

Connectors hold the Romex securely in the box. If the outlet is at the end of the circuit, connect the bare ground wire to the green terminal screw at the bottom of the receptacle. (If the circuit continues, use a pigtail connection.) Connect the white neutral wire to the silver screw and the black hot wire to the brass-colored screw on the opposite side of the receptacle.

RUNNING WIRES

Once you start running wire, keep in mind that it should be attached with plastic staples every 4½ feet or less along the run and attached within 12 inches of any box, cabinet or fitting. And when you run wire into a box it must be secured at the box with either a self-locking tab on a plastic box or connector clamps with screws. One thing that can trip up the beginner is not leaving enough wire inside the box. It's natural to cut off the wires at a length that looks reasonably long enough to attach a receptacle or fixture. But the code is specific on requiring a minimum of 6 inches of wire as measured from the outside edge of the box. One-quarter

Use connectors to hold the cable securely in the box.

Connect the wires.

To finish up, bend the wires accordion-fashion and push the receptacle into the box. Secure the receptacle with screws at the top and bottom.

Push the receptacle into the box and secure with screws.

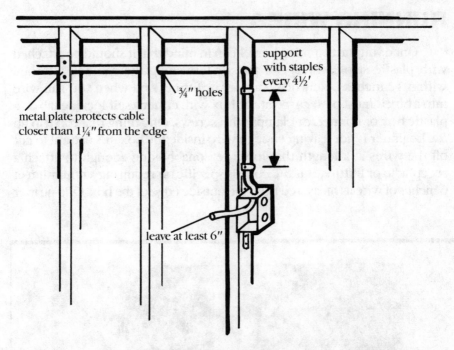

support
with staples
every 4½'

¾" holes

metal plate protects cable
closer than 1¼" from the edge

leave at least 6"

*When running wire, make sure wire is stapled every 4½ feet or less along the run.
Be sure to leave enough wire in the box–at least six inches.*

to ½ inch of Romex sheathing must be showing inside the box. If you
don't have enough wire coming into the box, after an inspection you
may find yourself redoing all your box connections, pulling wires and
restapling.

Make sure you don't use too many wires inside a box. The code
provides formulas and charts for figuring the number of wires allowed in
various sizes of boxes. For example, you can have 10 "wire ends" of
14-gauge wire in a 1½-by-4-inch box, or 9 wire ends of 12-gauge wire. All
bare ground wires together count as one wire end. And any wire running
continuously through the box without a splice is counted only as a single
wire end.

You can also go by the space required per wire end inside the box.
You need 2 cubic inches for each 14-gauge wire end, or 2.25 cubic
inches for each 12-gauge wire end. (However, you need to reduce the
count by one wire end for each switch or receptacle put into the box.)
The space available is now often stamped inside plastic boxes. In some
cases you can solve a space problem by using what's called a mud ring,

or raised cover. With an existing metal box, you can also use what's called an extension box for additional wire space.

Another point to remember when running wire is that where Romex cable is installed closer than 1¼ inches to the edge of a joist or stud (i.e., other than in the center of a 2 × 4), you need to protect it with metal nailer plates. Also, it's a good idea not to run Romex "through the air" for more than a foot or so. If you are bridging rafters, for example, first tack down a scrap piece of lumber across the space and staple the cable to it.

The NEC requires a continuous ground wire to be run through the older flexible metal conduit called greenfield. If you need to pull more wire though existing greenfield or conduit, keep in mind that there are limits to the number of wires allowed. The number allowed goes by wire size and insulation on the wire (either TW or THHN). Conduit is sized by what's called nominal trade size, which can be confusing. What they call a ½-inch conduit will have an outside diameter of ⅞ inch and inside diameter of ¾ inch. This size conduit can take up to 7 wires of 12-gauge (or 9 wires of 14-gauge) with TW insulation. Or, it can take 10 wires of 12-gauge (or 13 wires of 14-gauge) with THHN insulation.

REWIRING A HOME

Electrical projects come in two categories for an electrician: new work and rewiring. Rewiring entails doing wiring on existing systems, and this is the kind of electrical work that most homeowners get into.

If you live in a house that's over 20 years old, chances are good you'll have up to three "generations" of wiring in that house. In other words, it's likely that three sets of owners have monkeyed with the wiring. As a result, there may be as many as a dozen problems in the system that would make an inspector see red, ranging from simple things such as loose fixtures to serious, dangerous situations such as bare wires hanging in the air. The following are typical code violations you might find in an older home.

WIRES

You might find mixed wire sizes in a circuit. This can be okay if the added wire is larger, such as 12-gauge wire added to a circuit of 14-gauge wire. You can always go to a larger-sized wire in a circuit, but never go smaller. For example, if you have a circuit of 12-gauge wire protected by a 20-amp circuit breaker, you should never add smaller, 14-gauge wire to that circuit. It's too small for the intended load. Also, circuits should not contain wire that doesn't have proper insulation and that is not approved by Underwriters Laboratories Inc.

This box is too small for the number of wires used. Other problems include the loom stripped back from the wire and the absence of connectors, wire staples and box cover.

CONNECTIONS

You might find improper connections such as twisted wires covered with tape, or splices in the open air, outside of a box. Wire nuts should be used for connections, and they should be inside an acceptable junction box.

You might also find improper terminal connections, either on electrical devices or in your service panel. Some service panel terminals may accept two wires, but usually only one wire should be clamped under a terminal screw. Wire should be wrapped clockwise around the screw on receptacles or switches so the screw snugs down on the wire as it's tightened.

SWITCHES

Here most problems are with three-way switches (two switches controlling a light fixture) or four-way switches (three or more switches controlling a light fixture). If they've been installed by a homeowner, chances are 9 out of 10 they're connected incorrectly. These can be

The BX cable here runs under (instead of through) the joist, and the cable clamps are inadequate.

The Romex cable here is inadequately secured by wire staples.

Here's an example of a wire spliced outside of a box.

Shown here: a three-wire outlet without the proper ground connection and cover.

confusing to connect, and the best thing to do is go by good diagrams. One good reference is *Step by Step Guide Book on Home Wiring*. If switches are installed upside down, correct them; they may cause a problem in an emergency.

FIXTURES

Sometimes you'll find fixtures incorrectly installed without an electrical box behind them. Multiple light fixtures should be wired in *parallel* – in other words, with the black wire from the first fixture connected to the black wire of the next fixture, and the white wire from the first fixture likewise connected to the white wire of the next fixture and so on. If you buy used fixtures or electrical supplies to replace those currently in your home, be cautious. They may not be allowed under the current code. For example, let's say you acquire an older recessed lighting fixture and install it. You probably will need to take it out after the inspector sees it. The code requires recessed ceiling fixtures to have thermal protection, which cuts out the current above a certain temperature, and older fixtures don't have it.

CIRCUITS

Overloaded circuits can result from undersized wiring, too big a load or too large a fuse for the circuit (for example, a 30-amp fuse or breaker in a 15-amp circuit of 14-gauge wire). Overloads are definite fire hazards. Another danger is not having enough receptacles for the amount of appliances you're using. This can lead to the use of multiple-headed extension cords, or "octopuses," which are common causes of electrical fires.

I'd say that an average homeowner could easily handle projects involving the *replacement* of outlets, switches or fixtures. Replacement equipment is often available in blister packs with instructions on the back. However, *additions* to existing circuits or adding new circuits require specific know-how and probably a permit.

Any work on the service panel should be handled by a professional, unless you know *exactly* what you're doing. But if proper safety precautions are used, beginning do-it-yourselfers could handle one-to-one replacement. An experienced do-it-yourselfer could handle that, plus adding to existing circuits and possibly adding new circuits, as well.

My best advice is that you should do your homework before you start. Call the local electrical inspector to verify local laws. In many states it is illegal for someone to work on another's electrical system without a license. If you take out the permit yourself, some states require that you also do the work yourself.

STOCKING YOUR ELECTRICAL TOOL KIT

Besides the tools you probably already have, a minimum electrical tool kit might include:

- a straight-shank screwdriver
- lineman's pliers with flat jaws and wire cutter
- Channellock pliers
- needle-nose pliers
- neon test light

If you plan to do a lot of wiring, consider buying such tools as a wire stripper, screw hole tap, larger straight-shank screwdriver, small electrician's pliers, six-inch Crescent wrench, volt-ohm meter or clip-on amp tester and fish tape, to pull wires with.

You may need special supplies such as custom plate covers, three- or four-way switches, special electrical boxes or outlets for appliances. If you can't find them, check with a wholesale house. They may sell to you for cash. If they don't carry what you need, they may be able to direct you to a source. You can also ask an electrical contractor if he or she either has what you need or will get it for you.

LEARNING THE SHORTCUTS

There's an easier way to do almost everything; electrical work is no exception. If you need to run new wire through existing walls, for example, a fish tape is helpful. But if the wire is less than six feet long, you may not need it. When running wire, first make sure you know where you're going. My advice is to measure, remeasure and measure again. You can get yourself small-diameter "aircraft" bits for your drill, which are about a foot long, to help you explore the area and do your measuring. Open up the walls where boxes must go. If the wire is less than six feet long, you may be able to push it through. If not, try coat hangers, doweling, even string with a washer at one end. Drop the string through, then pull back up a heavier string or rope attached to the cable. Some other home wiring helpers:

- Die-cut sheet metal devices known as madison clips or box clamps are essential for mounting boxes between studs in either wallboard or plaster walls.

• Special wire-pulling lubricants are helpful when pulling wires through conduit. One is called Wire Slick. (The job is also easier if you pull out all the old wires, add the new wire and pull the entire bunch back through.)

• Pigtails are used when connecting more than one wire to one terminal. Loop one wire – the same size as the largest wire in the box – under the screw, allowing up to six inches to extend beyond the screw. Connect other wires to this pigtail with a wire nut.

When doing your own electrical work, put safety first and never guess. Check, double-check and triple-check your work before, during and after your project. Wiring can be tested while the current is off with a continuity tester – either a volt-ohm meter or signal device. Neon test lights can be used to check whether wires, outlets or switches are live. Always shut off the current at the main switch on the service panel. Turning off switches and circuit breakers may not be enough. For example, switches may be fed from fixtures, and neutral wires may be shared by more than one circuit. In some cases you can get shocked by white wires assumed to be off. You can also get a shock from neutral wires if you interrupt their path back to the service panel. Always assume the wires are hot, and work accordingly. Also remember to wear basic protective gear for hands, eyes and ears. If you're not sure of what you're doing, or if questions arise, seek competent help.

If you need to hire an electrician, first try to get recommendations from friends, neighbors and relatives who have had work done. The contractor they suggest may not be the low bidder, but at least you have an idea of his or her professional ability. If you start from scratch, get formal written proposals from at least two contractors.

Look for a fair shake, rather than a bargain. Often the low-bid contractor may not be a bargain in the long run. Electrical contractors have an obligation to point out hazards they see that should be repaired, even though you may not want to have the work done. If you have questions about your own electrical projects, or projects you plan to have done for you, call local electrical code officials or your power company. It's their job to make sure wiring in your community is done correctly and safely.

PART 6

PROJECT SHORTCUTS AND SLICK TRICKS

CHAPTER 21

JOHN A. GORDON:

HINTS FOR PAINLESS PAINTING

On a pleasure scale from one to ten, a week's holiday in the Caribbean would be a ten for most of us, watching TV might be a six, cleaning out the garage a three and painting might rank a one — possibly a two. "Yet there can be nothing more satisfying than looking at a paint job successfully completed," notes John A. Gordon. "The trick is to learn the basics, then do everything you can to make it as painless as possible."

Many professionals consider John the guy to go to with a question that has to do with paint and painting. He spent a lifetime working for big-name paint manufacturers before teaching paint technology at the University of Missouri and Kent State. He now is director of the Center for Coatings Technology

223

at Eastern Michigan University in Ypsilanti. From his office there, he talks about ways to make painting less of a drudgery while getting better results.

The reason many people groan at the thought of painting either the inside or the outside of their homes is that the job can be messy, expensive, time-consuming and frustrating. I've gone through all the problems myself, but there are ways to get in control of any painting project.

The big thing, of course, is not to get your mind set in the wrong gear and think that painting is mainly applying the paint. The truth is that planning and preparation account for most of the work, so it's good to set your expectations accordingly. Once you get into a project, there are ways to save time spent on preparing surfaces, on cleaning up and on repainting, plus some ways to keep from spending more money than you have to in order to get the job done.

CUTTING PREPARATION TIME

Getting all chalking, flaking or peeling paint off the surface you're about to repaint is a must. Consider using your garden hose or a rented pressure washer on the outside of your house. Unless you are using latex, wait until the surface is completely dry before starting to paint. If you have mildew problems, use a bleach solution, one pint per gallon of water, to kill the mildew and bleach out the stains. If you don't kill mildew, it can grow right under your new coat of paint.

Inside the house, you can use shellac to seal water stains. Water-borne stains will bleed right through any latex paint. (I once experimented

When embarking on any painting project, realize that preparation, not applying the paint, is the biggest part of the job.

to see how many coats of latex it would take to cover a water stain. I gave up after 15 coats!) Shellac dries quickly. Use alcohol, not mineral spirits, to clean it from brushes.

Remove wall items you don't want painted, such as electrical plates. It's quicker and easier than trying to mask everything with tape. Cover up what you can't remove. For example, tie garbage bags over fixtures such as chandeliers. Use care when painting around exposed wiring.

Glass can slow you down. Some folks don't bother covering glass, saying it's faster to scrape the paint off later. You can stick wet newspapers on glass, but it can dry out and fall off. I use dry newspaper over glass with masking tape around the edges.

CUTTING CLEANUP TIME

Try to avoid unnecessary cleanup when your painting is interrupted or finished. Line roller trays with plastic; you can even slip a plastic garbage bag over the tray. A lining not only makes cleanup easier, but also prevents the high pH of latex paints from interacting with the aluminum tray. If you use plastic lining, buy a gridlike roller screen that fits inside the tray over the plastic. The screen keeps the plastic from wrinkling and the roller from slipping.

Put paint tools and trays inside a garbage bag to keep them from drying out if you have to stop painting for a few hours or overnight. Small plastic sandwich bags work great for brushes and also help them keep their shape. For rollers, you can use Ziploc storage bags, plastic wrap or large, plastic food storage bags.

BRUSHES AND ROLLERS

To speed brush cleanup, try not to get the bristles wet beyond about half of their length. When you're painting overhead, paint will drop down into the brush. To remove this paint, wash the brush, then comb it out with a bronze wire brush, the kind used for cleaning barbecue grills.

One trick to cleaning rollers is to use the stream of a hose nozzle. By turning the hose on full blast and directing the spray to the side of the roller, it will almost spin itself clean. Of course, you must do this outside, and you should wear old clothes and avoid spraying shrubbery or your house.

SPATTERS

It's easier to cover up than to clean up. When mixing paint, prevent spattering by putting the can inside a cardboard box or a garbage or grocery bag. Any flying paint will be neatly confined. To keep paint from running down the side of the can, you can buy special plastic lid devices that fit over the rim. You can also fashion your own by cutting a semicircle in a coffee can lid to within about one inch of the edge. Then use the inside edge to wipe your brush.

Buy plenty of drop cloths. Canvas lasts longer than plastic and soaks up paint, but 3-mil plastic works fine. Make newspaper "paths" to and from your work area so paint sticking to your shoes won't be dragged through the house. Also get enough masking tape. You are buying it to save time, so buy a good brand that's at least an inch wide. If tape comes in contact with some paint solvents it can glue itself to the surface. Pull off the tape as soon as the paint has set. Between jobs, store tape in the refrigerator or at least keep it out of direct sun.

To clean solvent-borne paints off of your hands, try ordinary salad oil. (Solvent-borne paints include oil-based paints, varnishes and urethanes.) It takes the paint off and won't irritate your hands like other solvents. Salad oil can also help you remove solvent-borne paint spilled on wood finishes that are sensitive to other solvents.

SAVING ON PAINTING TIME

There's no point in painting if you don't really have to. For example, if you have small water stains on a ceiling, experiment to see if you can get by without painting. Mix up a water-bleach solution and apply it with a small spray bottle, using normal safety precautions. The stains may disappear, saving you a paint job. Here are some other shortcuts that can save on painting time:

- Lay screens on top of sawhorses to confine splattering while you're painting them. Or use two sponges, pads or rollers directly opposite each other on each side of the screen. You can also set boards across the second rung on your stepladder to support screens or storm windows while you paint.

- Attach a carpenter's nail apron to the top of your stepladder to store small items such as putty, nails or screws that you may need while painting.

- Quart-sized or smaller paint cans are hard to carry and easy to tip over. Put the small can inside an empty gallon can. It's easier to carry and if it spills, you can simply pour the paint back into the little can.

- If you're thinking of buying any mechanized painting equipment, buy a power roller for interior use. The first time I used one, I painted a living room, dining room, hallway and bedroom in one day.

TRIMMING PAINTING COSTS

There's no need to throw away expensive solvent after one use. Pour it into a metal can and cover it. After the paint particles settle out, pour off the clear solvent for reuse. You can do this a number of times. To test, rub some between your fingers. When it feels sticky, throw it away.

Brushes can also be expensive to replace. If you have brushes that are dried out and hard, try this. Soak them overnight in water-washable paint remover. Then clean and comb out with a bronze wire brush. This overhaul works best with brushes that have been used with oil-based paints.

When storing paint, blowing into the can before sealing helps the paint last longer. It adds carbon dioxide, reducing the oxygen level that causes paint to skin over. You can even throw in a small chunk of dry ice to increase the carbon dioxide level. But don't blow into cans of moisture-cure urethanes (most of today's polyurethanes) because your breath contains moisture.

Another trick for storing paint is to use plastic wrap. Push it into the can, down to the paint, and seal it around the edge with your finger. If paint does get lumpy, strain it through old nylon stockings or panty hose. Just hang the paint can above an empty can and pour it through the nylon. We do this often in our lab – it works great.

If you want to keep full cans of paint for long periods, store the can upside down for a month, then right-side up the next month, then upside down, and so on. This moves the paint's pigment back and forth, and keeps it from settling out.

When to throw paint out? Some corrosion-inhibiting pigments can react with paint over time, turning it into a semisolid gel. Once this happens, the paint is finished. Also, once latex paint freezes and looks like cottage cheese, you may as well throw it away and save your time.

AVOIDING REPAINTING

There are several tricks that will help you avoid the headache of repainting a newly painted surface. When using latex, for example, be sure the temperature is above 50° F. (Latex won't form a film at lower temperatures.) With solvent-borne paint, be sure the temperature is at least 5° F above the dew point. If it's not, water may condense on the surface as it cools while the solvent evaporates. When that happens you end up with an uneven color.

Painting over new galvanized metal can be a problem. If possible, let it weather for a year. Next best is to treat it with a preparation material such as Galva-Grip. Never use solvent-borne paints such as alkyd resins. They turn into soap at the metal's surface and lose their adhesion. Use an acrylic or vinyl-acrylic paint instead.

When buying brushes, get nylon bristles for latex. (The high pH of latex will ruin expensive hog-bristle brushes.) Good nylon-bristle brushes can be used for solvent-borne paints, but hog-bristle brushes are best if you can afford them. Don't be casual about buying roller covers. Get quality covers with a nap length to match the surface to be painted.

One fear most people have is that they'll end up buying more paint than they need. As a result, they're often just a little bit short. Assume that almost all paint will cover about 400 square feet per gallon at a normal 4-mil thickness. Latex goes on so easily it's possible to stretch it too much. You could cover 700 square feet per gallon, but you might have to put on a second coat to finish the job. The approximate coverage you can expect is usually listed on the paint can label. Adjust these figures for the application method you are using: for brush or roller, waste is about 10 percent; airless sprayers lose about 20 percent and air sprayers waste 40 percent of the paint. Remember, too, that rough, textured or porous surfaces take more paint than smooth, sealed areas.

CHAPTER 22

ROBERT SNIDER:

GETTING ALONG WITH GLUES

Gluing problems are always expensive. Any piece of furniture or other project becomes high-priced junk if the glue joints fail, regardless of fancy design or finishing.

Whenever we encounter glue failure, most of us occasional-project builders venture offhanded guesses as to what went wrong. And most of the time we blame the glue: wrong kind of glue, glue no good, glue too old. But, says Dr. Robert Snider, when a woodworking glue fails to do the job, the problem can be linked to a dozen or more reasons besides the glue itself.

Dr. Snider, a chemical engineer, is a leading glue expert at Franklin International, where he has worked for the last 45 years. Further, he is a home craftsman and well aware of glue problems experienced in the home workshop. "Gluing success boils down to using the right glue properly," he explains. "Getting the right glue is the easy part; using it correctly is the big challenge."

Most home projects are done with ready-to-use adhesives that include the liquid hide glues, aliphatic resins and polyvinyl acetates. However, the latter two are the most commonly used. Aliphatic resins are the yellow glues such as Franklin Titebond and Elmer's Professional Carpenters Wood Glue; polyvinyl acetates are the white glues such as Franklin Evertite and Elmer's Glue-All. Although neither is waterproof, the yellow aliphatic resins are water resistant and stronger than the white glues. Both glues set in about one hour and cure to full strength in about 24 hours. One advantage of the yellow glues is that they tend to clog sandpaper less during finishing.

Various adhesives work either by drying, cooling, chemical reaction or a combination of these methods. The yellow and white glues work by drying, that is, by losing water from the glue line. After the glue is spread, parts are pressed together until the glue sets. During this time, the glue-and-water mix penetrates the pores of the wood surface. As the water goes through the pores, glue is retained on the wood fiber walls. The glue gains strength as the water leaves this adhesive film.

TROUBLESHOOTING GLUE PROBLEMS

The first step in troubleshooting glue problems is to make sure you are closely following the directions of the glue manufacturer. A good rule of thumb for any gluing is that a thin glue line or tight joint will give you a stronger and less noticeable joint. See that the moisture content of the wood is close to what it will be in later use. Also make sure the joint has been made with sharp tools for a clean fit.

The more common gluing problems are outlined below, along with some suggestions on how you can avoid them.

LOW GLUING TEMPERATURES

Low temperatures slow setting time. For example, the time the glued wood needs to stay clamped in cold shops during winter may be twice that needed in the summer. Below certain critical points, low temperatures can cause a loss of joint strength because the glue can't form a continuous film as it dries. For the white polyvinyl acetates, this point is about 55° F. For the yellow aliphatics, the minimum use temperature is about 40° F.

WEAK DOWEL JOINTS

Some woodworkers put glue in the bottom of the hole and hope that when the dowel reaches the bottom of the hole, glue will be forced up around the dowel. For a good dowel joint, the dowel must fit loosely enough to allow the glue to come up around it, the dowel must go to the bottom of the hole and adequate glue must be applied. The best procedure is to apply glue to both the sides of the hole *and* the dowel. Grooved dowels allow the glue to come up in the grooves, but that doesn't guarantee that glue will be outside the grooves. A good fit is one where you can push the dowel in with a finger, but it's not so loose that it wobbles in the hole.

STARVED END-GRAIN JOINTS

Glues can soak into the end grain more than into the rest of the wood, resulting in a "starved" joint. To help prevent this, you can "size" the end grain with a mixture of glue diluted with water. Dilute just enough so that when it's applied, glue drops don't form at the lower edges of the wood. Another method, somewhat less effective, is to coat the end grain with full-strength glue, allow to dry 5 to 10 minutes, then recoat with glue and assemble.

SUNKEN GLUE JOINTS

If the glue joints in your finish work are sunken below the wood surface, chances are good it was caused by working the wood too soon after gluing. This happens because as wood absorbs moisture from the glue, it swells along the glue line. If the wood is planed before the moisture has left, more wood is removed near the glue line than elsewhere. Though the surface will appear smooth, a shallow channel results along the glue line after drying. To prevent this, let the glue (and wood) dry completely before finishing. A minimum of three days at room temperature is needed for complete drying.

IRREGULAR SURFACES

This problem is a cousin to the one above. If you are edge-gluing lumber, try to make sure each of the boards has relatively the same moisture content. If, for example, one board has 10 percent moisture and the boards next to it are at 4 percent, you are asking for an irregular surface. If you glue and plane boards with unequal moisture content, the boards with higher original moisture content will shrink more than the others. This will leave an irregular surface at the juncture or glue line.

BLACK GLUE LINES

Glues with a pH of less than 7 will absorb iron from steel, and this dissolved iron will then react with certain woods, such as oak, walnut, mahogany, cherry and other colored woods, and form a black glue line. This is less likely to happen with the yellow glues than the white glues.

Coffee cans are a common source of iron contamination. It's a good idea to use plastic or glass containers for storing glue to prevent these iron stain problems.

STAINS CAUSED BY GLUE

Glue stains result when spots of glue on the wood surface fill the wood pores. This prevents stain or finish from being absorbed by the wood, and the result is light-colored spots. The key is to remove excess glue properly.

One way is to remove it with a damp sponge or rag immediately after it oozes out. Be sure the sponge or rag is moist enough so you can avoid applying a lot of pressure, which can drive glue into the wood. Or, after a half hour or so, when the glue dries to the consistency of cottage cheese, you can use a scraper or metal spatula to remove it.

GLUE SOFTENING

Sometimes applying a finish to glued lumber can cause a small ridge at the glue line, or even weaken or open the glue joint. Wash-off solvents may also soften the glue and cause joint failure. The trouble can be corrected by changing to a solvent-resistant glue, or changing the finish or solvent. Liquid hide glues resist most solvents (except water), followed closely by the aliphatic resins. Polyvinyl acetates are affected by a number of active organic solvents such as acetone or methyl ethyl ketone.

DULL WOODWORKING TOOLS

If dull cutting tools such as saws, bits or blades are used, they can loosen but not remove a layer of fibers on the surface of edges to be joined. When this happens, the glue may not penetrate through the debris to solid wood. You can usually tell if this is causing weak joints if the glue line of a ruptured joint is coated with wood fibers. Sharpening your cutting tools will often help increase the strength of the glued joints because sharp tools will remove the fiber layer.

IMPROPER CLAMPING

The purpose of clamps is to bring boards being glued into close enough contact to produce a thin, uniform glue line and hold them until the glue is strong enough to hold the assembly together. If boards fit together perfectly, you wouldn't even need clamps. But because machining of wood is never perfect, a certain amount of clamp pressure must be used. Usually 100 to 150 pounds per square inch (psi) is needed, but applying pressure uniformly is actually more important than the amount.

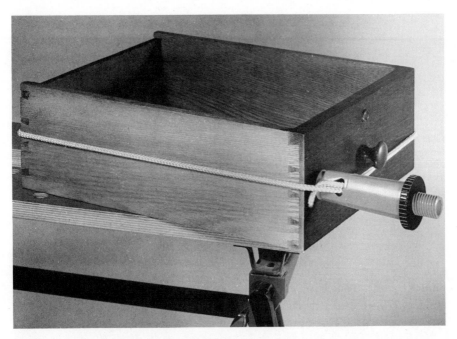

Clamping affects gluing results. If machining was perfect–and it never is–clamps wouldn't be needed. The ideal pressure when clamping is 100 psi or more, but uniformity of pressure is the key. This device, from Black & Decker, is called a cinch clamp and is used with a 10-foot length of rope.

When gluing veneers it's best to use only enough pressure to get good contact so you can avoid "show through" or "telegraphing" of imperfections from the lumber beneath.

POOR GLUE PENETRATION

This problem is common when repairing previously finished projects. It's difficult, if not impossible, to reglue dirty joints or those filled with old glue. With the exception of some antiques, first dismantle and clean the joints. Remove old paint, wax, dust, oil, grease and glue. (Warm vinegar will generally soften the most stubborn glue.) Then dip the parts to be glued in warm water and let them dry completely to help open the wood pores and allow glue to enter more freely. Warming the parts on top of a radiator or in the sun also helps open up wood pores.

IMPOSSIBLE APPLICATIONS

Although it's a good idea to dismantle furniture to be repaired with glue, some antiques such as rung-type chairs and furniture held together with wooden pins or wedges shouldn't be taken apart. To repair loose

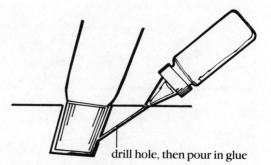

One way to avoid taking apart old antiques for regluing is to drill a small hole down to the joint and force glue into it with an oil can or squeeze bottle.

drill hole, then pour in glue

joints in these, you can try to use a toothpick to work the glue into the joint. Or you can drill a $\frac{1}{16}$-inch hole at an angle to, or alongside, the joint and force glue into it with a small oil can, plastic squeeze bottle or glue syringe (available through mail-order woodworker supply firms).

CHAPTER 23

ROBERT SCHARFF:

CHOOSING AND USING FASTENERS

Psychologist Abraham Maslow once said that people who are good only with hammers see every solution as a nail. "You certainly don't have to be that narrow-minded about fasteners today," observes Robert Scharff. "In a well-stocked hardware store or home center you'll be able to find a fastener to handle just about any kind of challenge."

Scharff, of New Ringgold, Pennsylvania, is a self-made put-it-together expert who has explored the world of fasteners for more than 30 years. A longtime home shop enthusiast who regularly examines the latest fastener offerings at major hardware trade shows, he knows a new fastener when he sees one. "I was always being asked by homeowners about what to use where. Choosing fasteners used to be a real challenge for the uninitiated. But it's getting much easier; more of the most useful fasteners are getting into the stores, with some good packaging that shows you how they work."

Still, Robert says there are tricks of the trade that can help you when using almost any fastener. Some make the job easier; others help prevent fastener failure.

Over the years I've observed that the average homeowner often misses the boat by either using the wrong fastener or installing a fastener in the wrong way. Finding the best fastener to use is half the battle. The other half is installing it right. Two places where this is especially true are in fastening items to walls and to masonry. That's where some people get really stumped.

One reason for the confusion is that there are so many variables. For example, if you ask me what's the best way to hang a shelf above your fireplace, I can't tell you unless I know what the wall's made of, how thick

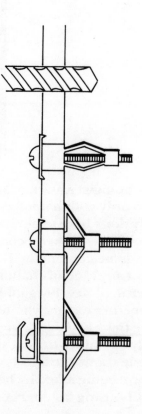

Molly brand fasteners are great for hanging lamps, curtain rods, shelving, brackets, racks and planters from hollow walls. A hole is drilled, the fastener is tapped in and the screw is turned until tight.

it is, what kind of shelf you plan to hang and what you plan to put on the shelf.

A second reason for confusion is the pure number of fastener types. Most of those for hollow walls actually go through the outside surface and anchor themselves on the back of it. But most solid wall and masonry wall fasteners anchor themselves against the inside of the hole. The shell expands and grips as the fastener is tightened. Some fasteners usually used for masonry walls can also be used for hollow walls. These include plastic, nylon expansion and nylon drive anchors. They are usually inserted into predrilled holes and expand as either a screw or a threaded nail is driven into them.

Generally, though, if walls are hollow and covered with drywall, you'll need to use a hollow-wall fastener. An example is the Molly bolt invented over 60 years ago. These hollow-wall fasteners come with a slotted metal sleeve or tube that has a bolt going through its center. This bolt threads into a nut or collar on the inside end. To install, you insert the anchor in a hole drilled through the drywall, then tap lightly to seat the flange or lip against the face of the wall. When the bolt in the center is tightened, it pulls the far end of the fastener inward, causing it to expand or "mushroom" behind the wall. When fully tightened, the fastener is locked permanently in place. Then the bolt can be unthreaded and pushed through the bracket or fixture to be mounted, then screwed back into the anchor for final tightening.

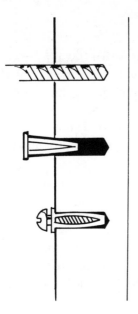

Nylon expansion and nylon drive anchors are all-purpose fasteners for both hollow and solid walls of various materials from wood to concrete. The hole should be made the same size as the fastener shank.

If, on the other hand, you have a solid wall such as plaster or cinder block, one choice is a plastic-lipped anchor. You first drill a hole, then push the anchor into the hole until its flange is flush against the surface. Then, as you insert and drive in a screw, the anchor expands, locking itself firmly in place inside the hole.

SELECTING FASTENERS

Fasteners should always be able to support the heaviest loads that will ever be placed on them, and do so with a reasonable margin of safety. A good rule of thumb is to use a safety factor of 4-to-1 for general fastening. In other words, if you want to hang something on the wall, use a fastener with a holding power four times as heavy. So if you want to hang something weighing 25 pounds, use a fastener with a holding power of 100 pounds. If there's the possibility that what you hang may be affected by vibrations, then go with a 10-to-1 ratio.

If you want to hang something on a hollow wall, you must first see if you can drive fasteners into the studs before you can determine which fastener you'll need. There are electronic stud finders available to help you locate studs, but there are other ways. Try tapping the wall lightly. A solid sound usually indicates you are over a stud. If that doesn't work, try measuring out from a corner to find studs, usually 16 or 24 inches on center. You can also drill small holes in the wall until you find a stud. Or, take off the baseboard; a stud is usually behind the place where two wall panels meet.

TOGGLE BOLTS

The main disadvantage of the toggle is that if you remove a fixture, the wings will drop off and disappear inside the wall. But the toggle fixture hanger is a great money-saver in remodeling. Its wings spread the load and are useful for attaching junction boxes and light fixtures to ceilings. The tie-wire toggle bolt is also helpful. It has a spade-end bolt, with a hole to run a wire through, and works great for installing suspended acoustical ceilings.

MOLLY BOLTS

These have a sleeve that stays in the wall after installation so you can withdraw and replace the original bolt. The disadvantage is that, for Molly bolts to work, they must be correctly sized for the wall thickness. To double-check the thickness of your wall, you can insert a bent wire or crochet hook and pull it back so the bend or hook catches the inside of the wall.

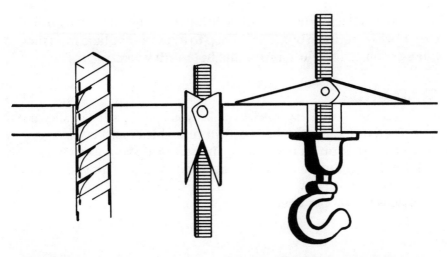

Toggle bolts need an oversized hole to admit the folded wings. The assembly is pulled back to hold the wings on the inside of the wall while the bolt is turned and tightened.

ANGLED PICTURE HANGERS

If you need to hang a picture, keep in mind that the hangers that are cemented in place, or have an adhesive back, have limited load capacity. Angled picture hangers have more holding strength – up to 100 pounds in the bigger sizes. Before driving these into plaster, make an X with two pieces of masking tape where the nail will enter the wall to keep the plaster from chipping.

DRILLING THE HOLE

The holding power of a fastener in a solid masonry or concrete wall depends on your making the right kind of hole. The easiest way to drill a good hole in brick, stone or concrete is to use a carbide-tipped bit and at least a ⅜-inch drill. Carbide bits are brittle, so maintain a steadily increasing pressure as the bit enters the wall. Don't let the drill ease up or run idly in the hole. And when drilling hard materials such as tile or porcelain, use water or turpentine as a coolant.

When using a masonry drill bit, it's important to keep the hole free of dust. Bits with a flute or twist along the body will remove cutting dust.

If the hole is deep, you can avoid getting dust in your eyes by using an empty plastic squeeze bottle as a pump to blow out the hole from time to time, or you can try flushing out the hole with water.

STAR DRILLS

If you have just a few holes to make, you can use what's called a star drill. The cutting end of the star drill resembles four chisels joined at their edges to form a cross (star). The star drill should be struck only with a heavy drilling-hammer or sledge, and should be rotated after each blow. A piece of tape wrapped around the bit will help you know when the hole is the proper depth.

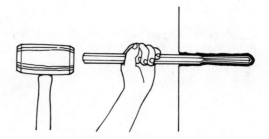

Hand drilling holes in masonry walls can be done either with a portable electric drill and carbide-tipped bits or with a star drill and a hand-drilling hammer, as shown here. Be sure to wear safety goggles no matter which method you choose.

WOODEN DOWELS

To fasten things in masonry you can use sections of wooden dowels, either purchased or made yourself. First make a hole with either a carbide bit or star drill. With a hammer, drive in the dowel flush, then drill a pilot in its center, slightly smaller than the holding screw you plan to use. Use a dowel that is slightly oversized, and grease it, if necessary, to make it go in easier.

If you want to drive lag screws into hard masonry, you can use soft lead lag screw anchors, also called expansion shields. To install these, drill a hole the same size as the outside diameter of the shield. Then insert the lag screw through whatever is being attached and into the anchor. To save drilling time, buy short anchors (one to two inches long) if they will do the job.

USING NAILS

If you're using small nails, they can be hard to hold on to. One trick is to use a magnetized tack hammer. If you don't have one, convert your nail hammer by coating the head with double-faced tape and sticking the tack to it. You can also hold a small nail by first pushing it through a piece of light cardboard or even a small pocket comb. A handy way to position a small nail is with a holder made by attaching a pencil clip to a nail set. Put the nail between the clip and the base of the nail set.

If you have a lot of brads to drive, consider buying a brad driver. In fact, some electric staplers can be converted to drive brads. If you are driving them by hand into tough hardwood, you can drill a hole in the wood using a bit made from a brad with the head removed. The nail will go in more easily if dipped in paraffin. You can keep paraffin handy by drilling a hole in the end of your hammer handle and pouring hot paraffin into the hole. When it cools you have a ready supply.

Quench-hardened cut nails, used for fastening wood to concrete mortar or masonry, can break, chip and shatter. Be sure to wear safety goggles and start these nails perfectly straight. Hit the nail squarely with a tapping, one-two stroke with a large ball-peen or hand-drilling hammer. Never use a nail hammer; its face could chip and cause injury.

USING SCREWS

As a general rule, select screws so that at least two-thirds of their length will go into the base material. Try to have the threaded part at least ⅛ inch shorter than the thickness of the bottom piece being fastened. For softwoods such as pine or spruce, drill a hole only half as deep as the threaded part of the screw. For hardwoods such as oak, maple or birch, drill the hole as deep as the screw.

If a screw is difficult to turn, back it out and enlarge the hole. Wax or paraffin rubbed on the screw will take most of the effort out of driving. A candle is perfect for this purpose. Never use soap because the moisture in the soap will rust the screw, weaken the joint and cause discoloration of paint or varnish finishes. Don't use oil, either – it will penetrate and stain the wood grain for some distance around the screw head.

There's not a house existing that doesn't have a least one screw hole that has become oversized because the wall material has given way. If you have this problem, try this: Remove the screw and push fine steel wool into the hole, packing it in with a screwdriver. Now redrive the screw. You can also try putting glue on splinters, toothpicks or burned-out wooden matchsticks and drive them into the hole. Let dry and then redrive the screw.

USING BOLTS

Buy bolts long enough so the nut goes all the way onto the threaded part and leaves a little thread showing. When drilling holes for bolts in wood, make them exactly the same diameter as the bolt. Try to use washers under both the head and the nut. Whenever possible, install bolts in metal parts so their heads are up. This way, if the nut is shaken off, the bolt is more likely to stay in place.

You can use lag bolts (lag screws), whenever wood screws or nails are too short or too light. To anchor them properly, first drill a hole slightly larger than the diameter of the shank, to a depth that is equal to the length that shank will penetrate. Then drill a second hole at the bottom of first hole equal to the "inside" diameter of the threaded shank. Make this second hole half as deep as the threaded section.

COTTER PINS

Cotter pins are used to secure screws, nuts, bolts and pins. A cotter pin should fit neatly into the hole with very little side play. There's actually a preferred way to bend back the prongs of the pin. Bend one prong over the head just to the opposite edge of the bolt; bend the other down alongside the nut, just short of touching the washer.

CORRUGATED FASTENERS

A useful fastener, especially for miter joints, is the corrugated fastener. Also known as the wiggle nail, it's made of 18- to 22-gauge sheet metal with alternate ridges and grooves. It can be used to fasten parallel boards together (as for tabletops), to make any type of joint or as a substitute for nails where nails may split the wood. For easier driving, buy yourself one of the special nail sets that are available. Otherwise, use a medium-weight hammer and evenly distributed blows, with the lumber set on a solid surface.

CHAPTER 24

HOMER FORMBY:

RESTORING AND REFINISHING FURNITURE

There's a hot new trend in advertising these days. The president of the company gets in front of the camera and explains how he's making the employees work hard and how he personally guarantees the product—whether it's fried chicken, electric shavers, popcorn or personal computers. Ads like these helped make Lee Iacocca an American hero.

If you think Colonel Sanders started it all, you're wrong. One of the first was a guy whose soft, Southern drawl makes you instantly think of the workshop—and fixing up furniture. Homer Formby started making a name for himself and his products nearly two decades ago. While copywriters crank out lines for other executive media stars, Formby has mostly spoken off-the-cuff on something he knows a lot about: furniture refinishing.

Formby grew up in a family of furniture craftsmen. He spent his childhood in a workshop. He remembers that at age eight he spent long hours learning how to hand-rub wooden surfaces until the wood glowed and felt like satin.

Before the 1940s were out, he had amassed a chain of antique shops where he kept 40 craftsmen busy restoring old furniture. But the writing was on the wall; skilled restorers were, as he says, "gettin' scarce as hen's teeth." So, after seven years of trial and error, he came up with a refinisher that would easily remove varnish, lacquer or shellac from old furniture without ruining it. Today his products line the shelves of more than 30,000 home centers and hardware stores across America.

He still spends most of his waking moments telling people how to avoid common hang-ups of furniture refinishing. He's what you might call narrow-minded about specific products and techniques, but for good reason—he sincerely believes in them. At age 62, he's a virtual gold mine of refinishing tips, tricks and shortcuts. (If you have a question on furniture refinishing, you can write Homer Formby directly at P.O. Box 667, Olive Branch, MS 38654.)

If you ask me what I've learned in the last 50 years, I'd probably tell you that just too many people still end up using the wrong techniques and actually ruin fine furniture with harsh chemicals that are difficult to use, messy and time-consuming. Really, I guess I've spent most of my life trying to bring restoring techniques into the twentieth century. If you've heard that refinishing furniture is hard work, you've been talking to people who are still doing it the hard way! I'd say that the key to refinishing success is using the right product, some easily learned know-how and a little effort.

GETTING STARTED

Rescuing some heirlooms may not be that difficult. Often old furniture is covered by a buildup of pollution, and all that's needed to restore its appearance is a thorough cleaning. To check this, rub the dirtiest spot on the piece with furniture *cleaner*, not polish, on a cotton cloth. Try several times, letting the cleaner dry between applications. If you can clean the spot well, and the wood grain turns out clear, don't bother with refinishing.

Homer is dead-set against dipping or stripping furniture because it removes the wood's patina and can also loosen joints. Use refinisher instead and work it into an area the size of a dinner plate.

What if the finish is dark, ugly, badly marred or "alligatored"? In this case, you'll probably need to refinish it. Old furniture will naturally get dark. It's called ambering, caused by years of exposure to light. But don't let that discourage you; it's the finish, not the wood, that's discolored.

REFINISHERS AND PAINT REMOVERS

Once you decide to refinish, try to avoid dip tanks and strippers if possible. Stripping takes away the the glow brought on by age, or what we call the wood's patina. It may also loosen the joints, and then you'll be forced to hire a professional to reglue it.

Today's furniture refinishing products take most of the work out of the job, as well as eliminate the mess of stripping. They remove varnish, lacquer and shellac. Paint or synthetic resin finishes call for a paint remover. To determine which type of finish you have, moisten a cotton ball with nail polish remover and touch a glossy area of the finish in an out-of-the-way place. If the cotton ball sticks, your finish is varnish, lacquer or shellac. You need a refinisher. If the cotton ball doesn't stick, then you need a paint remover.

My own furniture refinisher formula is applied with fine steel wool. Pick a small area to work on, about the size of a dinner plate. Then just overlap the areas until you're done. An old paint brush trimmed to a stubby length will help you work the refinisher in carved and fluted areas.

There'll be some swirls and streaks. But just rub fresh refinisher with steel wool from one end of the piece to the other, going with the grain. Then wipe it with a clean cotton cloth and let dry for 30 minutes. The final step is buffing well – but not hard – with dry steel wool.

I recommend avoiding paint removers that require a water rinse. The water can cause wood to warp or mildew – even loosen veneer and wood joints – and open the wood grain. Look for a heavy-bodied paint remover. Shake the container. It should feel like there's molasses in the can.

Apply paint remover with a brush in six-inch strokes. You'll get the most out of it if you brush only in one direction. Once the bubbling action stops, lift the old paint off with a wide putty knife. Don't scrape or gouge the wood, and repeat as needed. You'll also get a better job if you do it when the temperature is between 65° and 85° F.

STAINING SAVVY

When should you stain? Simply when you want to change the wood's color. You can also use stain to even up different wood colors. And staining new wood helps bring out the grain. Deciding which stain to use can be frustrating. But you won't go wrong by sticking to a few basic principles:

- Try brush-on pigment stains. They're best for most uses, especially on unfinished furniture.

- If you have a small job such as a spice rack, jelled wiping stains applied with a cloth are ideal.

- Stick with a stain that contains a pigment instead of a dye. Dyes fade more quickly in sunlight, plus both dye and alcohol stains can leave marks if you don't apply them uniformly.

The real trick to staining can be presealing if you are working with softwoods such as pine, fir or poplar. How do you tell if you've got softwood? Easy. Just push your fingernail into the wood. If it dents easily, it's softwood. If it doesn't, it's probably a hardwood such as maple, oak or walnut. (Poplar is technically a hardwood but, like softwoods, will dent. It is one of the most-used woods in old furniture.)

If you're working with softwood, it's critical to first apply a thin coat of wood seal with a brush or cloth. Wood seal can be the key to getting a rich, even finish. It's a colorless formulation of clear resins and polymers. It helps slow up the speed that stain penetrates, helping you control the color better and avoid streaking. Stains will penetrate unevenly on unsealed softwood, leaving streaks, blotches or uneven color.

Even if you are working with a hardwood, a wood seal can help you do a better job of staining certain problem areas, such as knotholes and unfinished corners, edges or sides.

APPLICATION

To get the right color stain, don't go by the name, but by a stain chart. A maple stain from one company can be much different than another company's maple. Once you've got your stain, apply it darker than you want it. Then use a soft cotton cloth or tissue to wipe off the excess after a few minutes. This way you can get exactly the right shade.

What's a good staining job? If your project looks like it's been stained instead of looking like natural wood, you've used the wrong stain. The grain should be highlighted by the stain, not hidden by it.

PRESERVING THE FINISH

Put a protective coating over stain. Varnish is a classic finish for sealing and protecting stain; polyurethane is used when you want a hard-wearing surface, such as a tabletop. I prefer coatings that contain tung oil.

Once a project is done, keep it clean! This may sound odd, but there are two kinds of dirt. One kind is water soluble – most food and drink falls into this category. The other kind is oil-soluble dirt, such as greasy spills and body oils. To clean water-soluble dirt, wipe with a dampened cloth. To get rid of oil-soluble dirt, wipe with a cloth dampened with a furniture cleaner – not polish.

In my years of working with furniture, I've come up with three don'ts. All these things can speed the destruction of a fine finish:

- Don't wax furniture, especially with waxes containing silicone.
- Don't wipe wood with ammonia or other harsh cleaners.
- Don't keep wood in direct sunlight if you can avoid it.

USING HOME REMEDIES FOR DAMAGE

There are lots of home remedies you can use when furniture is accidentally damaged. Some of the best ones are products you already have:

Toothpaste: It's a gentle abrasive, ideal for rescuing wood furniture damaged by water spots and rings (caused by moisture trapped underneath wax). To remove the water marks, simply squeeze toothpaste onto a wet cotton rag and buff the spotted area. For stubborn rings, you can combine toothpaste with equal parts of another gentle abrasive, baking soda. Buff until the spot disappears. Then, with a clean cloth, continue buffing until you can see yourself.

Nail polish remover: Ugly char marks from cigarettes don't have to ruin a good piece of furniture. Just dip a cotton swab into nail polish remover and rub it lightly across the burn. This will dissolve the black residue. If any remains, scrape it gently with a small knife. If a slight hollow is left, you can fill it in with a mix of equal parts of remover and clear nail polish. Apply one coat at a time with the nail polish brush. Let each coat dry between applications, and have patience. It might take seven or eight coats to get the job done.

Colored crayons: If you have a scratch marring your coffee table or other furniture, you can try covering it up with a crayon that matches the finish. Just melt the crayon over the gash until the depression overflows. You can melt it with a soldering iron. Or tie a nail to a pencil, heat it over a flame and put the hot nail to the crayon. After filling the gash, let the wax cure for a half hour, then gently shave off the residue with a credit card.

A colored crayon can help cover up a scratch. Melt it over the gash, let cure, then shave off the extra with a credit card.

Cedar chips: Wood acquires a musty odor over time. In fact, it's one way to be certain that a piece is old and not a reproduction. It can be tough to get rid of the odor, but you can effectively mask it. Start with about a pound of red cedar shavings, not western cedar. Put the shavings in the toe of a nylon stocking, tie the end and cut off the excess. Then tack the sack along the back of a drawer. If there are no drawers, tack it on the back or underneath the piece.

FINDING FURNITURE TREASURES

Remember, a piece of furniture doesn't have to be 100 years old to be a treasure worth restoring. I've come across a lot of 50-year-old reproductions worth as much or more than some antiques 100 years old. You can spot real treasures just about anywhere. Here are some things to look for:

• furniture that has good lines, molding and turnings

• furniture with joints that are dovetailed (interlocking), not held by staples or nails

• furniture made of solid wood, with no particle board on the back or bottom

• furniture that doesn't need much structural repair.

FINISHING YOUR FURNITURE

By investing a few hours of your time, you can turn unfinished furniture into beautiful decorator pieces and cut your furniture costs in half, Homer says.

Today you can buy beautiful oak furniture, unfinished, and get excellent results by finishing it yourself if you take the finishing process step-by-step (1) prepare the surface and seal it, if necessary; (2) stain and (3) finish.

First, sand the piece lightly with fine sandpaper or garnet paper. Then clean it with denatured alcohol, lacquer thinner or a commercial paint remover wash on a cotton cloth. This removes dust left from the sanding, and also removes dirt, glue or other imperfections that can show up on even factory-fresh furniture.

Next use a wood seal, if necessary, to keep the stain from soaking in unevenly. Use color charts to select the shade of stain closest to the color you want. Then finish with varnish or polyurethane.

PART 7

PLANNING FOR THE BIG PROJECT

CHAPTER 25

2 × 4 TEACHERS:

LESSONS FROM THE ENERGY CRISIS

Every home that's ever been built started out in someone's mind. What to build, where to build and especially how to build it are tough questions in themselves. But throw in soaring energy costs, with no relief in sight, and panic sets in.

That's what happened to home builders during the early 1970s. The panic of the energy crisis was compounded by a proliferation of new and often untested methods of designing homes for energy efficiency. If you were building, you struggled to learn the potential of concepts such as passive solar, active solar, envelope homes, underground homes, bermed homes and superinsulated homes. Plus, you had the nagging fear that you might miss something among the new energy-saving building materials and products that were being introduced at a fast and furious pace.

After the dust settled, builders found they had learned a few things about energy-saving concepts, say teachers at owner-builder schools across the country. These teachers have watched hot building ideas come and go. And they are among the first to know when new concepts move into mainstream home construction. The folks who run these schools say that owner-builders are in surprising agreement now about general approaches for designing energy-efficient homes. In a nutshell, interest in active solar space heating has waned, although the principles of passive solar and superinsulation have gained a strong foothold in the thinking of today's owner-builder.

Though the search for the perfect solution is not over, they say one thing's certain: If you're planning to build a low-energy home, the know-how available today can put you light years ahead of home builders of the early '70s.

SEEKING COMFORTABLE EFFICIENCY

Shelter Institute, a pioneering owner-builder school in Bath, Maine, opened its doors just when the first big energy crunch hit. "Back then," says Patsy Hennin, cofounder, "home builders were thinking 'We'll give up anything to make it through this energy problem.' That's not the case anymore. They're not as hyper about saving energy as they used to be. They're demanding high energy efficiency, but aren't willing to give up comfort to get it!"

Owner-builders showing up at Shelter Institute now take it for granted that any house that's built will be energy efficient. "They do, however, want to know what the options are," Patsy says, "and they want to be in charge of selecting them. Now they can base their priorities on knowledge, rather than going into a panic and resorting to a primitive life-style."

Maureen McIntyre, director of the Colorado Owner-Builder Center in Boulder, remembers the crisis mentality of those times. "But now owner-builders are much more relaxed, plus they have gotten much more sophisticated about building energy-saving homes. It used to be," she says, "that builders would brag about how their solar homes would overheat. But not anymore. The techniques have been so refined that you can literally design and build a house now, in most areas, that doesn't even need auxiliary heat . . . the house can take care of itself, without some of the early problems."

After the dust settled from the energy crisis scare, energy efficiency became a given. Now owner-builders want a comfortable, well-designed house as well as an energy-efficient one.

The view that a more straightforward approach is being taken on building energy-stingy homes is held by teachers at other owner-builder schools. If you were a builder in the early '70s, you were into experimenting, says Will Beemer, codirector of the Heartwood Owner-Builder School in Washington, Massachusetts. "We saw quite a few back-to-the-earth types searching for ways to build their $5,000 underground home. Now the builders we see are more savvy about energy efficiency and know they don't have to go to extreme designs to get it."

At Cornerstones, the owner-builder school founded by Charlie Wing in Brunswick, Maine, potential builders are leaning more toward convenience, aesthetics and quality. "Before," observes Barbra McCandless, school administrator, "folks were primarily just interested in a low-energy-consumption, self-sufficient life-style. Now they want a home that's easy on energy, but one that's built the way they want it."

FINE-TUNING PASSIVE DESIGNS

Building schools across the northern tier of the country generally accept the concept of an energy-efficient house incorporating passive solar techniques. It's not thought of as a new, experimental or pioneering effort anymore.

Leslie Miller, program coordinator at the Northwest Owner-Builder Center in Seattle, Washington, says that at first builders were more interested in active-solar systems. "But most folks around here have come to realize they don't have to spend a lot of money on complicated high technology to conserve energy."

If an active-solar system is used, she says, it's usually to help preheat water before it goes into the water heater. "Builders here are also keen on the concept of using thermal mass with typical building materials such as floor tile, masonry walls or ⅝-inch Sheetrock in the right place. They aren't going for overhead glazing like they were at one time. It hasn't proven out too well in this area. Generally, we'll see vertical glass on the south, and maybe a skylight or two that can be opened for ventilation."

Maureen McIntyre says the interest in active-solar systems has faded. "The feeling is that the up-front costs aren't justified for the usable BTUs you get out of it. But interest has remained strong in hybrid designs incorporating what could be called low-tech active systems.

"For example, some builders here are putting in radiant floor systems using collectors. Some are installing hydronic systems that collect actively, but discharge passively through polybutylene pipe in the floor slab. Others are laying concrete block sideways, and pouring a slab over them to channel warm air under the floor with low-volume fans."

Patsy Hennin says builders they see have favored passive-solar designs all along. "In many areas," she says, "they just aren't able to justify active-solar systems financially. It boils down to taking the perspective of 'What can we take most advantage of on our site for both heating and cooling?'"

Superinsulation is popular with owner-builders throughout the country. The good news is that the basic concept and techniques can be worked into almost any house plan.

Will Beemer concluded that active-solar is fine for hot water, but doesn't recommend an active-solar system for space heating. "Passive systems work better. We tell builders here to stick with vertical glass and stay away from sloped glazing, unless it's a greenhouse, because of weatherproofing problems.

"We also tell them not to get into fancy mechanical systems that may break down, especially if they are building in a rural area. There's no question you will have some problems. But if a builder likes the idea, and has someone nearby who can install it and make the service calls, we say go ahead."

"You can build anything, as long as you can make it work," is the motto at Cornerstones. Says Barbra McCandless, "We stress a passive-solar orientation, but the design itself can vary from contemporary to traditional, as long as the details are worked out. We also have seen a change in ideas on where to put glass and how much to use. Builders started out socking as much glazing into the south side of the house as they could. But those homes became 'cookers.' Now less glass is being used to avoid those heat control problems that resulted in having to keep your shutters closed all day to control the temperature."

INCORPORATING
SUPERINSULATION TECHNIQUES

Updated state building codes have demanded higher levels of insulation. Still, in many cases, builders go even further. When the state of Washington, for example, instituted a code requiring R11 walls, R30 attic and R19 floors over a crawl space, most folks attending the Northwest Owner-Builder Center in Seattle wanted more. They leaned toward a R19 wall using 2×6 studs, or R11 in a 2×4 wall with insulated sheathing on the outside, and R40 in the attic.

Building schools have observed the shock waves from superinsulation concepts, but the push for more insulation doesn't mean builders are abandoning passive solar. Rather, they are looking at ways to incorporate superinsulating techniques into passive-solar designs. "It decreases your dependence on solar gain to reduce heat costs," explains Barbra McCandless.

Interest in superinsulating is strongest in Canada. "It's the only way to go up here," claims Harry Pasternak, program director for the Thousand Islands Institute, an owner-builder school near Picton, Ontario.

"Research in Canada shows that both active and passive solar don't work that well up here. After seeing the figures, most of our builders go superinsulated. The beauty of it is that it doesn't require any solar gain. There's no sloping glazing, only fat walls, fat ceilings and fat floors."

Pasternak likes to refer to these homes as "Rudolf Doernach structures," respectfully crediting the first person who built such a home (back in 1954 in Stuttgart, West Germany) and heated it with one baseboard heater. Doernach, he notes, was the originator of the concept that has spawned such labels as superinsulation, Zero Heat Loss, Low-Cal or Saskatchewan houses.

"But the best part," he emphasizes, "is that the techniques can be applied to almost any home plan. You don't have to make your house long and skinny, short or tall. Whatever your design fantasy, from Cape Cod to Frank Lloyd Wright Prairie Design, you don't have to change it. You can build it exactly as you want it; the only difference is that the walls will be thicker."

Pasternak says Canadian builders have successfully used superinsulation techniques to build homes that can almost be "heated by burning paper cups in the fireplace," a cost of $100 to $200 a year. These homes typically contain R30 insulation in basement floors and walls, R40 in upper floor walls and R50 or R60 in attics or cathedral ceilings.

Wall thickness, he says, generally runs in the 8- to 12-inch range, with both single- and double-wall construction being used. "Those builders who believe wood is a good insulator use a single 2×10 or 2×12 stud wall; those who don't, go with a double wall." Pasternak says builders are getting picky about brands of insulation; Canadian research shows the performance of some brands can vary by as much as 25 percent from stated label claims.

CHOOSING A HEAT BACKUP

When heating costs can be wrestled down to the level of a water bill, what systems are builders choosing? Barbra McCandless says most people building in Maine use wood as a primary heat source with electrical heat backup. "Homes are being so well built now that folks can heat them with only a cord and a half of wood per winter. This makes electrical heat an economical backup system."

Wood heat is likewise favored by builders at the Heartwood Owner-Builder School in Massachusetts. However, Will Beemer points out that it may not be a first choice with a superinsulated house. "Wood heat, with a chimney and outside air coming in, sort of defeats the purpose of superinsulation. While wood heat is fine for conventional construction, the consensus is that all-electric is best for superinsulated houses."

Blair Abee, director of the Owner Builder Center in Berkeley, California, says that even if a builder can get all the heat needed by using passive-solar and wood heat, codes in some jurisdictions may still require a traditional backup system. "In this case," he observes, "people will often put in electric baseboard heaters, more for the building department than anything, and perhaps never use them or only use them a few days a year."

It's the same story farther north at the Northwest Owner-Builder Center in Seattle. Says Leslie Miller, "Right now the code here requires a backup system, so people are having to spend quite a bit on systems they may never use. Some are going with heat pumps, some are using high-efficiency natural gas furnaces. Many like small electric baseboard heaters that can be controlled room-by-room. In any case, if wood stoves are used, they're not just plunked down in one corner of the house; they are put right in the center and the house is designed around it."

"Tankless water heaters aren't that popular here," she continues. "The feeling is that it's hard to get one to do the job for the entire house, so you need one at each point of use. That drives the cost way up."

Downsized, direct-vented furnaces are popular with builders at the Colorado Owner-Builder Center, as well as with superinsulated home builders attending the Thousand Islands Institute in Ontario. "If they use electric baseboard heaters in a superinsulated home," notes Harry Pasternak, "they can get by using only about $\frac{1}{15}$ the wattage required in a conventionally built home."

DESIGN TIPS FROM THE PROS

Contrary to what might be expected, home sizes haven't shrunk that much, according to these owner-builder teachers. Says Blair Abee, "Builders around here are often going larger. One of the reasons you build your own home is because you have a good idea of what you want, but don't want to pay the going rate for it. So you look at some way to get involved to be able to get that home for the money you can afford."

"Top-of-the-line homes, those costing about $250,000, seem to have come down about 500 square feet in size," notes Will Beemer. "But owner-builders have always tended to build somewhere around 1,500 to 2,000 square feet. Actually, the tendency is to design something bigger than you can actually pull off. So we say to build small and add on later."

Owner-builder schools generally don't follow too closely on the heels of hot new trends and usually don't parcel out the latest cutting edge home building technologies. "There is really no ultimate answer," explains Patsy Hennin. "Every new trend should be thought through to see what it has to offer for a home in a specific location. The best may be a careful blending of the old and new, all chosen for the site you plan to build on.

"Don't put something into your house unless you have a reason for it. Understand what the reason is, even if it's just because you feel like trying it. But don't do it because somebody told you that was 'The Way.' If you don't understand it, hold back!"

She says the same thing holds for the overall design. "More exotic designs can work, but if your design's too different, you may end up being stuck with a white elephant. Instead of building an underground home, for example, maybe you could build a nice home into a hillside. It's a nice compromise and your home can have tons of resale value."

Most schools maintain a "wait and see" attitude, telling owner-builders to be especially cautious about becoming a guinea pig for someone else's ideas. Blair Abee notes that a number of ideas that surfaced since the energy crisis simply didn't work or were too expensive or impractical. "It's come around to the idea that simpler is better." He points out that rock storage bins have generally been found to be impractical, at least in his area, as have Trombe walls.

"The air envelope house," adds Will Beemer, "is also a good example of an idea that's faded. They were the rage for three years around here. We built one; they work, but are more expensive than conventional houses. Now no one is building them."

Still, the teachers at these schools, as well as the builders, are keeping their eyes open, putting the current crop of new ideas under the microscope. Ideas such as shade or shutter night covers for windows, jet fans for moving air and one-gallon flush toilets have been accepted with open arms. A small sampling of concepts now being watched from coast-to-coast:

Canada: double load-bearing 2 × 4 stud walls, staggered either 36 inch or 48 inch on center; they promise to save half or more on both materials and labor

Massachusetts: airtight drywall systems using gaskets behind the drywall to bypass conventional plastic vapor barriers

California: panelized construction, including 8-foot or 10-foot prebuilt wall sections, to eliminate need for special equipment and to make assembly easier.

Regardless of which ideas survive, folks at owner-builder schools say that one of the best things to come out of the energy crisis is a new home-building tool that can be used by any builder: computer modeling. It's inexpensive, takes advantage of skilled know-how and let's you preview energy costs before you build.

"The problem always has been that energy-saving building techniques change relatively fast," explains Will Beemer. "There's always a lot of arguing going on. We advise using computer modeling to get a picture of energy costs before building. But we also suggest that folks think ahead to how their life-styles may change in the future."

CHAPTER 26

STEVE NORTHWAY:
LONG-DISTANCE BUILDING

Building at long distance presents a whole new set of challenges, on top of what ordinarily is enough of a job for first-time builders. If you don't meet the extra problems head-on, you can find yourself faced with escalating costs and a home that's much less than you had hoped for.

But distance doesn't have to mean misery, says Steve Northway, an experienced North Country contractor accustomed to building for out-of-towners, sometimes those living thousands of miles away. "There's really no reason why you can't build a place wherever you want and have it be a pleasurable experience," he says. "It boils down to being alert, using the right approach and putting in more effort up front!"

Steve is a partner in Nor-son, Inc., a Brainerd, Minnesota, designer-builder firm. Brainerd is about 160 miles north of Minneapolis, at the heart of a booming summer vacation area dotted with lakeshore homes owned by residents from nearly all

50 states. Most of those homes built over the past 10 years were projects of Nor-son and a half-dozen other area contractors who face the problems of long-distance building every month of the year.

If you're a city dweller used to freeways and skyscrapers, you might expect contractors working in the land of woods and lakes to be unsophisticated "boondocks builders." Despite their location, it's possible to find a professional firm such as Steve's, which employs dozens of carpenters as well as full-time architects, so they not only can do the building, but give you as much design help as you need. And they're experienced in working with absentee owners living in one place and putting up a vacation home miles away in another.

We've watched the concept of a shoreline vacation home shift from low-budget A-frames to substantial, often elegant structures most of us would be proud to call home year-round. A few of the ones we've built have set the owner back as much as $375,000. Let's say you have this dream of building a cabin here on a lake. Well, for most people that's not going to be a cabin, but a complete year-round home. Once you get serious, you need to start thinking about what the resale value might be. And you've got to build for resale today.

BUILDING FOR INVESTMENT

The whole idea of vacation homes has changed. More people are looking at the vacation home not only as a place to get away, but as a genuine real estate investment. And more people are building with the idea that their "cabin" will eventually be their main home after they retire. In fact, if someone tells me they want a low-cost vacation home, with no insulation, I try to steer them away from it. It doesn't cost that much more to insulate well. You might be talking $1,000 or $2,000 more. For one thing, it doubles the time you can use your investment. For another, you'll likely get that money back whenever you sell your home.

More expensive summer places, along with an abundance of new restrictions and regulations, are making the owner-builder who puts up a "shack in the woods" a rare bird, I'd say. It's still done, but nowadays if you don't live in the area, it's worth thinking twice about building or trying to coordinate a group of subcontractors yourself. I don't blame anyone for wanting to save money, get involved and learn some things. But from what I've seen, trying to handle the whole job of being your own general contractor from a distance has the potential to become a nightmare. I've seen people try it and many of their projects just get out of hand.

As an absentee supervisor, it gets really tough to site the home properly, coordinate the work and keep a handle on the quality of the work being done when you're gone. The biggest horror stories I've heard involve people who try to build entirely on their own. The house gets too low or high in the ground. Or the house is set too close to the lot lines or too close to the lake. The local contractor knows the regulations and how our zoning and planning committees think. Sometimes half of what we do is keep people out of trouble!

ADVICE FOR THE DO-IT-YOURSELFER

If you're pressed for money, a contractor generally will take your project to any stage you want. We can just put up the shell and get it under lock and key. Or we can put up the shell and finish off critical areas such as a couple of bedrooms, bath and kitchen. This way the house is livable and you can work on the rest at your convenience. There are always a bunch of guys around with Skilsaws and levels in the back of their pickups ready to bid on anything that comes along. In most cases, if you try to be your own general contractor, you'll end up with one of these low bidders and actually create problems right from the start! Trying to coordinate the whole show when building a distant vacation home may not save you much money over the long haul, plus you may be courting serious scheduling problems. Find yourself a good general contractor. If he's doing his job, he'll work for you, the owner, to maintain quality of work throughout the project.

Many subcontractors will charge an individual more than they will charge me as a general contractor. The reason is you're only giving the subcontractor one job in a lifetime, as opposed to hundreds sublet to him by area contractors. A local contractor also knows who's good and who's available. By not knowing the workmanship of the subcontractors, you can end up with the bottom of the bucket. If you have the time, you can do your own finish work, things that don't require much day-to-day coordination.

FINDING THE RIGHT CONTRACTOR

I think the selection of a contractor could be the most important decision you make on your entire project. So how do you find the right outfit? My advice is to narrow your selection and check out a few of the most promising builders. Then, if you want to put some work into it, spend your time checking those guys out.

You may also need to consider getting help in coming up with a plan, or even modifying a blueprint to fit the climate or your personal taste. It's great if you have a plan to show a contractor. But even if you don't, a good contractor should be able to help you get your ideas down on paper. On the one side, the contractor's job is to streamline the owner's dream house with what is feasible and appropriate construction for the area. The owner's job is to convey his expectations. The more input, the better.

A good contractor will work to ensure quality throughout the project. He knows the local subcontractors and can get the best people for the job.

If you are starting completely from scratch, you might consider a designer-builder firm with an in-house architect. Here are other tips:

References: Check with the firm's past customers, preferably by going to see their homes and asking them what they thought of the contractor's work. We like to have people spend a full day looking at three or four of our homes. And we leave them alone with the owners so they can talk freely.

Credit: Check the contractor's credit references to see if the guy pays his bills. You don't want to wind up getting a lien on the place after the job's done. You can check with the Better Business Bureau for any complaints, or the Contractor's Board and suppliers. It's possible that you might pay a general contractor in good faith and wind up with the subcontractors who didn't get paid coming back to you. Check the mechanics lien laws in your state. And always ask for a release of lien from the contractor before the final payment.

Service: A larger contractor generally will be able to spend more time with you than the one-man show where the owner is also out there pounding nails. This doesn't mean you should automatically write off an aggressive young guy who's trying to get established, however. Just make sure he'll give you the service and workmanship you expect.

Insurance: Check to see if the contractor carries workman's compensation and liability insurance to protect you from personal-injury lawsuits and disasters on the job. If a guy comes to backfill your basement and it caves in, you might be stuck if the contractor doesn't have insurance.

Workmanship: Ask about which subcontractors will be used. They're the ones doing the work. It's rare that anyone ever asks about who we use, but workmanship can vary tremendously. For example, I could give you a ranking of the plumbers around here, starting with the best to the worst. Those on the lower end can do plumbing, but it probably wouldn't be quite right.

Guarantees: In some states, such as Minnesota, a contractor has to stand by a structure for 10 years. But if the contractor goes out of business, where does that leave you? This is a good reason to use an established firm. Some contractors also offer a homeowner's warranty program. If the original builder is gone, the coverage can pay another builder to correct any problem.

Prices: Before you close the deal, make sure the contractor gives you a solid price. It should cover everything, including a specific allowance for carpeting and well drilling. Have him spell out what add-ons, if any, will be allowed at the end of the project. Also make sure that any changes will be made by specific written agreement between the contractor and yourself.

Quotes: A common stumbling block is interpreting bids. You just can't assume that because you show all the contractors the same plan, they will all be bidding on the same thing. In fact, you can expect a wide variation on workmanship, materials and service. Try to find out what a low bidder is actually giving you. Some people who automatically accept a low bid might think they're saving $3,000, but end up fighting with the contractor throughout the whole project.

Most problems that come up will be from poor communication or misunderstandings. Document everything before you start. Try not to leave anything open for questions to come up. We use a 20-page spec sheet to nail down every detail so everybody knows what's expected.

LIFE DURING THE BIG PROJECT

You might have heard about big projects—building a house, putting up a cabin or even redoing a basement—that go sour. It's one of the saddest pictures of all: a half-done project that's abandoned or brought to a screeching halt not because of an accident, lack of money or skill, but because of a breakdown in human relations.

It's one of the things folks don't talk about much. Maybe they figure it's too personal. Although George Nash talks here mainly about relationships between a man and a woman during large projects, you can project his advice to include father and son, mother and daughter, sibling and sibling.

George teaches shelter design at Vermont Institute of Community Involvement and lives with his large family on a rundown hill farm that he is slowly rehabilitating. Several years after he graduated from Wesleyan University with a degree in English, he found himself restoring to useful life a derelict old house in northern Vermont, and since then he has worked as a carpenter, contractor, housing consultant and homesteader. His examples relate to renovating an old house, but the project could be any major undertaking.

A house cannot be experienced separate from its householders. Even if you contract out the entire renovation, it becomes impossible to maintain any distance between yourself and it. Unless you hire an architect, approve the plans and leave for South America

Remember, too, that after a project starts is not the time to make changes. Settle on a plan and stick with it. Often it looks like something would be easy to change, but once you make it, you might find out that it leads to two or three other changes. Soon things can get out of control. The key to having a good long-distance building experience is to find a contractor with whom you have good rapport and who understands just what it is that you want.

for the next six months (some people do this and are thereby diminished by the emptiness they build into their lives), you will find yourself inexorably eaten up by the idea of the house.

It becomes all-encompassing, your womb. If you have hands-on involvement, it can also become a tomb. At first the house is a welcome thing. You are full of energy – enthusiastic and blissfully unaware of how much work actually lies ahead. You embrace the work, constantly measuring in your mind's eye where the curtains are to hang, where the bookshelves should go, the woodbox behind the big old iron stove.

As the days wane and the nights grow sharp and clear, your horizons shrink. Getting the place closed in for winter becomes a consuming passion that is rapidly occupying every waking thought. You sit down at the breakfast table and eat insulation. A rainy day is a personal insult from a malevolent god. At night, lying in your bed, your head is in the cellar jacking up a rotten beam, your spouse wondering where you are.

This obsession has a tendency to destroy family or interpersonal relationships. Whatever tensions already exist become exacerbated. Life becomes an incubator for a host of new and increasingly virulent strains of discord between you and your loved ones. The usual pattern is for the woman to take care of cooking meals, raising children and household chores so that her mate is free to pursue the "all-important" work of rebuilding the house. She becomes his support system. He takes this for granted and explodes in frustrated rage the one night she asks him to cook dinner, to allow her a break from her routine. He forgets that it is

(continued)

LIFE DURING THE BIG PROJECT— *Continued*

her work that enables him to devote himself to his singleness of purpose.

Although cultural patterns are changing, most of us are the victims and products of our upbringing and tend to fall into role stereotypes. Girls were raised with dolls, boys with blocks. Women are conditioned to expect the man to know all about the hardware. Men assume that women are tailored for the household manager role. The man fixes a leaky faucet, the woman fixes dinner.

Even couples who consider themselves liberated will find themselves falling into this pattern of role designation. They begin by invoking efficiency as an unfortunate evil. Because the male is often the stronger and more agile with tools and because there is so much to be done, he is the one who runs the chain saw while she stacks the firewood. He measures and cuts the boards and nails them into place. She pulls nails out of old boards, picks up the rubbish and moves piles of building materials. He does the skilled labor and she is left to the menial tasks. After a while expediency becomes expectation. It is assumed that she will do those tasks in addition to her domestic duties, which are viewed as inconsequential. And hardly is there time taken to say thank you.

As the work increases and the days shorten, so do the resentments and tempers. The couple who can start off equally unskilled is at an advantage. A woman can learn to use a hammer as well as a man. A man can actually cook a dinner. Both can learn to use tools with equal skill. Flexibility is possible, because brute strength is not the main component of intelligent carpentry. I know of one woman who wired and plumbed the entire house while her husband worked to pay for materials. Most couples, however, do not have skills that are that well balanced. The care of children tends to complicate the equation. In most cases the man is definitely the one with the skills and the woman the one with the children. The time factor is an inescapable reality. It really is more efficient for him to do the work while she does the dinner. But ask yourself, what is more important – efficiency or your marriage?

AVOIDING PROJECT CASUALTIES

More than one relationship has been the casualty of a remodeling project. How do you avoid getting caught in this vise? The advice is easy enough to give but hard to implement.

To begin, you should sit down with your mate and try to state clearly what you expect of each other. Try to define the areas of responsibility and who will do what. My wife and I both started out with the idea that we could share the building and the housework. This seemed reasonable enough. I would be up on the scaffold nailing on the siding. She would be on the ground, cutting it to length. After a half-dozen attempts at forcing that board to fit the measurement, I found my patience wearing thin and she was deciding that carpentry really wasn't all that interesting.

We were both frustrated by our impatience. We knew that she would eventually learn how to use a saw. I only had a seven-year head start on her, but on-the-job training doesn't work when dark is coming on. She went and cooked supper. I cut the boards and nailed them myself.

That evening we talked about it and decided that liberation is a matter of situation rather than role. You don't have to be a carpenter in order to be liberated. It is a question of reciprocity. A house is not built in a vacuum of time and space. The needs of daily life are not suspended during its construction. The labors required to support a household are every bit as important and as critical as those necessary to move walls or nail boards.

A house is a vehicle for a higher purpose. We should build our houses around our lives, to shelter and contain us, to aid us in achieving the things we have been living for, not to live for the building of the house. A liberated person tries to see how he or she can best utilize the resources and givens of personality and skills to achieve the agreed-upon goal. These people realize that they have a contract, between equals, with all aspects of the work given equal value.

It's a good place to start. But it won't carry you all that far. Constant vigilance will be required to keep from slipping back into those old roles. You will have to keep the communication lines open; talk about things before they come to a head.

Don't bottle up frustrations or let too much slide. Knowing when to let up or when to lean a little harder is a delicate balancing act. How successful you are at it is a measure of the strength and viability of your relationship. Ultimately and simply, you have to *trust* each other.

Do not ignore this advice. There is nothing sadder than a house that has devoured the souls of its people, or than the emptiness of waking up at night and looking at a stranger lying beside you.

BOOKS FOR BUILDERS

Ching, Francis, and Dale Miller. *Home Renovation*. New York: Van Nostrand Reinhold, 1983.

Clark, Sam. *Designing and Building Your Own House Your Own Way.* Boston: Houghton Mifflin Co., 1978.

Day, Richard. *Do-It-Yourself Plumbing*. Davison, Mich.: Genova Products, 1987.

Feirer, John L., and Gilbert R. Hutchings. *Carpentry and Building Construction*. New York: Scribner, 1981.

Garrett Wade Tools Catalog. New York: Garrett Wade Co. (Issued annually and available through newsstands and bookstores, or can be ordered directly from the Garrett Wade Co., 161 Avenue of the Americas, New York, NY 10013.)

Juranitch, John. *The Razor Edge Book of Sharpening*. New York: Warner Books, 1985.

McCormick, Dale. *Housemending*. New York: E. P. Dutton, 1987.

McReynolds, Ray. *Step by Step Guide Book on Home Wiring*. Salt Lake City: Step by Step Guide Book Co., 1988.

Miller, Robert S. *Home Construction Projects with Adhesives and Glues*. Columbus, Ohio: Franklin International, 1983. (Available where Franklin glues are sold or from the company at 2020 Bruck St., Columbus, OH 43207.)

Roberts, Rex. *Your Engineered House*. Edited by Charlie Wing. New York: M. Evans and Co., 1987.

Roskind, Robert. *Building Your Own House, Part I*. Berkeley: Ten Speed Press, 1984.

Roskind, Robert and Owner-Builder Center. *Before You Build*. Berkeley: Ten Speed Press, 1981.

Schwolsky, Rick, and James Williams. *The Builder's Guide to Solar Construction*. New York: McGraw-Hill, 1982.

Spielman, Patrick. *The Router Handbook*. New York: Sterling Publishing Co., 1983.

Wagner, Willis H. *Modern Carpentry*. South Holland, Ill.: Goodheart-Wilcox Co., 1983.

Wing, Charlie, and John Cole. *Breaking New Ground*. Boston: Atlantic Monthly Press, 1986.

———. *From the Ground Up*. Boston: Atlantic Monthly Press, 1976.

Woodsmith magazine. Des Moines: Woodsmith. (A 24-page, bimonthly publication; available from Woodsmith, 2200 Grand Ave., Des Moines, IA 50312.)

PHOTOGRAPHY CREDITS

James Clark Studio, p.131
Minnesota Historical Society, pp. 105, 165, 221
A. F. Raymond photo, Minnesota Historical Society, pp. 1, 61
Rodale Press Photography Department, p. 253
S. M. Taylor photo, Minnesota Historical Society, p. 251
Alice and Robert Tupper, pp. 71, 73, 74, 76, 77, 78, 80, 81, 122

All other photographs by Gene Schnaser.

Additional photographs courtesy of:
Marc Archambeau, p. 58
Russ Barnard, p. 83
Bob Beckstrom, p. 175
Dave Chapeau, p. 207
Garretson Wade Chinn, p. 7
Duane Clarke, p. 145
John Connell, p. 167
Richard Day, pp. 195, 197, 198, 201, 202, 203
Black & Decker, pp. 29, 233
Formby's Media Resource Center, pp. 243, 245, 248
Don Gabriel, p. 67
John A. Gordon, p. 223
Charlie Huddleston, p. 131
Ed Jackson, p. 63
John Juranitch, pp. 47, 49
Arnold Kastrup, p. 53
Paul McClure, p. 9
Steve Northway, p. 261
Kim Rasmussen, p. 107
Brian Ringham, p. 115
Marlyn Rodi, pp. 37, 42
Milford Roubik, p. 187
Robert Scharff, p. 235
Howard Silken, p. 19
Robert Snider, p. 229
Patrick Spielman, p. 25
Alice and Robert Tupper, p. 75
Elias Velonis, p. 175
Jim Young, p. 125

INDEX

Page numbers in **boldface** type indicate photographs; page numbers in *italic* type indicate illustrations.

Rodale Press, Inc., publishes AMERICAN WOODWORKER™, the magazine for the serious woodworking hobbyist. For information on how to order your subscription, write to AMERICAN WOODWORKER™, Emmaus, PA 18098.